AF579226

Understanding Paintings

Frederick Malins

Understanding Paintings

The Elements of Composition

Phaidon

Phaidon Press Limited
Littlegate House, St. Ebbe's Street,
Oxford

First published 1980

Malins, Frederick
Understanding Paintings
1. Painting – Technique
2. Composition (Art)
I. Title
751.4 ND1475

ISBN 0-7148-2116-0 (paper)
ISBN 0-7148-2114-4
Phototypeset by Filmtype Services Limited, Scarborough

Printed in Great Britain by Morrison & Gibb Ltd, Edinburgh

I wish to express my gratitude to all those students, past and present, with whom I have so much enjoyed working and who have helped me so much in clarifying my ideas. I would also like to thank those friends and colleagues who have not only made the production of this book possible, but have made it a pleasure. I particularly wish to thank Elwyn Blacker, Mark Ritchie, and my editor Sally Foy; my erstwhile colleague Terry Nilssen-Love, and Brian Sherwood. For typing and retyping I am indebted to Peggy Finch and Ann Williams, and for library facilities to Elaine Scott.
Finally, my thanks go to Margery Malins, without whose continued help and encouragement the book would not have been possible.

CONTENTS

TONE

COLOUR

DRAWING

COMPOSITION

INTRODUCTION

This book is based on a series of lectures given over several years to various generations of art students and as part of University extra-mural courses in Art Appreciation, for adults wishing to understand more about the basic grammar which underlies works of art. The aim of the book is to create a greater degree of such an understanding.

All paintings and drawings consist of certain visual elements, used singly or in combination, in different ways. The ways in which these elements are used will depend on which different pictorial qualities the artist chooses to emphasize in order to express his own personal vision.

Looking at a painting results in a complex visual experience. Distracting elements such as association (a painting of a landscape may be liked/disliked because it reminds the viewer of an experience associated with such a landscape) and all literary elements must be disregarded if we are to recognize and understand the pictorial qualities – rhythm, balance, movement, or pattern, all playing their greater or lesser parts in creating a unity of composition and thereby producing an aesthetically satisfying result. These qualities are created by the judicious, imaginative and inventive use of the basic visual elements, Point, Line, Tone, and Colour.

In the following pages a wide variety of paintings are analysed in order to see some of the different ways in which these elements have been used by the Old Masters as well as the artists of today. In this way we can appreciate the common factors in the paintings of artists as diverse in time as Piero della Francesca and Juan Gris, or the drawings of Pieter Breughel and Vincent van Gogh.

The basic elements of composition are considered in logical sequence, examining some of their possibilities and limitations.

Chapter one looks at some of the various roles played by the simpest mark – the point – literally our starting point. Its simplest role is to define a position in space, but it can also be used in other ways, such as to create pattern or a feeling of movement.

Subsequent chapters consider the point moving to describe a line and the vastly increased possibilities that this opens up. The versatility of line has been exploited by artists from earliest times. Linear perspective, as a means of opening up space, is our next consideration; this was a very popular device during the Renaissance. Another responsibility of line is the creation of the law and order of geometry – that underlying logical construction of so many classical works of art.

The tonal element used to create the dramatic chiaroscuro of Caravaggio or Rembrandt is equally capable of being used to produce the pattern of the Bayeux Tapestry or the powerfully modelled forms of a Leonardo *Virgin and Child.*

But it is perhaps colour above all which is the most important single element in the painter's repertoire. Paul Klee recognized this when, after visiting colourful Tunisia with the painter August Macke, he wrote: 'Colour and I are one. I am a painter.'

Chapter six explains the basic facts about colour, examines its three-dimensional nature and looks at some of the ways in which hue, value and chroma have played their different roles – or played similar roles in the hands of different artists.

Rossetti, for example, uses almost no colour at all to convey purity, spirituality and asceticism, whereas Gauguin's colour scheme in *Nevermore* suggests sexuality, paganism and a lost luxury of living. Artists as far removed in time as Claude Lorraine and Claude Monet both use colour, in their individual ways, to create the effect of space and light.

The next section looks at drawings in the light of previous chapters, *seeing* the point, line, perspective, geometry, and tone as the means of expressing those particular aspects of reality or experience which the artist wishes to convey.

In conclusion, we take one painting only and analyse it from several different viewpoints. This process of analysis enables us to dissect the design or composition (the organization of the basic *visual* elements) in order to *see* the underlying structure. Analysis enables us to look deeper and thereby gain deeper understanding.

It may be argued that this process of visual analysis is a rather objective way of looking at what is essentially a subjective experience, and that the analytical process, by its nature, tends to overlook the wood by concentrating on one leaf of one tree. Furthermore, it may be felt that to attempt to increase appreciation by conscious study (rather than by simply gazing dreamily and open-mouthed) may be a hazardous process, more likely to result in a self-conscious attitude than to develop pictorial consciousness on a deeper level. But an understanding of the formal elements of design leads to their understanding becoming accepted – becoming part of our subconscious faculty after having been consciously pursued.

Knowledge deepens subjective response, and there is no reason to suppose that understanding will diminish this response – and equally no reason to suppose that the essential mystery of art will be lost by the pursuit of knowledge. The mystery will remain: the life of the tree will be no less mysterious if we study its leaves.

> 'In the course of time, the human mind has penetrated many mysteries in their essence and in their mechanism – the rainbow, thunder and lightning, gravity and so on. But they are still mysteries for all that'. J. Itten. *The Art of Colour.*

Of course, paintings and drawings are products of the artist's personality and are highly subjective, the results of *feeling*, however objective the intention. Further understanding of the artist's work would involve further understanding of the artist's life, where and when he lived, his formative influences and experiences, in fact the psychological make up and background of each individual – a daunting prospect, and one which I am not qualified to attempt.

But a start may be made in our search for understanding by *looking at* pictures. We all *notice* paintings but we take them for granted, like everything else, as part of the world around us. *Looking at* involves a positive conscious effort. Learning something about how to look, and to a certain extent what to look for, is what this book aims to describe. Since the book is essentially about looking, explanations are presented as far as possible by visual means, with a minimum of text, but many illustrations and diagrams.

Frederick Malins
South Nutfield
1980

THE POINT

Paintings and drawings consist of marks arranged in a meaningful way on any suitable surface. These marks can be made by various means including the use of charcoal, chalks, pigments, inks, and more recently, aerosol spray – in fact any medium, singly or in combination with other media, that will make a visible mark. The surface may be the wall of a cave or church, skin, bark, paper, or telephone kiosk – any of the endless variety of surfaces used throughout history.

The simplest mark that can be made is the point, and so we begin by considering some of the ways in which it can be used. It has the ability to create pattern, to express rhythm and movement, to become a focus, or to produce areas of texture. But before looking at these different aspects we examine some basic principles.

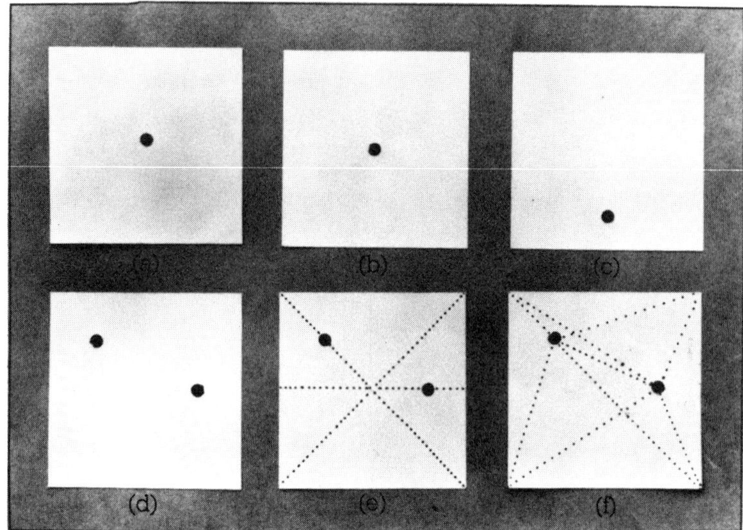

Visual and geometric centres (diagram)

When we look at a blank surface our eye roves over the area, looking for a place on which to concentrate. As soon as a mark is placed on this surface a relationship is set up between the mark and the boundaries of the surface: the tensions thus created appear to be held in delicate balance. Invisible but nevertheless felt 'magnetic' forces seem to stretch from the corners of the rectangle to the point.

(a) When the point is placed at the visual centre of the surface, a feeling of equilibrium results: the forces acting on the point are in perfect balance.

(b) But if the point is placed on the *geometric* centre, it appears to be slightly lower than it actually is and therefore to be pulled towards the bottom edge of the rectangle; the equilibrium is disturbed. To the artist the centre is the *apparent* centre and not the actual centre.

(c) If the point is brought still nearer to the bottom edge the effect of dropping out of the frame is increased and an uncomfortable feeling, due to the unstable situation, results.

(d) When two points are introduced the situation becomes much more complicated. Each point is held in tension by the forces acting from the four corners of the rectangle and between the points themselves.

(e) An effect of balance seems to result when the placing of the points is related to the invisible internal geometry of the rectangle.

(f) The dotted lines indicate the tenuous forces felt by the spectator as operating on these points.

The Point as position

The point may be used simply to identify or define a position or positions, as on a map or musical score – but as the eye moves from one point to another along different visual pathways different configurations and sensations result, and quite different characters are felt to emerge.

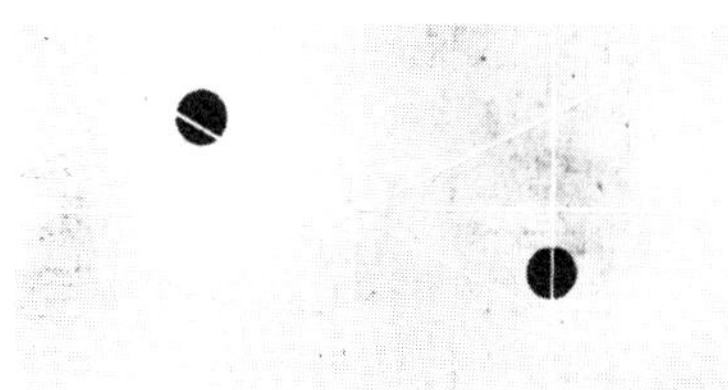

Le Rouge et le Noir: Paul Klee (diagram)

In this painting by Paul Klee we see two points held in balance both by the 'magnetic' forces generated within the rectangle and by the mutual attraction between the points. The introduction of colour into their relationship adds a new element to the balance of forces, the black point tending to exert a more powerful influence than the red. The superimposed diagram shows how the critical placing of these points relates to the internal geometry of the rectangle.

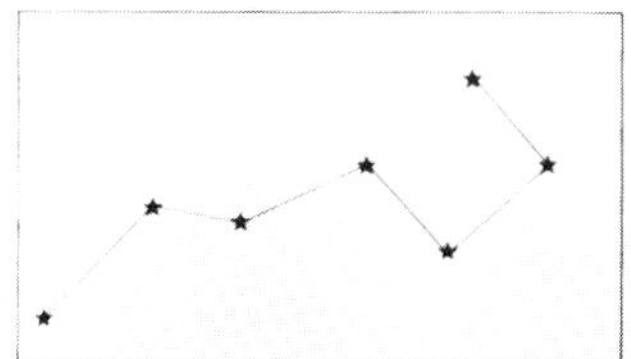

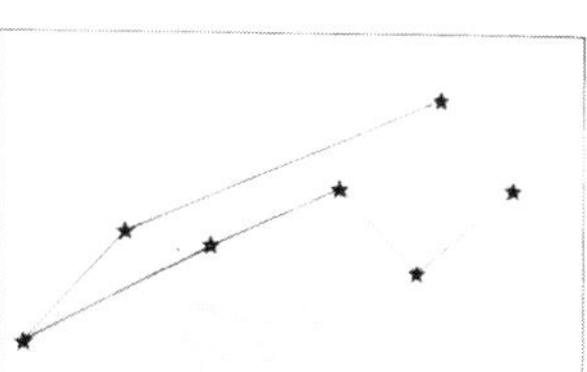

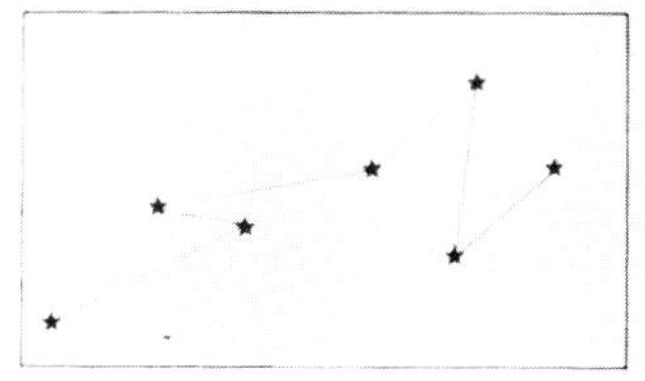

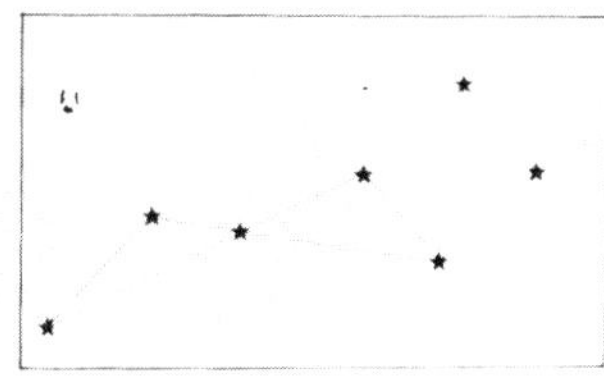

The Plough (diagram)

This star map shows the relative positions of the stars in the constellation known as Ursa Major, or 'the Plough'. The lines indicate some of the many possible visual pathways the eye may explore.

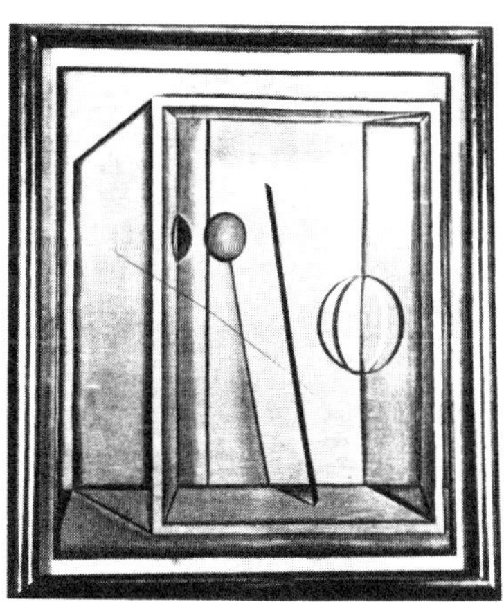

Metaphysical Still Life: Giorgio Morandi

In this painting the artist, Giorgio Morandi, has created an effect of three-dimensional space within the rectangle. This space is in effect inhabited by two points, separated by a line. The two points are the centres of the 'solid' sphere and of the skeletal sphere. These points are held in delicate balance, due to their careful placing – any alteration of the position of either would disturb the equilibrium of the whole.

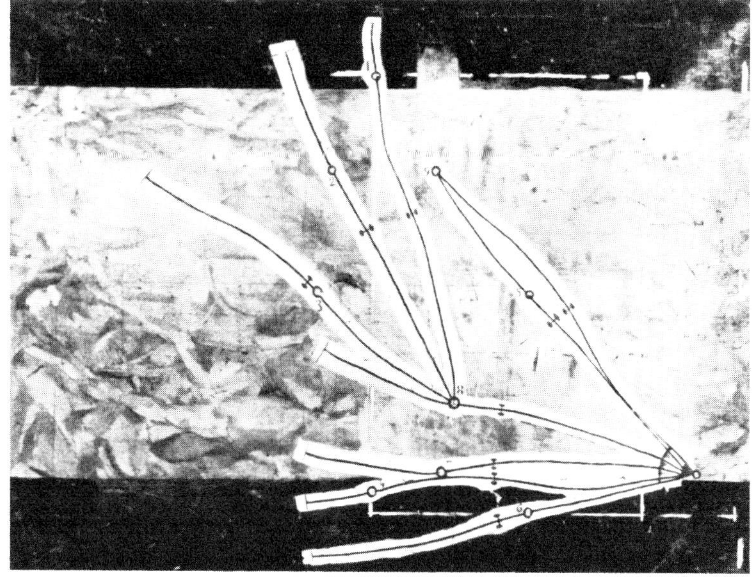

Stoppage Network: Marcel Duchamp

Duchamp uses the point in this way to identify positions in this map-like preparation for his work *The Large Glass.* The numbered points indicate the positions of elements to be placed in that work, and the nine lines of equal length radiating from the corner guide our eye along the visual pathways which Duchamp has determined.

THE POINT

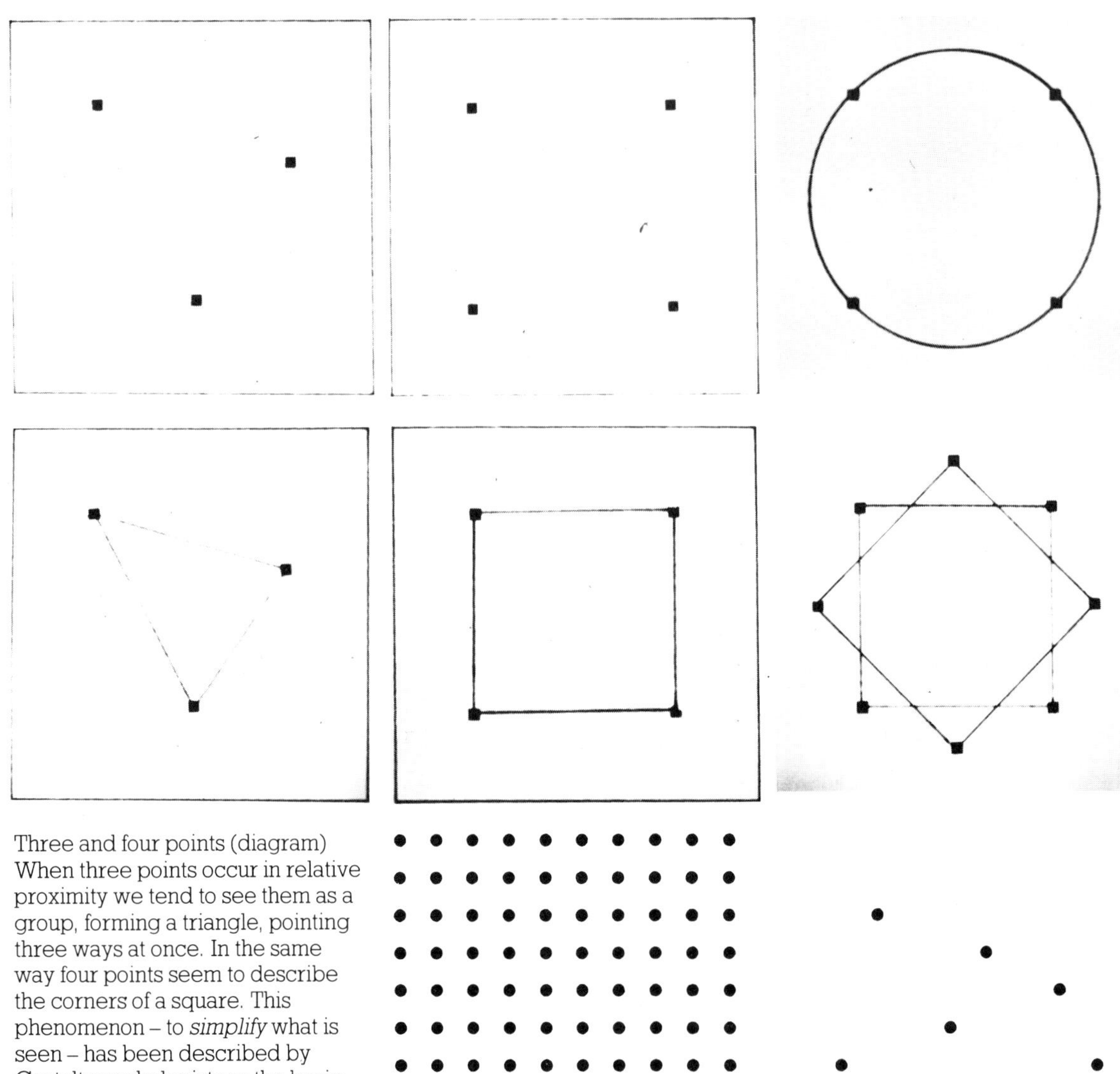

Three and four points (diagram) When three points occur in relative proximity we tend to see them as a group, forming a triangle, pointing three ways at once. In the same way four points seem to describe the corners of a square. This phenomenon – to *simplify* what is seen – has been described by Gestalt psychologists as the basic law of visual perception.

But the four points of the 'square' could equally well describe a circle and the 'circle' of points could have other, less simple, interpretations as shown. In general, units of similar size, shape, or colour tend to combine to produce visual clusters or groups.

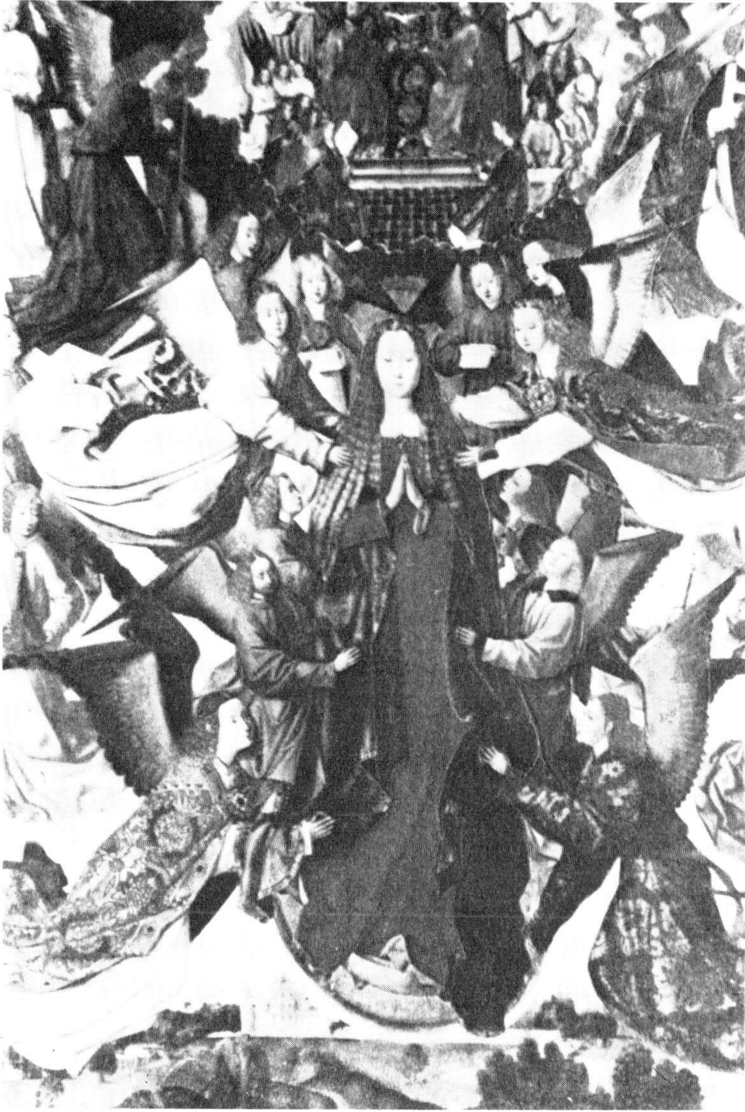

Mary, Queen of Heaven: Master of the St. Lucy Legend
In this painting by the Master of the St. Lucy Legend, it is difficult to see the organization or arrangement of the figures.

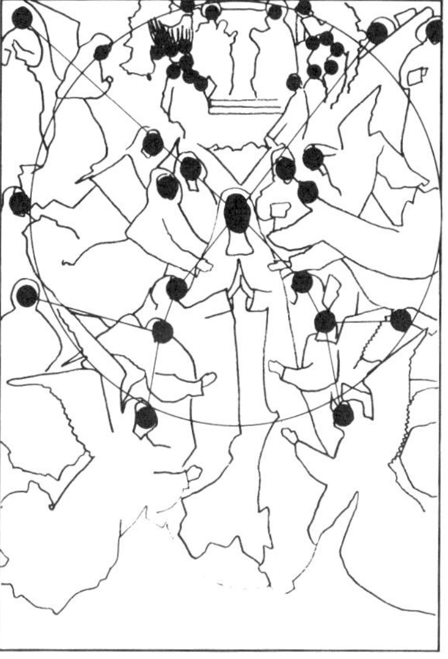

But when the heads are replaced by dots (above) the regular and symmetrical grouping of the figures around a central point is clearly seen. The symmetry is cleverly disguised by variations within the poses.

Visual clues (diagram)
Of course the orderly grouping of units in a picture is not always so obvious especially when visual clues are reduced to a minimum; however, one senses a kind of balance in this diagram (left) and the next shows why. An artist may organize the elements of a design in such a way that the basic simplicity is disguised – the result being that organization is felt, rather than made obvious.

THE POINT

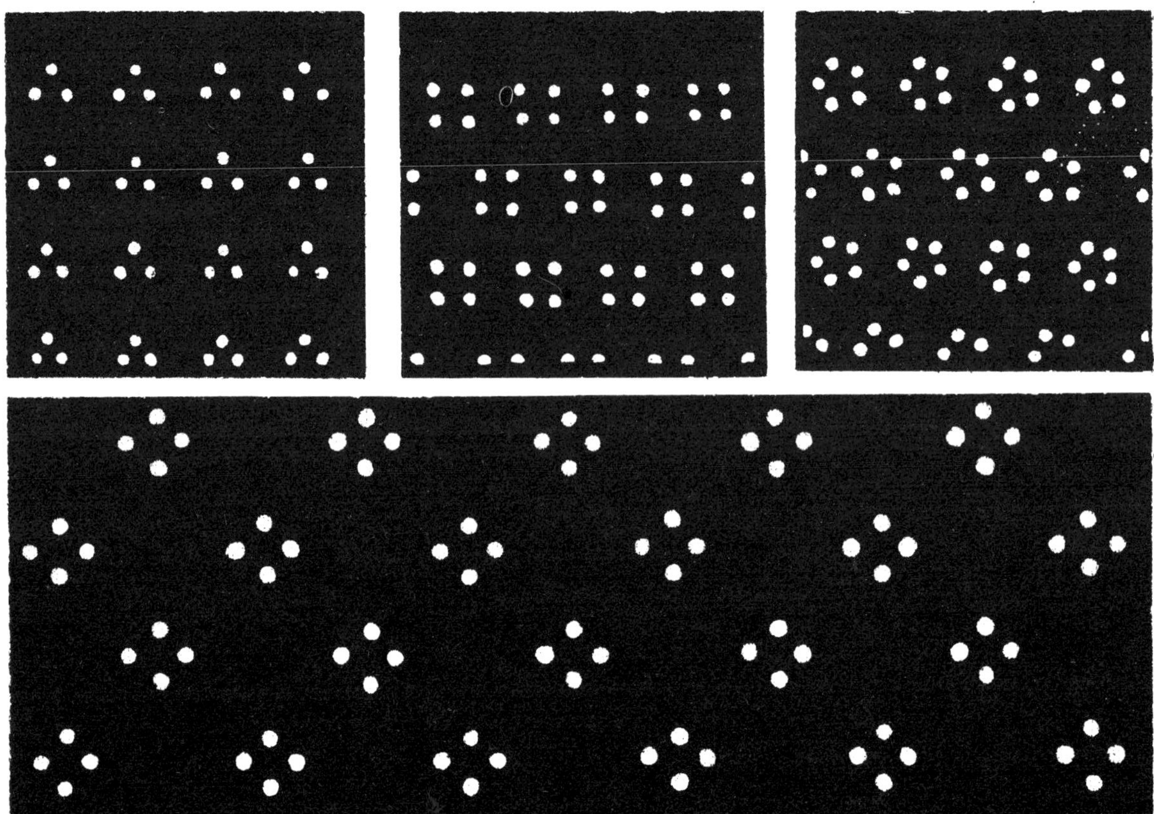

Patterns from Athenian vases (diagram)
From earliest times artists have used geometrical and pictorial motifs arranged in a regular and repeating sequence that we call 'pattern'. Whatever the reason for arriving at these decorative results it seems unlikely that they were produced simply for surface decoration, but more likely had a magical or religious function.

The four patterns illustrated derive from draperies painted on Athenian vases. Using three, four, or five points in regular and symmetrical grouping, the artists have produced richly ornamental effects from these apparently trivial motifs inherited from prehistory.

But very complex patterns can result from equally simple means. The artist may organize the design in such a way that the basic simplicity is disguised – so that the sense of organization is felt rather than made obvious.

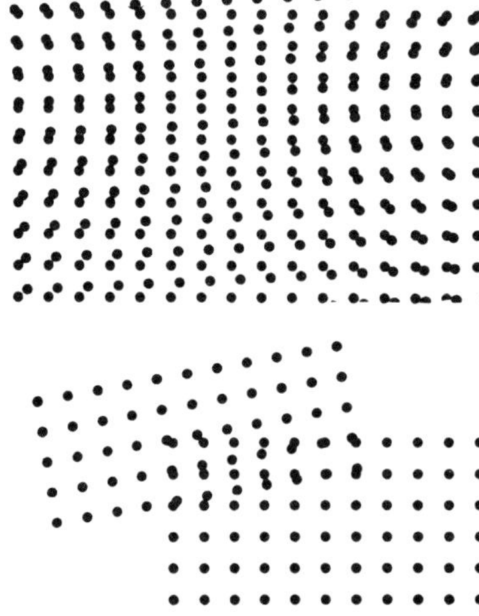

Superimposed points (diagram)
The diagram shows an extremely complex arrangement of points, apparently circling as pairs and separating again into individual units. Clearly there is some organization governing this grouping, but it is virtually impossible to understand the principle on which this pattern is based simply by looking, however visually sophisticated the observer may be.

Basic grid pattern (diagram)
In fact this complex rhythm results when we superimpose a regular repeating pattern of points on a slightly angled version of the same pattern. In this way the regularity is completely disguised, and a complex rhythm results.

The Point as pattern
One of the simplest ways to create a sense of pattern is by the regular grouping and repeating of similar units.

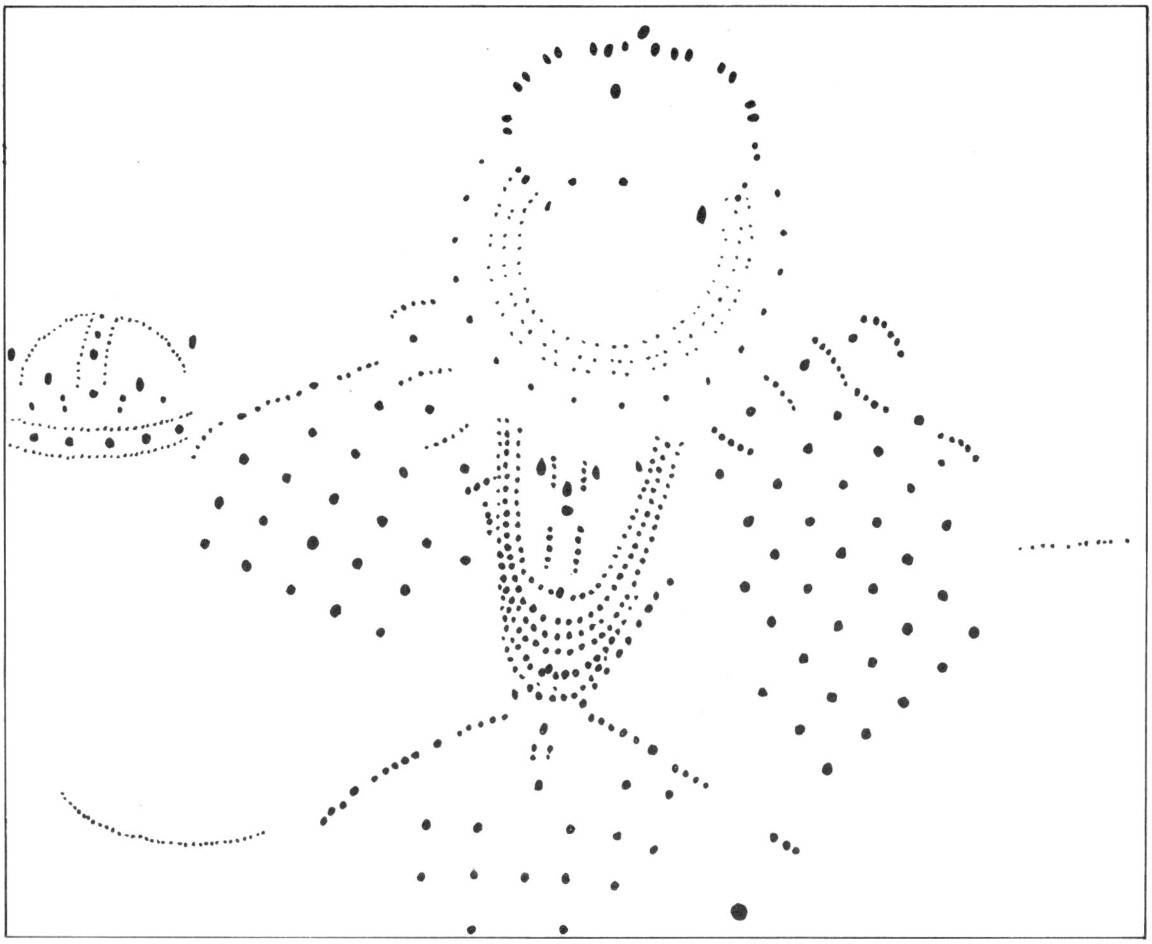

The 'Armada' portrait of Queen Elizabeth I (diagram)
In addition to the pattern value of the points representing the jewels, collar and crown in this diagram, the distribution of jewels on the sleeves is shown to be strictly two-dimensional – i.e. arranged on a completely regular grid which ignores the three-dimensional form of the sleeves.

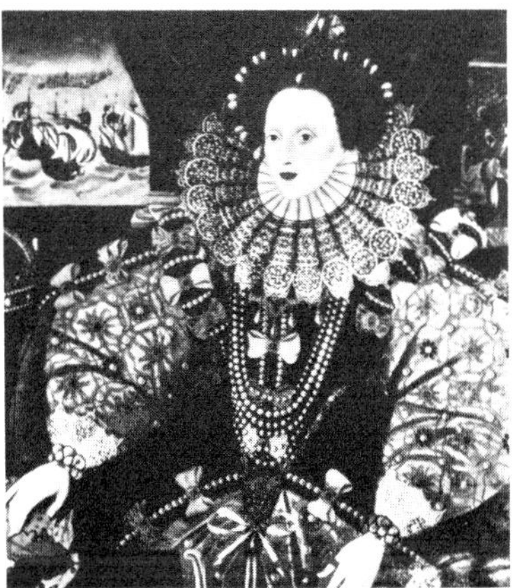

The regularity of this repetition accentuates the effect of rich pattern in the painting – a regularity which is not at all obvious, being disguised by the implication of form.

THE POINT

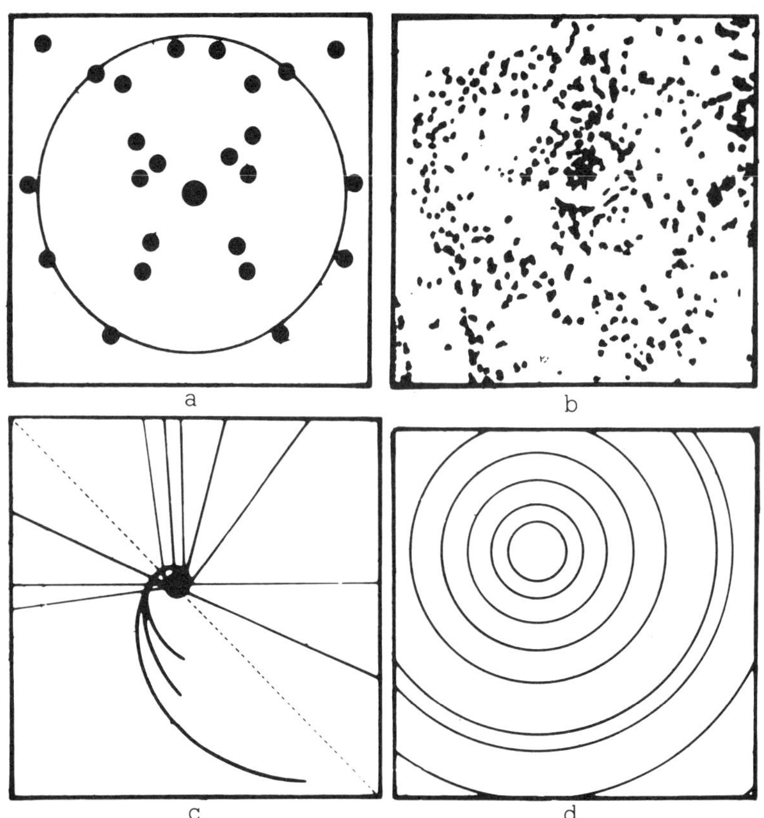

Focal points (diagrams)
The diagrams suggest some ways in which the point may become the focus of the design. The principle of radiation, inseparable from the idea of focus since it is the opposite concept, is of great antiquity. It occurs in Nature and may be observed in the rays of the sun or the arrangement of the petals of a daisy. It is a device employed by artists of all times and countries. The arrangements of focal points may be observed in the following paintings: a, *Mary, Queen of Heaven* (see page 15); b, detail of eye from *Portrait of Mr. A.L.* by Paul Klee (page 25); c, Giotto's *Kiss of Judas*, and d, Bronzino's Allegory (both on opposite page).

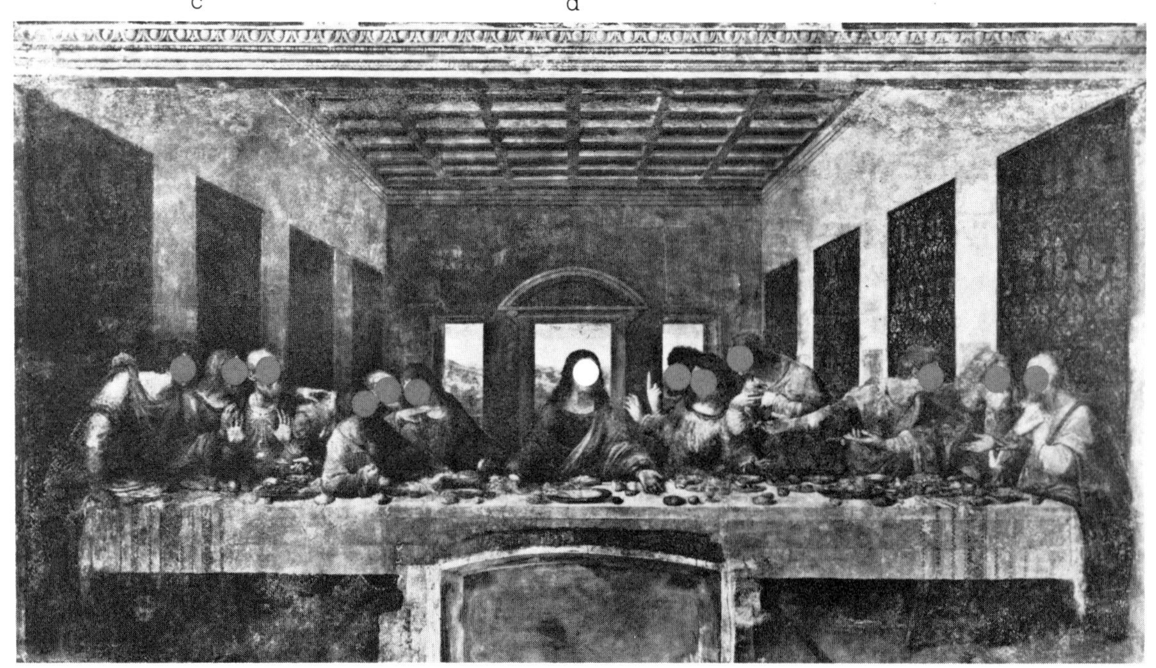

The Point as focus

In many compositions there is a main centre of interest, or focal point, possibly accompanied by subsidiary points, towards which the eye is directed by various subtle means (e.g. the direction of gaze of the figure, or the use of colour differentiation, or tonal contrast) and along various routes, so that we are tempted to explore the byways of the area as well as to arrive at the main centre or centres of interest. This visual journey may be made in a variety of ways depending on the starting point.

Venus, Cupid, Folly and Time: Bronzino (diagram)
In this allegory the action radiates from the kiss of the principal figures: the concentric circles show how the poses have been adapted to produce the result. Not only limbs but projections of gaze draw our eyes to the focal point. It is rather as if a spotlight is focused on the joined heads, leaving the perimeters progressively darker.

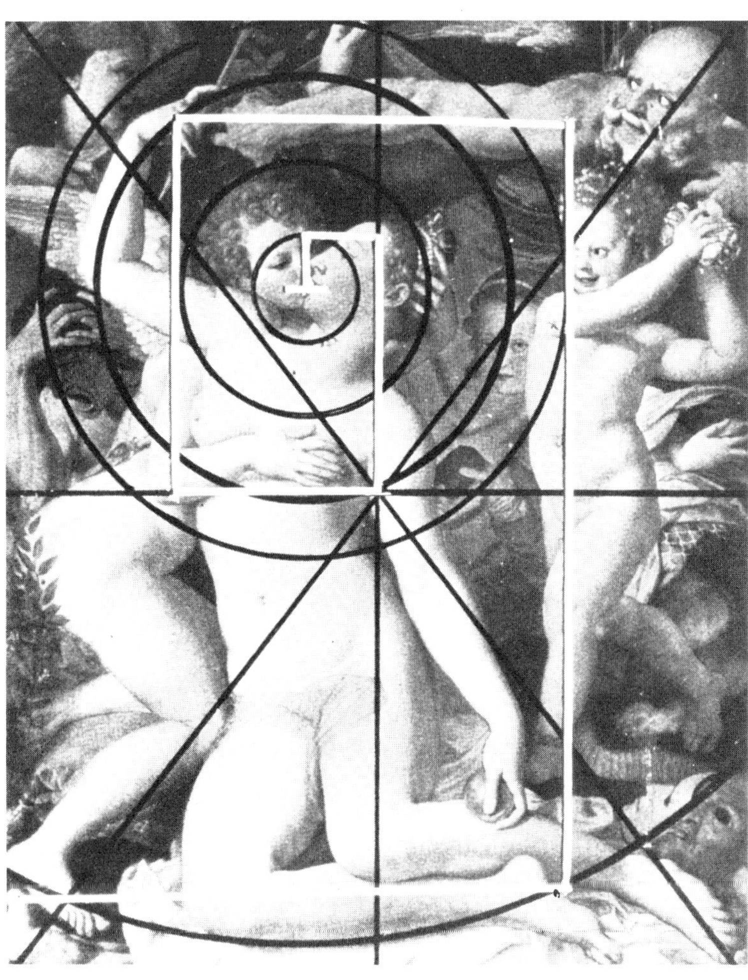

The Last Supper: Leonardo da Vinci (diagram)
Although this painting deteriorated badly (due to faulty technique) even during Leonardo's own lifetime, enough of its dramatic force remains to charge the composition with powerful emotions, in the midst of which the figure of Christ is silhouetted in lonely isolation. The head of Christ is the focal point of the composition. Not only do the perspective lines converge to meet at this point (or radiate from it) but the individual heads are balanced in groups of three around this centre.

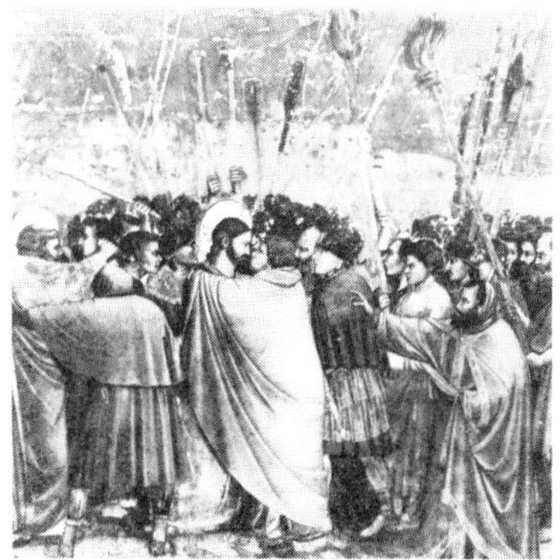

The Kiss of Judas: Giotto
The focal point of this painting again centres on the kiss: a very different kiss. This silent confrontation between good and evil is surrounded by staves, torches, noisy threats and angry gestures, all of which lead our eye inevitably to the timeless moment. (Compare it with *The Last Supper* by Leonardo da Vinci.) In many of his works Giotto expertly directs our eye to the main protagonists in his drama.

THE POINT

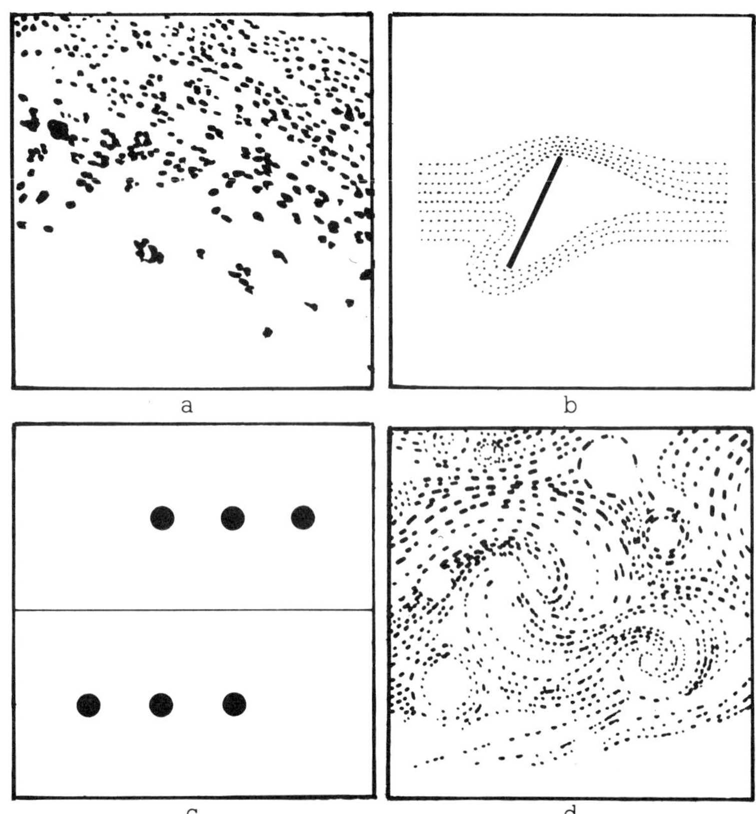

Movement of points (diagram)
(a) These points convey the feeling of existing on an undulating surface and create a rhythmic movement in depth (see Monet's *Field of Poppies*).
(b) Here the movement is clearly controlled – entering from the left, the moving particles meet an obstruction, diverge and eventually flow together again.
(c) This diagram suggests that all three points in the lower half have shifted to the left – a curious phenomenon, since it is only one which has been placed in a different position.
(d) Spiralling points move in a continuous, endless dance through space and time ... (see *Starry Night* by van Gogh, page 23).

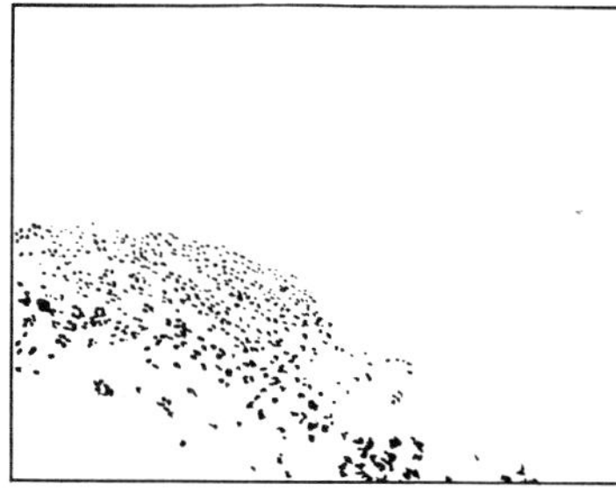

Field of Poppies: Claude Monet (diagram)
Groups of points, close together at the top, gradually separate and move further apart towards the bottom part of the picture, conveying a feeling of rhythmic flowing movement.

The Point as movement

Life without movement is inconceivable, and art is the reflection of life. Even 20,000 years ago the first artists, working in the recesses of their caves by the flickering flames of torches, were concerned with the idea of expressing the movements of the animals on the walls.

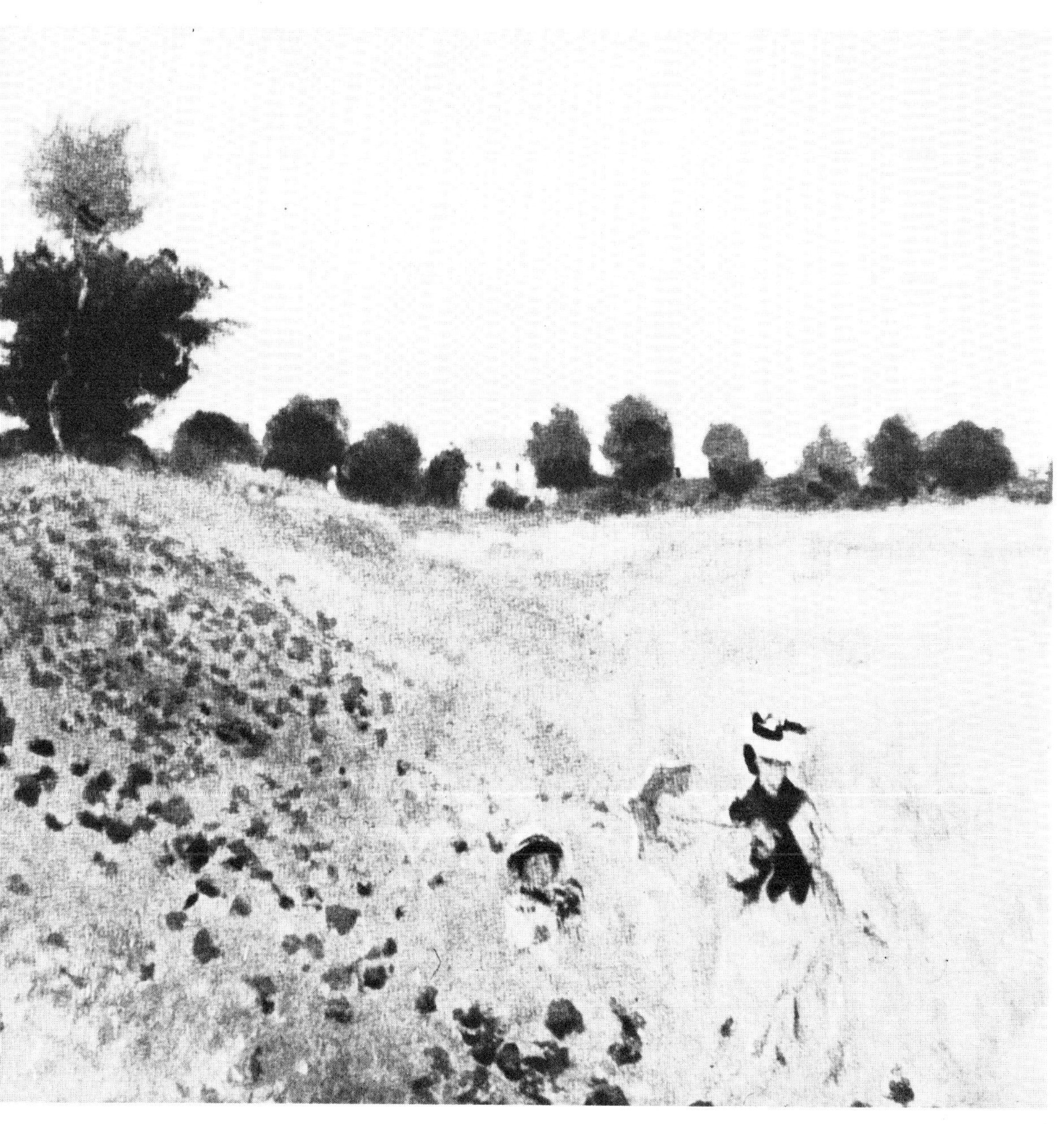

Field of Poppies: Claude Monet
In this painting by the 'Dean of Impressionism', which is full of fresh air and daylight, the red poppies – apparently clustering closer together as they approach eye level – help to describe the rolling movement of the pasture land. This sense of movement, an essential in painting Nature, is complemented by the relationship between the two figures at the top and bottom of the hill – the beginning and end of the journey through the poppies.

THE POINT

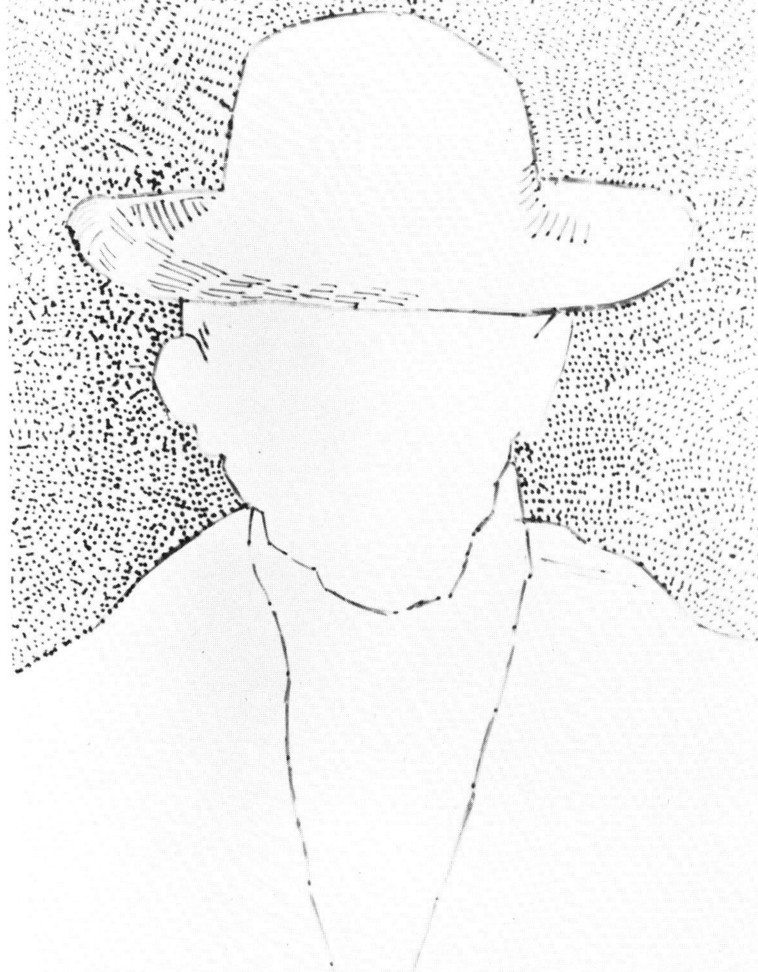

Peasant of the Camargue: Vincent van Gogh (diagram)
Working with reed pens, Van Gogh not only broke down the form into swirling lines, but treated space itself as an orchestration of spinning atomic particles – coalescing and separating in the constant agitation. Disturbed by the introduction of the peasant's head, the moving points re-arrange themselves to occupy the available space.

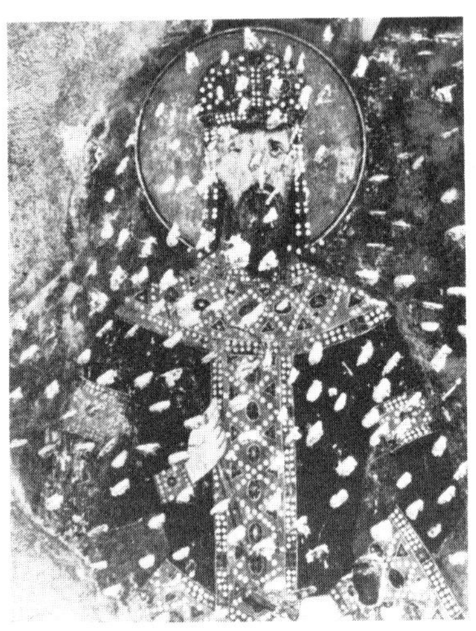

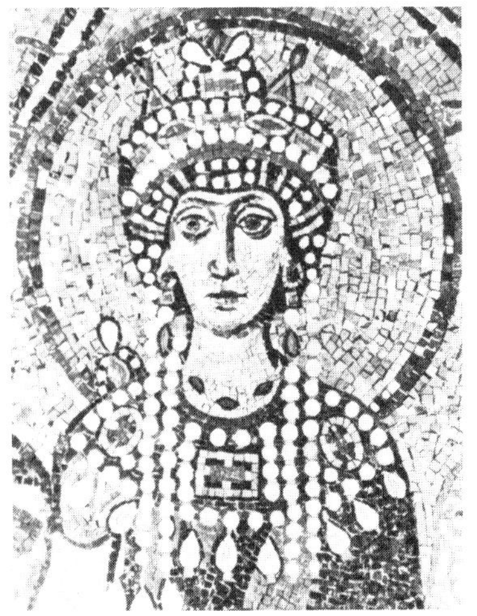

Mosaic of the Empress Theodora, Ravenna
This detail from the mosaic of Theodora and retinue in S. Vitale, Ravenna, not only demonstrates the pattern value of the point in the symmetrical arrangements of the jewelled headdress and collar, but also the myriad points of light striking the eye from the *tesserae* give a feeling of active movement and generally activate the whole composition by their dynamic placing – here the points create a combination of pattern and movement.

Fresco of King Milutin, Yugoslavia
In this portrait of King Milutin, founder of a monastery at Prizren, the light-coloured points that cover the painting are holes made to carry the coating of plaster which had subsequently been used to obliterate the frescoes. The result of this destructive hacking is the creation of a new pattern of points, flowing in an informal rhythmic movement superimposed on the original pattern of points, which was a pattern of strict formality.

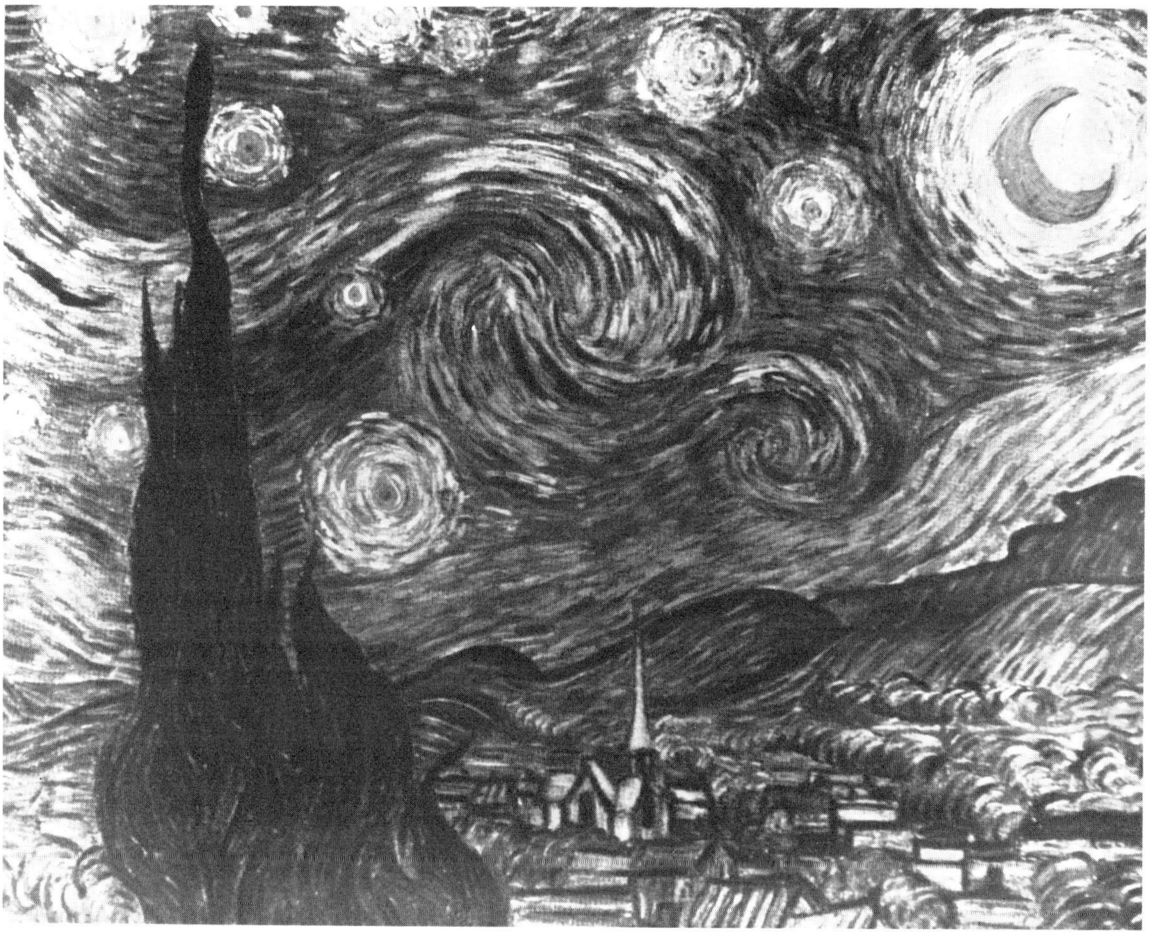

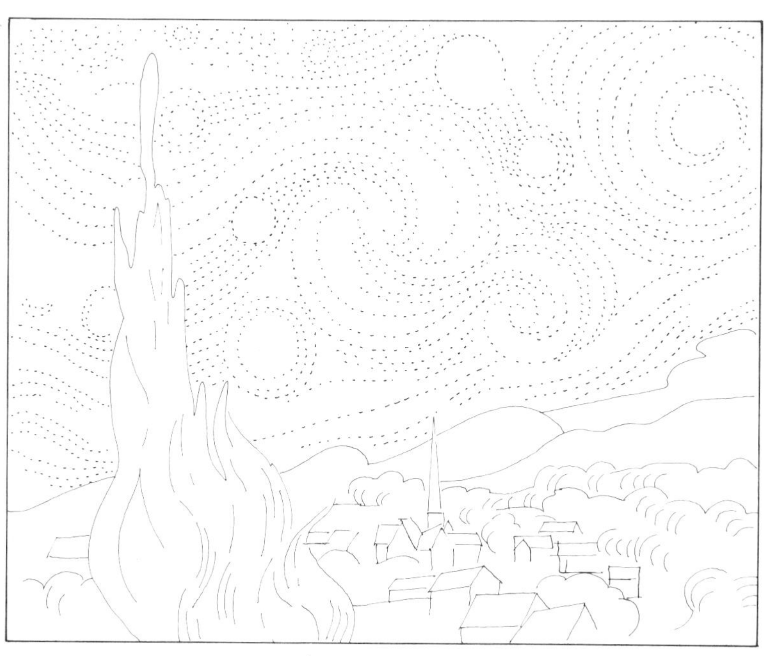

Starry Night: Vincent van Gogh
Myriad stars, organized into spirals, twist and turn across the sky – the points suggest the orbital patterns of the planets as they sing their way through the night sky.

THE POINT

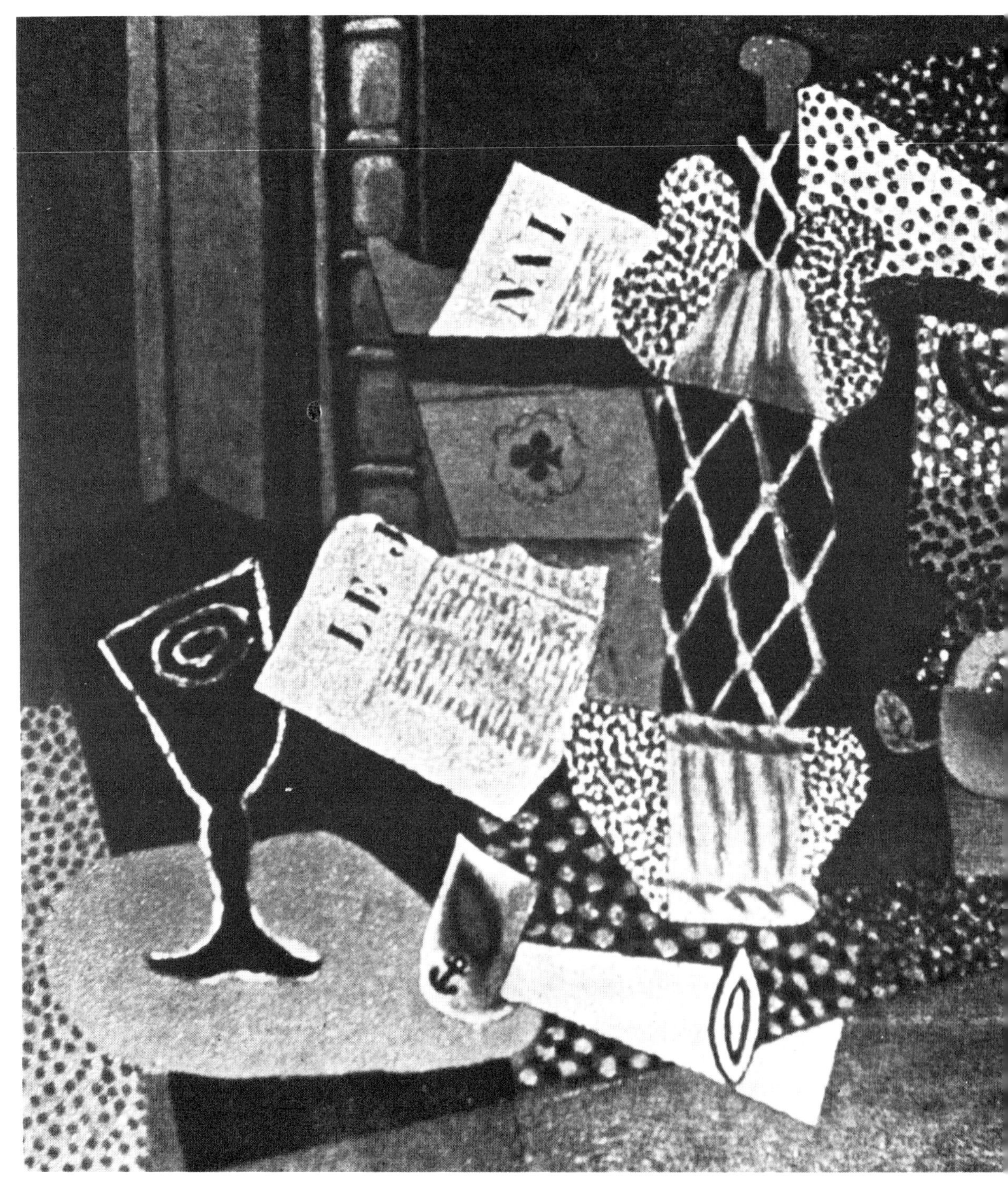

The Point as texture

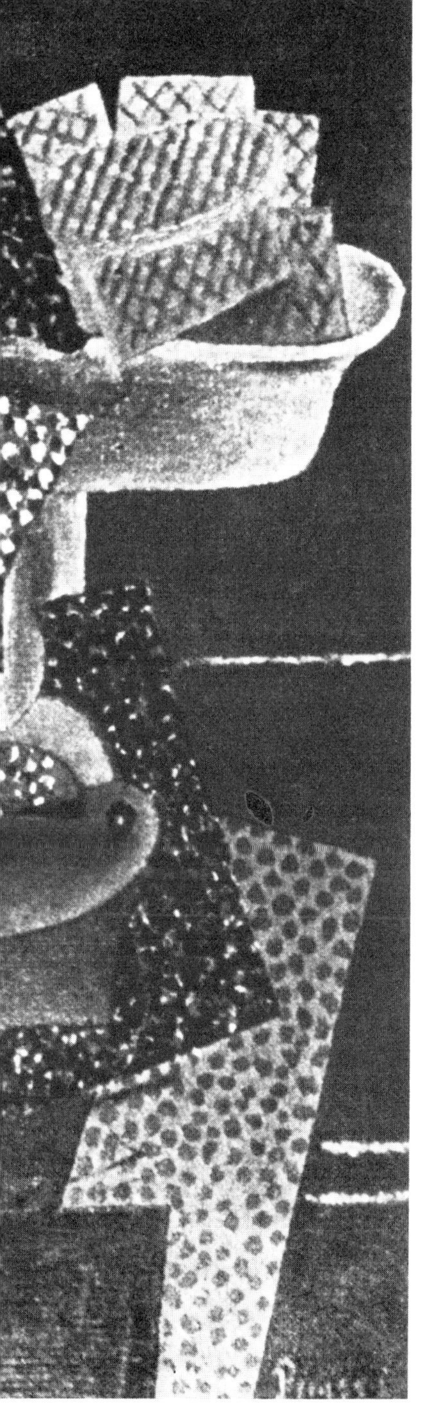

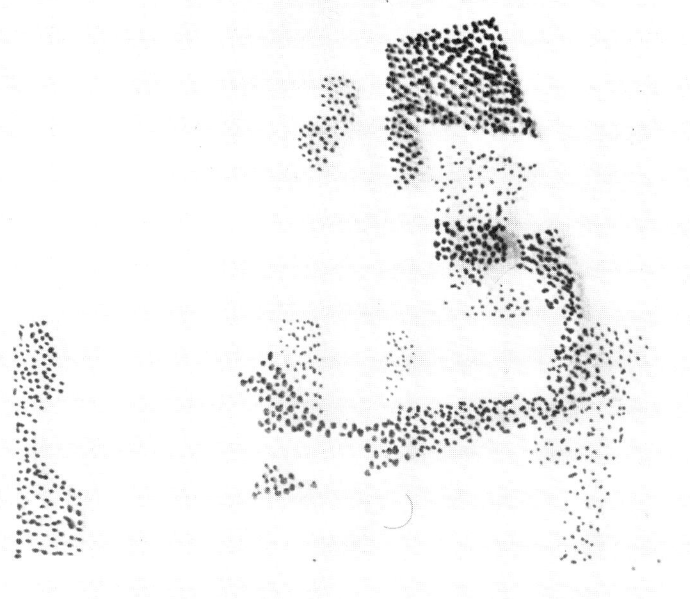

Still Life with a Bottle of Maraschino: Pablo Picasso
Both Picasso and Braque, during the period of Cubism known as Synthetic Cubism, used various means to introduce textured surfaces into their work. Newsprint, wallpaper, sandpaper, marble, and grained wood were some of the textured surfaces employed. Possibly owing something to the work of the Pointillists (see Colour), they also used the device of identifying specific areas of their work by covering the area with *points*, as seen in the analysis (above) of this painting by Picasso. The composition is derived from the 'papiers collés' frequently used by Picasso between 1912 and 1914 – this is a typical composition in the style known as 'Synthetic Cubism'. The reconstruction of the objects is achieved by the use of flat planes resembling cut-out papers, and the flatness is emphasized by various means such as the imitation of fragments of newsprint, or by stippling points of colour on the surface. The subject is still present in the painting but now plays a secondary role.

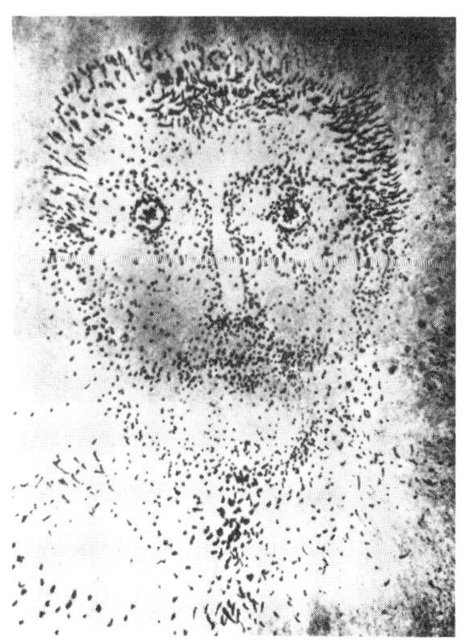

Portrait of Mr. A.L.: Paul Klee
Paul Klee experimented fully with all the elements of composition, including the point. In this one work, by an impressive economy of means, he conveys many of the qualities that the point is capable of expressing – e.g. movement, space, form, texture, and human emotion.

LINE

Because of its versatility line is indispensable to the painter, sculptor or designer. Lines can be active or static, continuous or broken, curved or straight, broad or delicate, light or dark. This rich linear vocabulary is employed to express various aims: to display emotion or movement, to delineate contour or structure, to describe pattern and texture. In addition, line may also evoke a feeling of space, through linear perspective (see Chapter 3); or to create geometric divisions (see Chapter 4); or to convey direct information, as in a graph or in writing. However, one would not expect to find any of these qualities of line used singly or exclusively by the artist, nor to find all the possibilities exploited in one work. Some of the qualities of line, such as the ability to describe form, can be clearly observed and appreciated in drawings, but it is in paintings that it has been most expressively used.

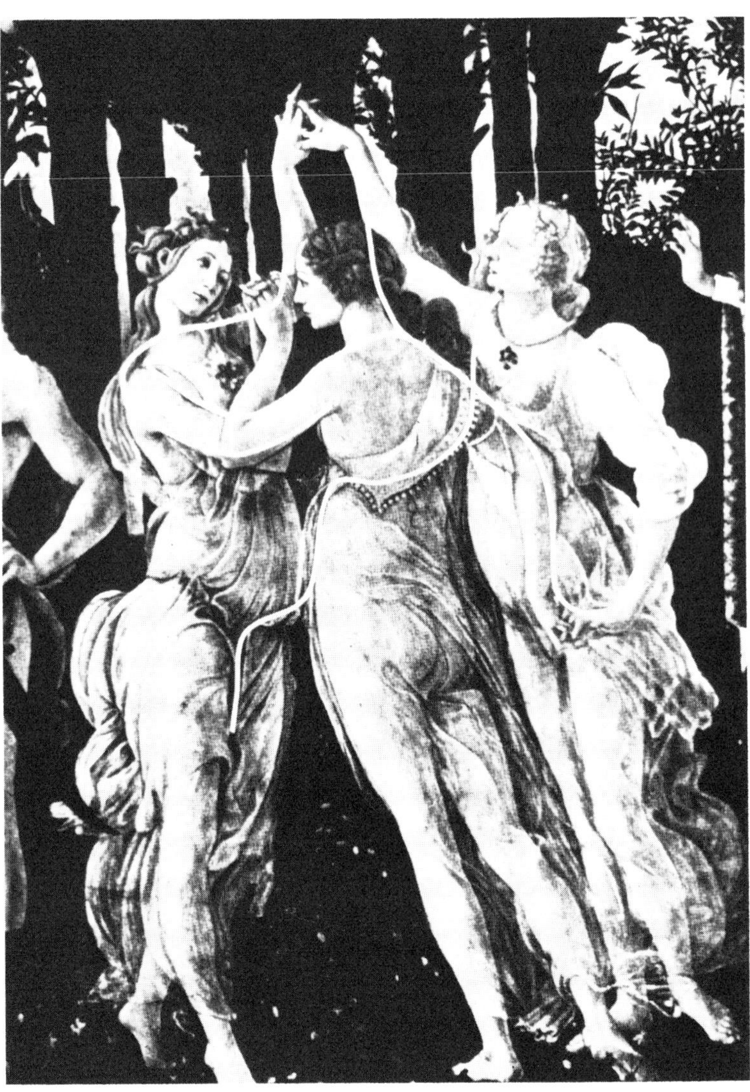

Primavera (detail): Botticelli (diagram) In *Primavera* the linear rhythms dance and interweave in counterpoint to produce a lyrical dreamy quality. Lines weave a hypnotic spell in praise of paganism.

Line used to express feelings and emotions

Botticelli and Blake were two of the great masters in the use of line to express feelings and emotions.

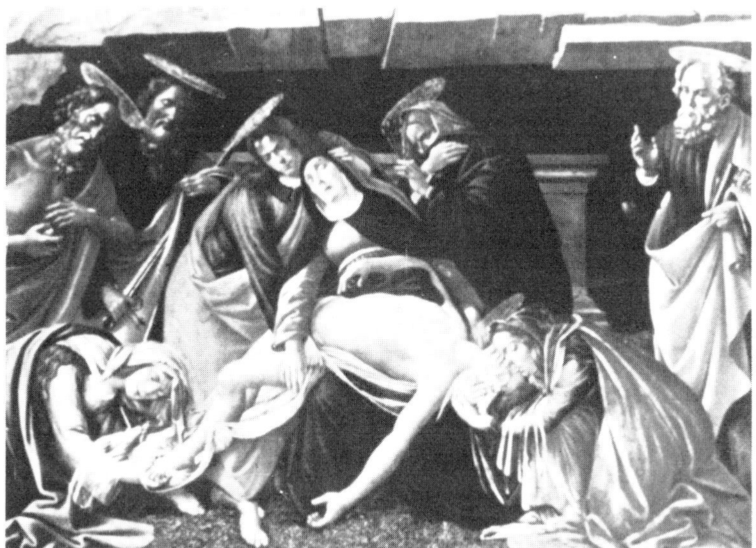

Pietà: Botticelli
No longer dreamy lines: here linear thrusts oppose each other at every turn, creating a harsh and disturbing quality.

Weeping Woman: Pablo Picasso
The harsh angular lines of Picasso's *Weeping Woman* are used to create and convey disturbing emotions. As the conflicting straight lines describe the grief of the woman, so they are used to create emotional disturbance in the spectator.

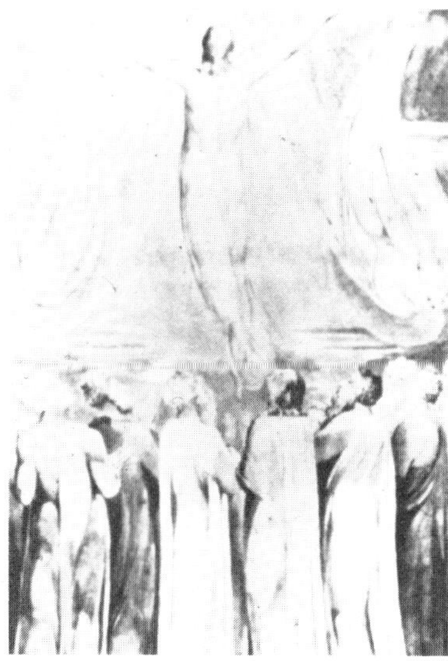

Ascension: William Blake
Blake's faith in line amounted to an almost religious belief – the harsh and wiry lines of rectitude became, for him, almost the straight and narrow path. In the *Ascension* Christ soars triumphantly to Heaven borne on upward-thrusting lines, emphasized by the downward sweep of the flanking angels.

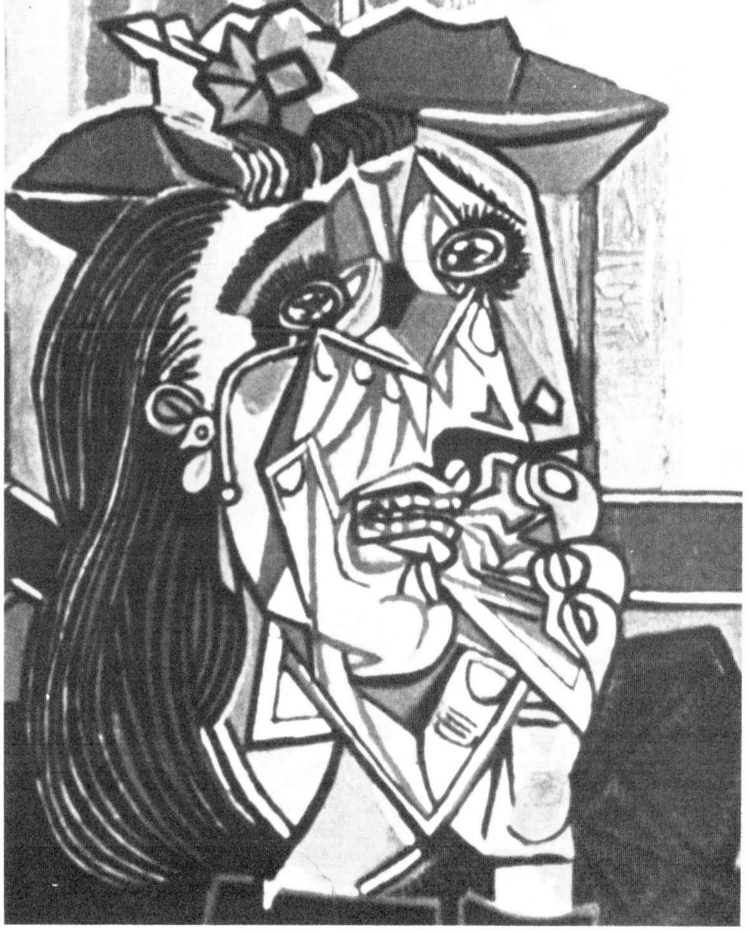

LINE

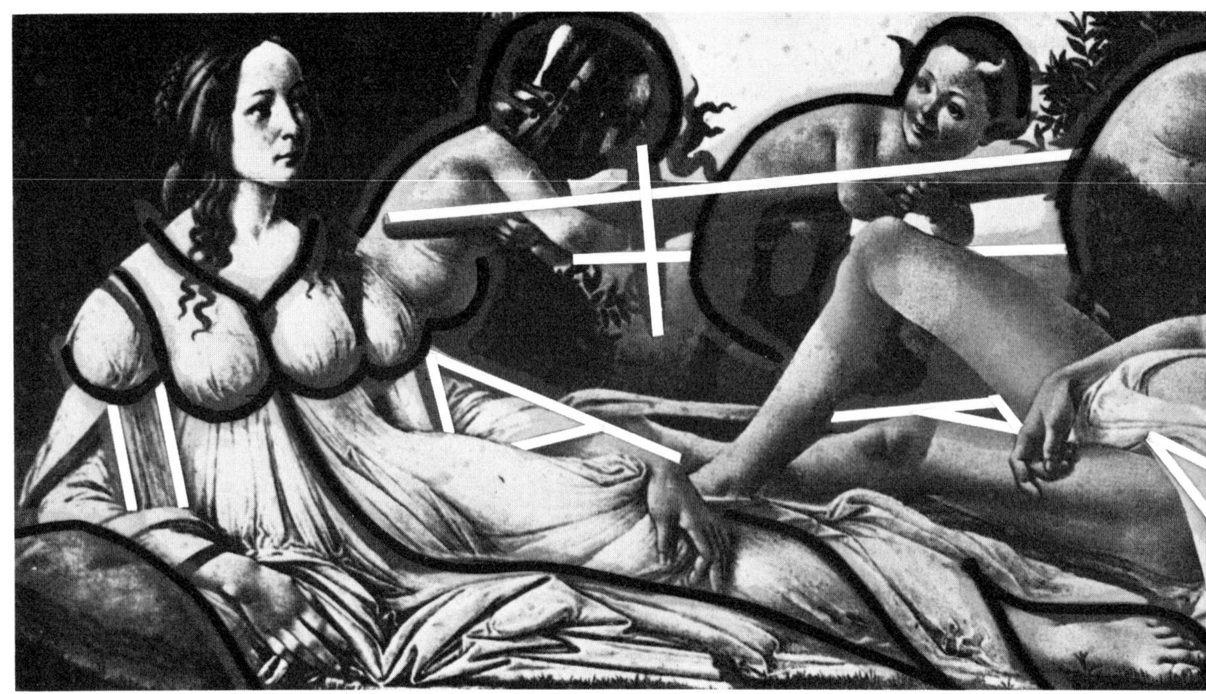

Mars and Venus: Botticelli (diagram)

Botticelli's *Mars and Venus* is a long horizontal shape in which the emphasis is on the languorous line, as befits the subject. But analysis of the curved lines (shown in black) reveals a complex linear construction. Whereas the figure of Venus is composed of sleepy and slow-moving curves, the three baby satyrs in the background – who have stolen Mars' lance and helmet – are based on a sequence of short jerky rhythms which rise to a crescendo. This is a fascinating composition of long, slow curves (inaction) contrasted against the minor theme of short sharp curves (action). The difference is rather like that between the slow motion of waves and the agitation of ripples. But the painting is not entirely made up of curves, as shown by the analysis of the straight lines (shown in white). In the foreground we find short and broken straight lines, incapable of exercising much authority, compared to the strong assertive lines of the background, which bridge the gap between the two main contestants. These straight lines help to underline and symbolize the content of the painting – the overcoming of Mars' strength and virility by the Goddess of Love.

Line as a compositional element

From the paintings we have already seen it is apparent that straight lines and curved lines convey different qualities. Now let us analyse how artists can exploit this difference.

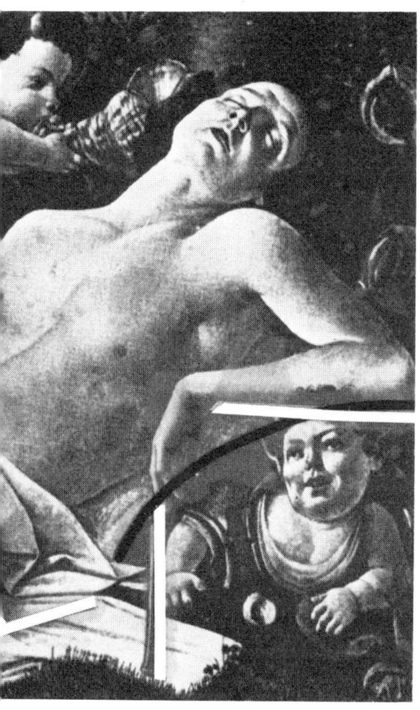

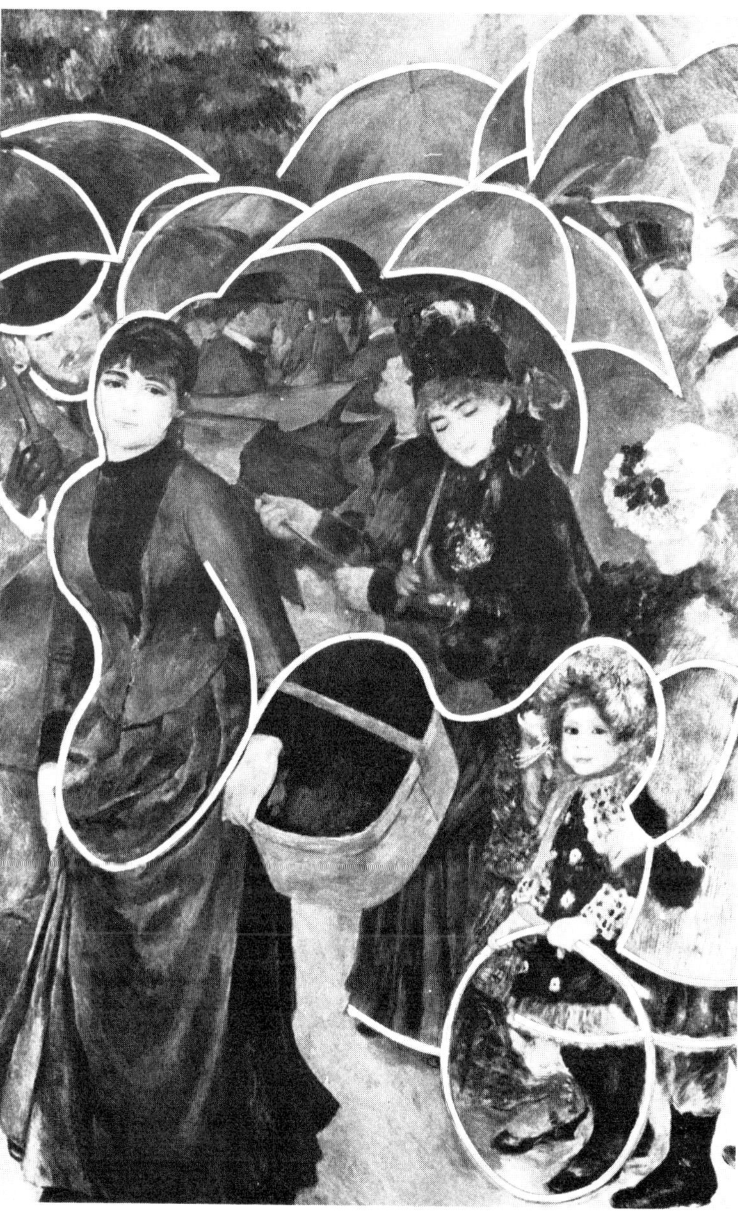

The Umbrellas: Pierre Renoir (diagram)

Although generally regarded as one of the Impressionists, Renoir became dissatisfied with their superficial approach to form and formal structure. In this painting, *The Umbrellas*, he has tried to impose a sense of order on the scene of a bustling crowd, which a true Impressionist would have seen as a much more casual arrangement dictated by individual circumstances rather than created by the artist.

An analysis of the curved lines shows how he has used the repetition of segments of a circle as a means of giving a sense of pattern and formal arrangement to the composition.

LINE

The Red Tree: Piet Mondrian (1909–10) is a representation of the linear aspects of the branches of a tree.

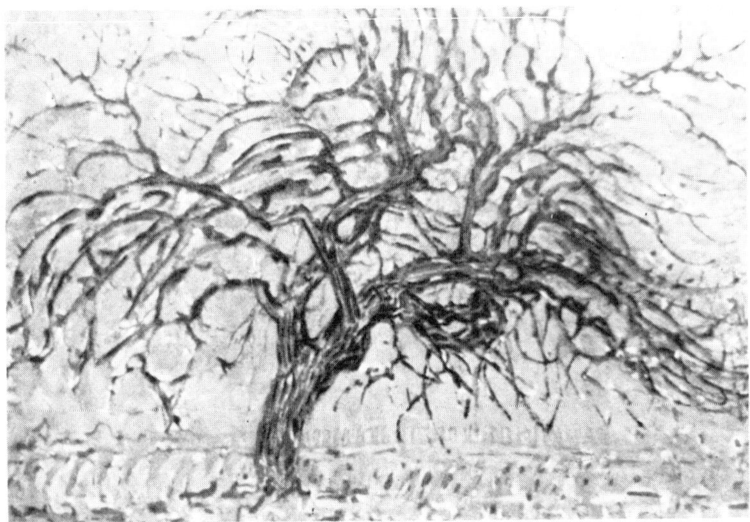

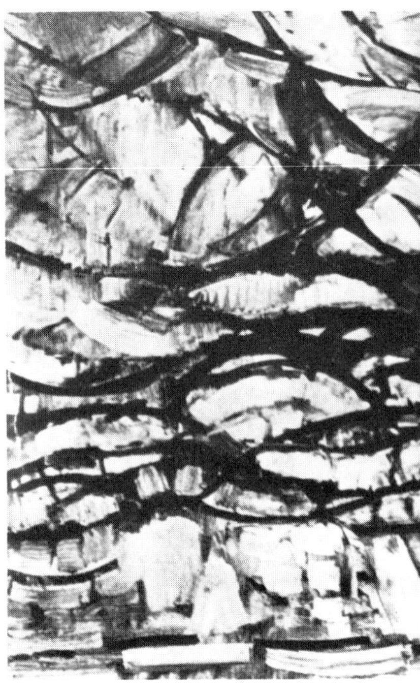

The Grey Tree: Piet Mondrian
A few years later, Mondrian had begun to simplify and organize the lines (branches) he has selected in order to emphasize their similarities of curvature. By using only those lines which are related in terms of curvature, Mondrian's analysis is moving him towards abstraction.

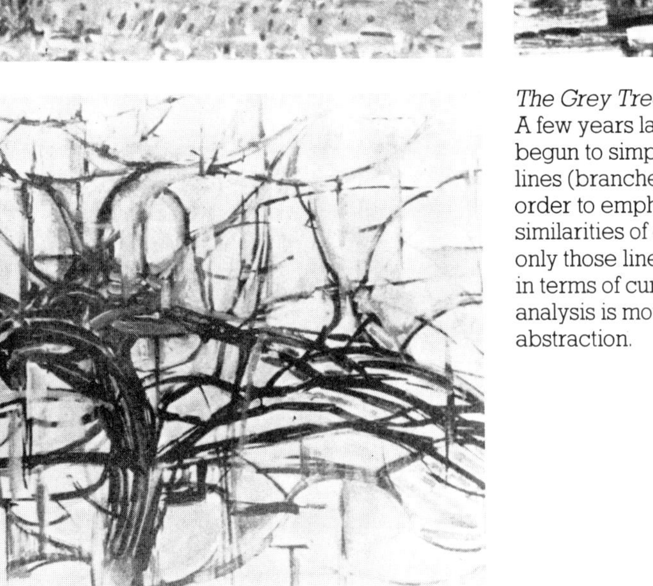

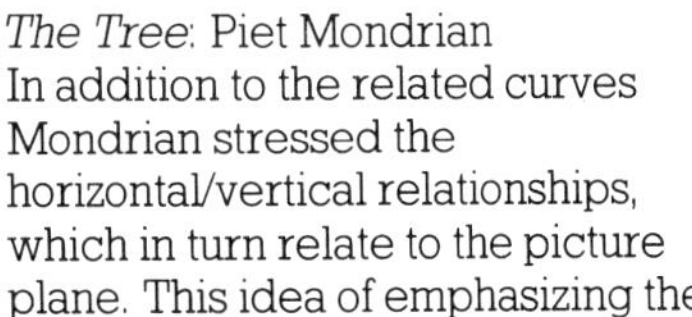

The Tree: Piet Mondrian
In addition to the related curves Mondrian stressed the horizontal/vertical relationships, which in turn relate to the picture plane. This idea of emphasizing the horizontal/vertical was originated by Cézanne and developed by Picasso and Braque during the Analytical phase of Cubism. Mondrian subsequently pursued this idea to its logical conclusion.

The line analysed

All painting is in one way or another an analysis (some analyses are, of course, more specific than others), and all painters select from the seen or imagined image those aspects of line/tone/colour necessary to give visual form to their concept. Mondrian and Klee both use line to analyse their image.

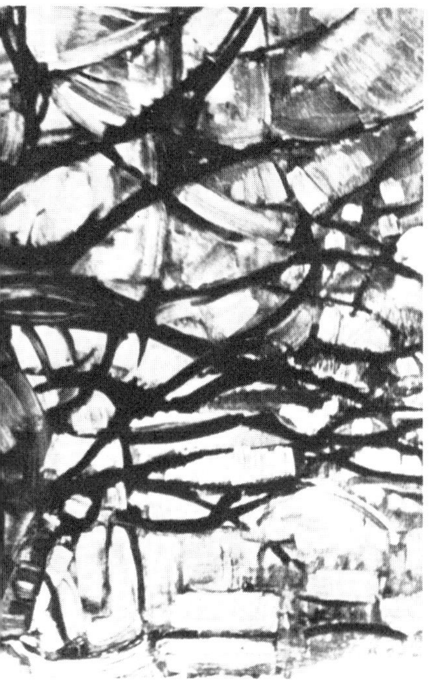

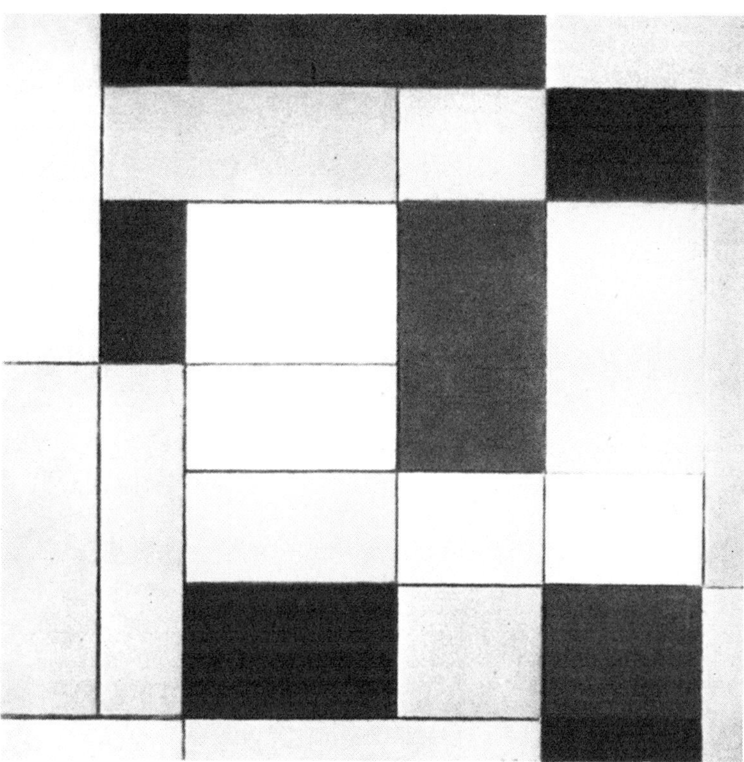

Composition in Grey, Red, Yellow & Blue: Piet Mondrian
His work shows a continuous and gradual move towards isolating the related lines of the composition still further, eventually arriving at a tightly knit linear analysis which emphasizes the vertical/horizontal elements.

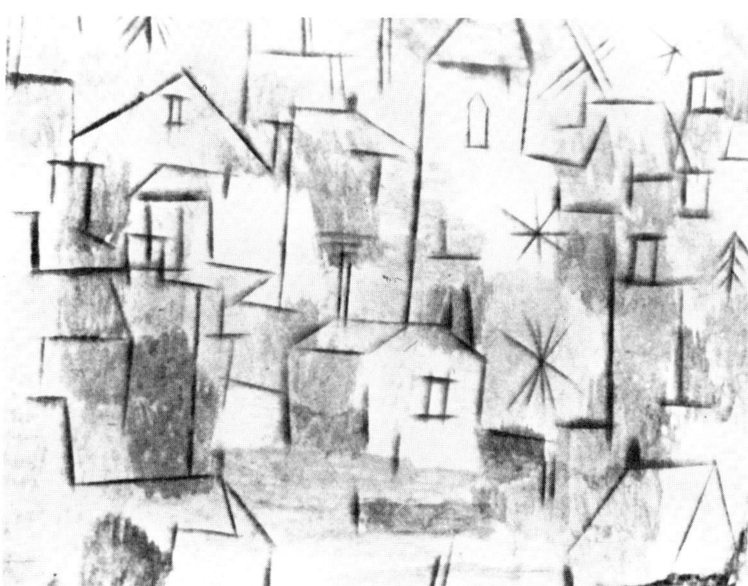

Houses in a Landscape: Paul Klee
Klee produced many architectural works. In *Houses in Landscape* he emphasizes the static quality of architecture by accenting the near verticals and horizontals. In his writing he suggests that there is no such thing as a purely dynamic architecture. Klee made a number of linear analyses of this work, reducing the composition to the straight line components in order to explain the function of the different linear elements. This analytical approach was a consistent feature of Klee's thinking and formed the basis of his teaching as well as of his own work.

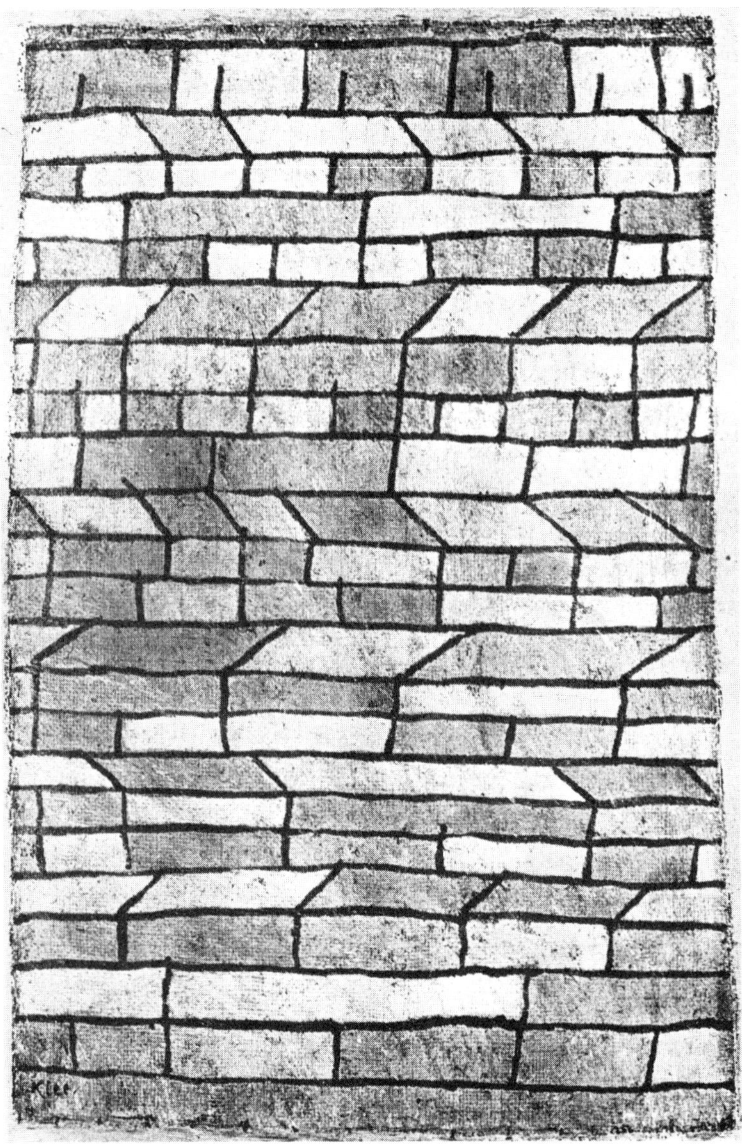

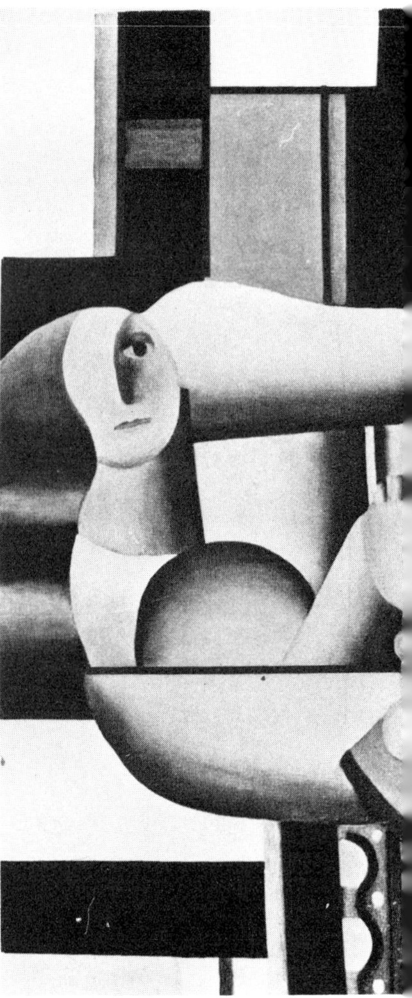

Group of Huts: Paul Klee
Very many of Klee's works are based on a linear structure – some more obviously than others. In this case Klee uses another favourite motif, that of exploiting ambiguity of spatial relationship. 'Some of the forms move outward, some inward.'

Line as structure

Throughout history many artists, including the Ancient Egyptians, have used a linear structure of framework as a set of guidelines to help in creating relationships throughout the composition. These lines are often based on simple geometric divisions of the area to be covered (see Chapter 4). But there are other methods of structuring a painting on a linear plan, such as by using a mathematical grid. However, a composition based on such a simple system as a brick wall could be rather obvious and predictable.

Klee dealt very fully with the structural concept in his lectures to his students and in his own work, examining the structural possibilities of organic forms, cellular and anatomical as well as mathematical. He wrote 'Regularly-measured multiplication is stagnant.' However, this predictable aspect of regular measurement may be easily overcome by distortion of the grid lines in various ways, e.g. twisting and warping.

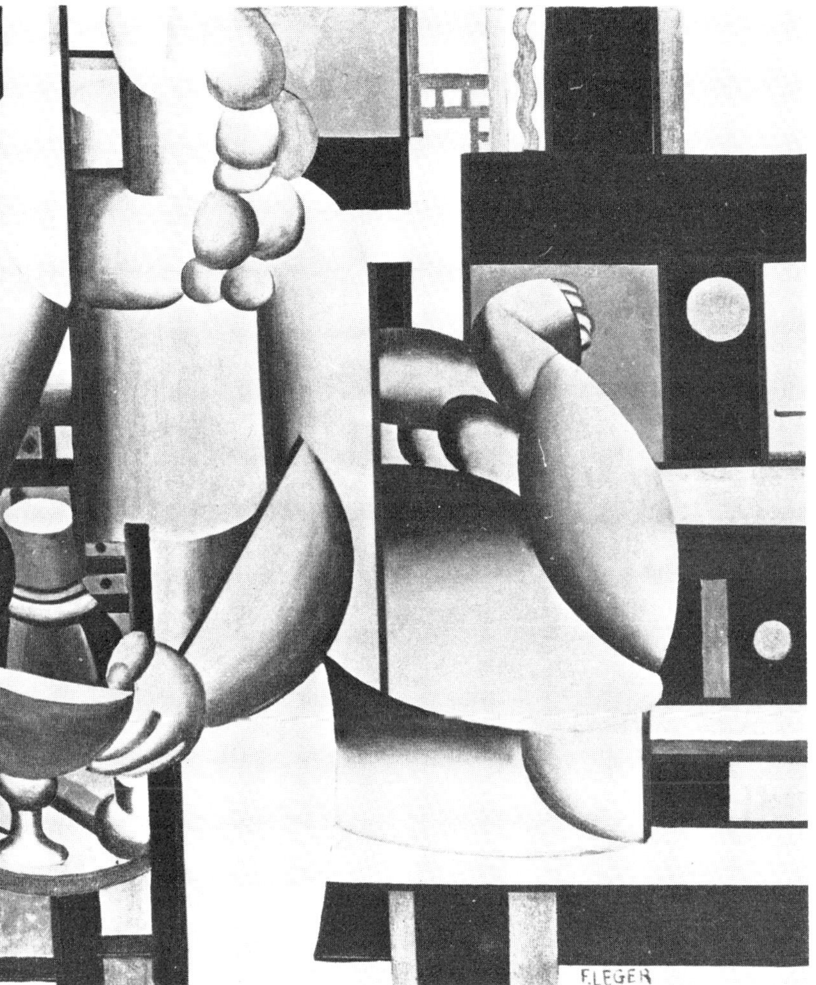

Two Women and Still Life: Fernand Léger (diagram)
Léger bases his work on a system of vertical and horizontal lines – a kind of scaffolding which holds the other elements into a firm composition. The severe formality of the scaffolding also reflects Léger's interest in machine-like forms, which can also be seen in his approach to the human figures, which appear as mechanized robots.

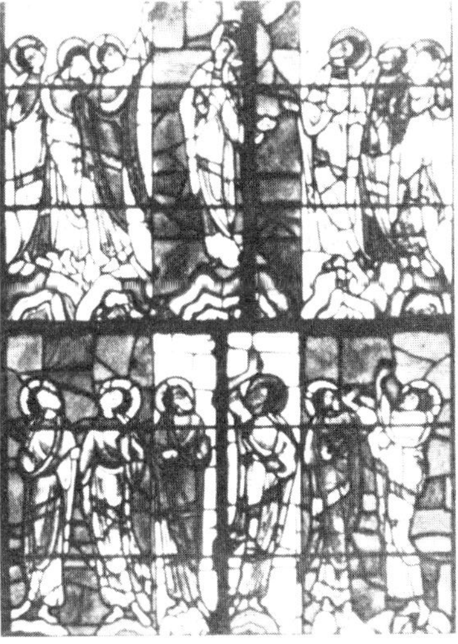

Assumption of Mary: eleventh-century stained glass window, Le Mans
In stained glass, the leading that holds the glass together forms a physically structural framework which, seen against the light, appears as a powerful linear element in the overall design – an element which must be considered by the artist both as part of the design and as part of the structure.

LINE

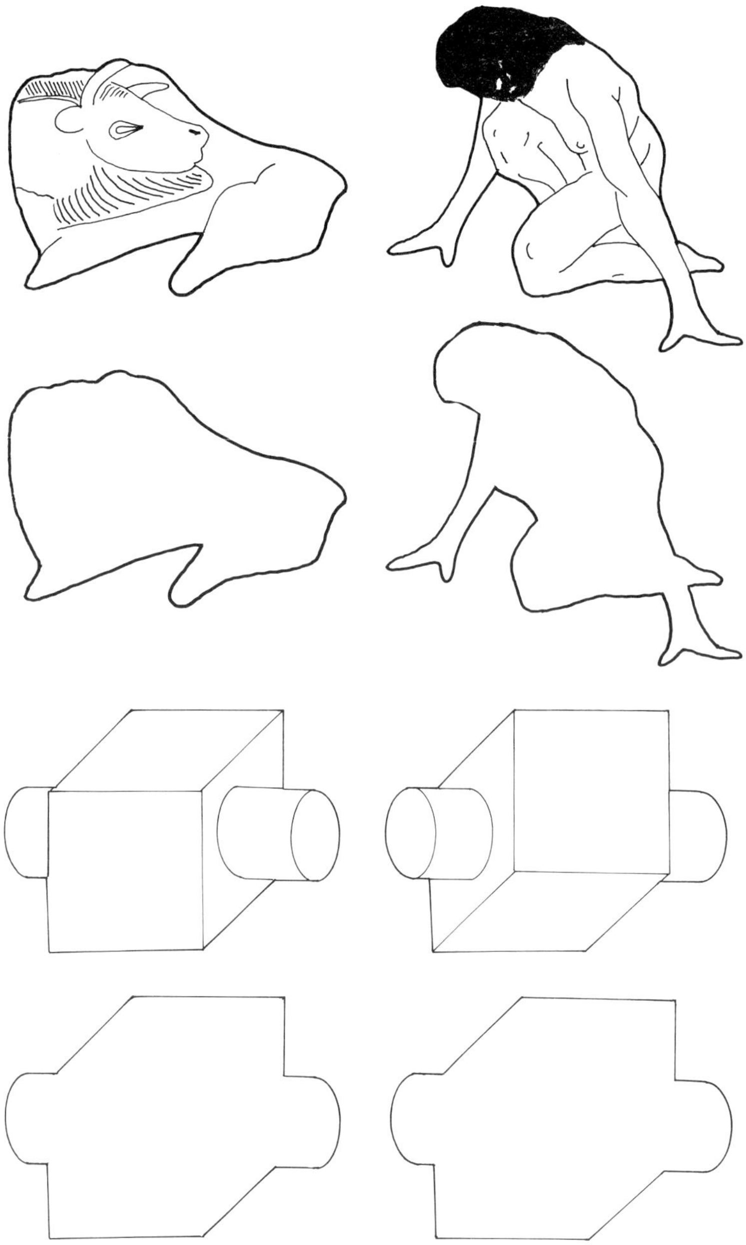

Outlines (diagram)
When four shapes are drawn by outline only, the first and second are virtually meaningless and have a superficial resemblance, and the third and fourth look exactly alike. It needs the addition of further lines to make clear that the first was carved by a Paleolithic man; the second drawn by Rodin; and the third and fourth are different views of a cylinder penetrating a cube–one seen from above, the other from below.

So outline provides only limited information, and additional lines

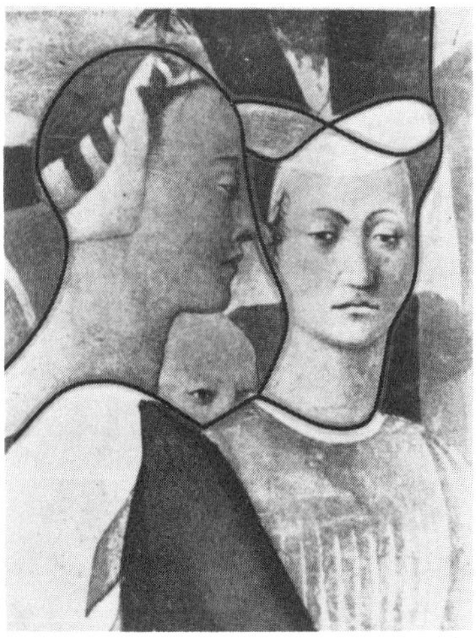

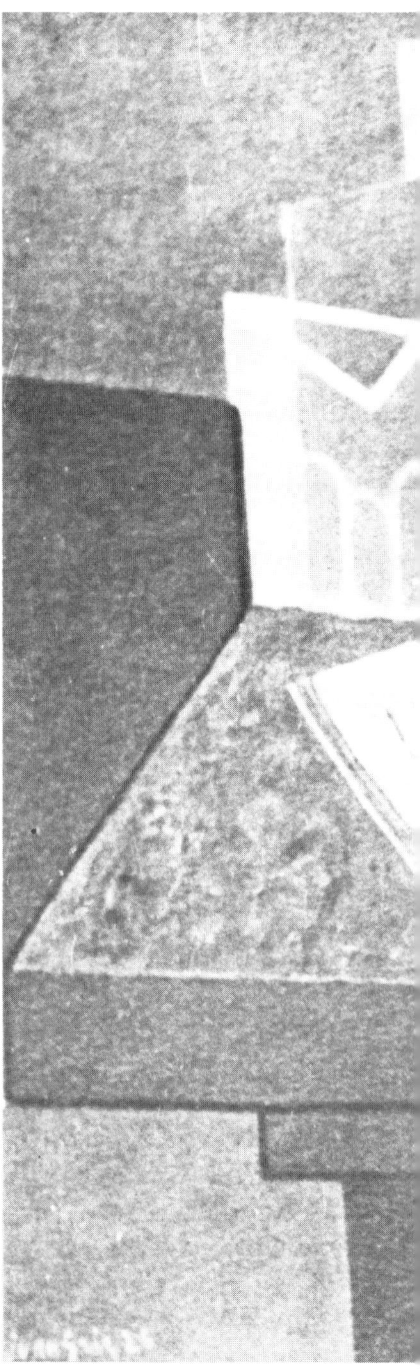

Attendants of the Queen of Sheba (detail): Piero della Francesca (diagram)

The Album: Juan Gris
Both Gris, a twentieth-century Spanish Cubist, and Piero della Francesca use line in the same taut classical way, using contours which are common to several forms or areas, so that one line belongs to tablecloth/book/guitar, or is a guitar/fruit bowl/tablecloth line. The interlocking contours are reminiscent of a jigsaw puzzle.

Line as contour

Lines can express the boundary edges of objects, stating where one thing begins and another ends; but this aspect is of very limited use to the artist, and has little practical application.

can provide further explanation. But drawing a line round an object, simply defining the edge and differentiating one thing from another, is not the way in which the artist works. He is not thinking in terms of words–naming the individual things and telling us their particular areas of occupation–but thinking in terms of visual relationships between the contours of one area and another. This approach can be seen clearly in the work of Piero della Francesca and Juan Gris.

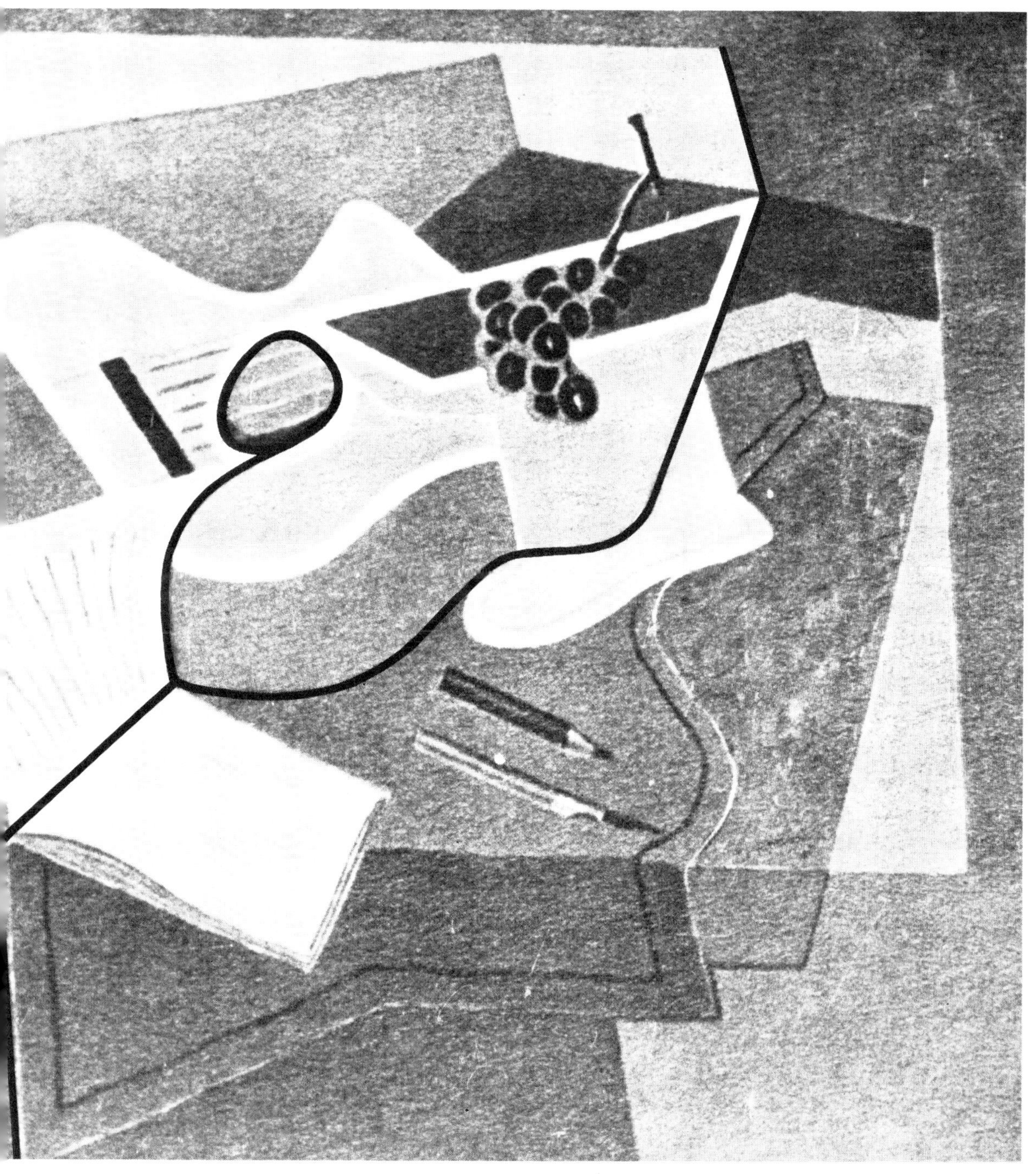

Line expressing transparency

The ability of line to describe form without the use of added tone is not particularly applicable to painting, but has a much wider application in drawing: similarly the use of line to express transparency tends to play a greater part in drawing than painting. But there are notable exceptions. Lines were used to indicate transparency by Paleolithic painters in caves, where one animal merges into and overlaps another and sometimes pregnant animals are shown with young inside them. Both Eskimo and Australian aboriginal artists (and Picasso!) have given us 'X-ray' views of animals, showing the bone structure inside the bodies.

Transparency implies interpenetration – one form penetrating another, which are both seen simultaneously. This idea was used by mediaeval artists as well as the Primitive painters already mentioned; but it was Picasso and Braque, in their Cubist paintings, who developed this idea to a much greater extent, and the simultaneous view became one of the most widely used devices of Cubism.

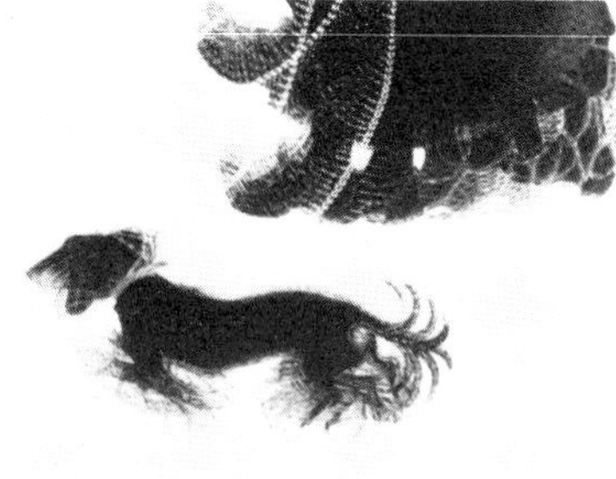

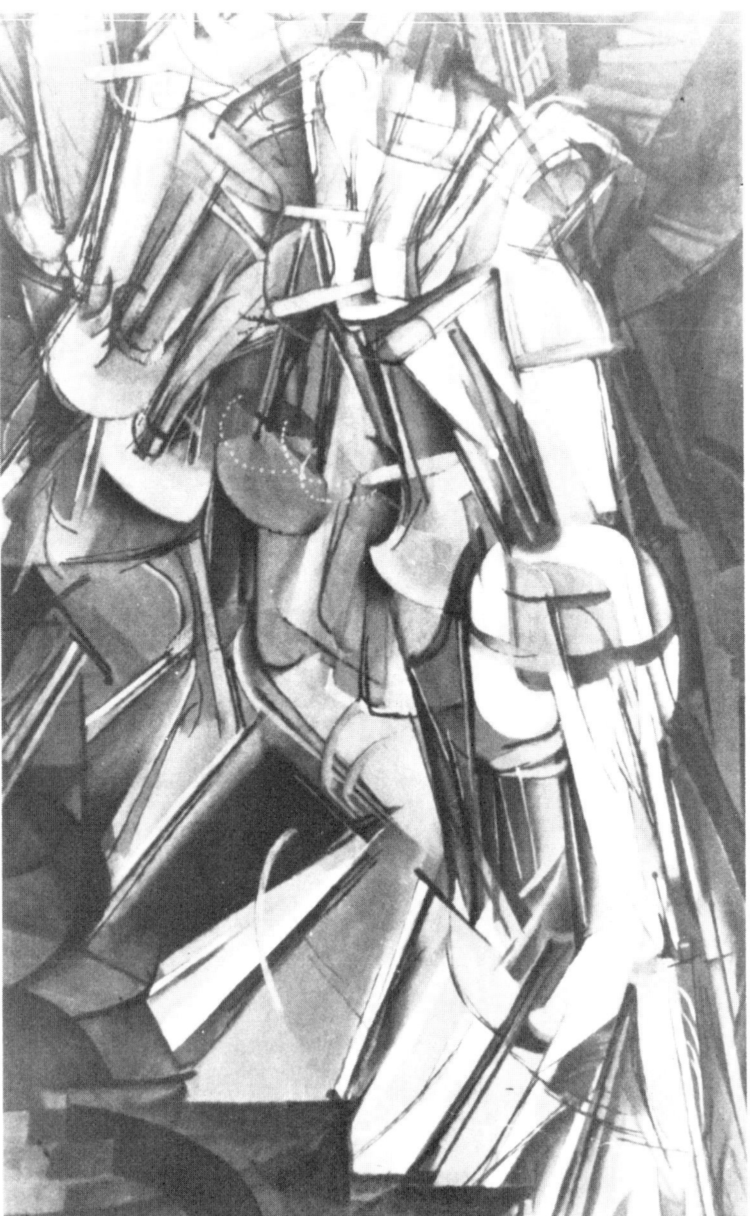

Following the Cubist lead, the technique of the simultaneous view was taken up by the Futurists as a means of expressing *movement* – multiple representation achieved by overlapping lines was used to suggest sequential action or space/time continuum.
Balla exploited this idea in *Dog on a Leash* (above). But perhaps the most famous picture to use the composite simultaneous views was Marcel Duchamp's *Nude descending a Staircase* (right). Here transparency is assumed in the interpenetration of form. Colour is almost as limited as in the previous painting, and so line is called upon again to play a major role, indicating the paths of moving parts and overlapping to indicate sequential shifts of position of the various planes.

Line as movement

We have seen that transparency may be used as a device to express or convey the sense of movement by superimposition of a sequence of images – but lines can convey movement in many other ways. A line generally results from something moving over a surface: the earliest man-made examples may have been a pointed stick used on wet sand, or a finger drawn across soft clay. Whatever the means, the kinetic element is inherent in line. (Writing is a good example of the suggestion of continuous movement that line is capable of conveying.) As part of its nature and origin, line moves. But there are many and varied kinds of movement and some lines are much more active than others.

Paul Klee made many diagrams explaining visually a variety of different ways in which line conveys differing qualities of movement, telling his students at the Bauhaus 'All figuration is movement, because it begins somewhere and ends somewhere'. These diagrams explore the movement of the pendulum, of gases and fluids, of movement and counter-movement of all kinds and their differing characteristics, frequently using the arrow as a graphic symbol to suggest directional movement.

Hieroglyphic Water Plants: Paul Klee
In this painting the pictorial elements are superimposed as a slow-moving rhythmic structure. In fact the painting suggests a musical score, with the plants as the notes and the undulating movement of the background as the staves – giving visual form to the restful sound of rippling water.

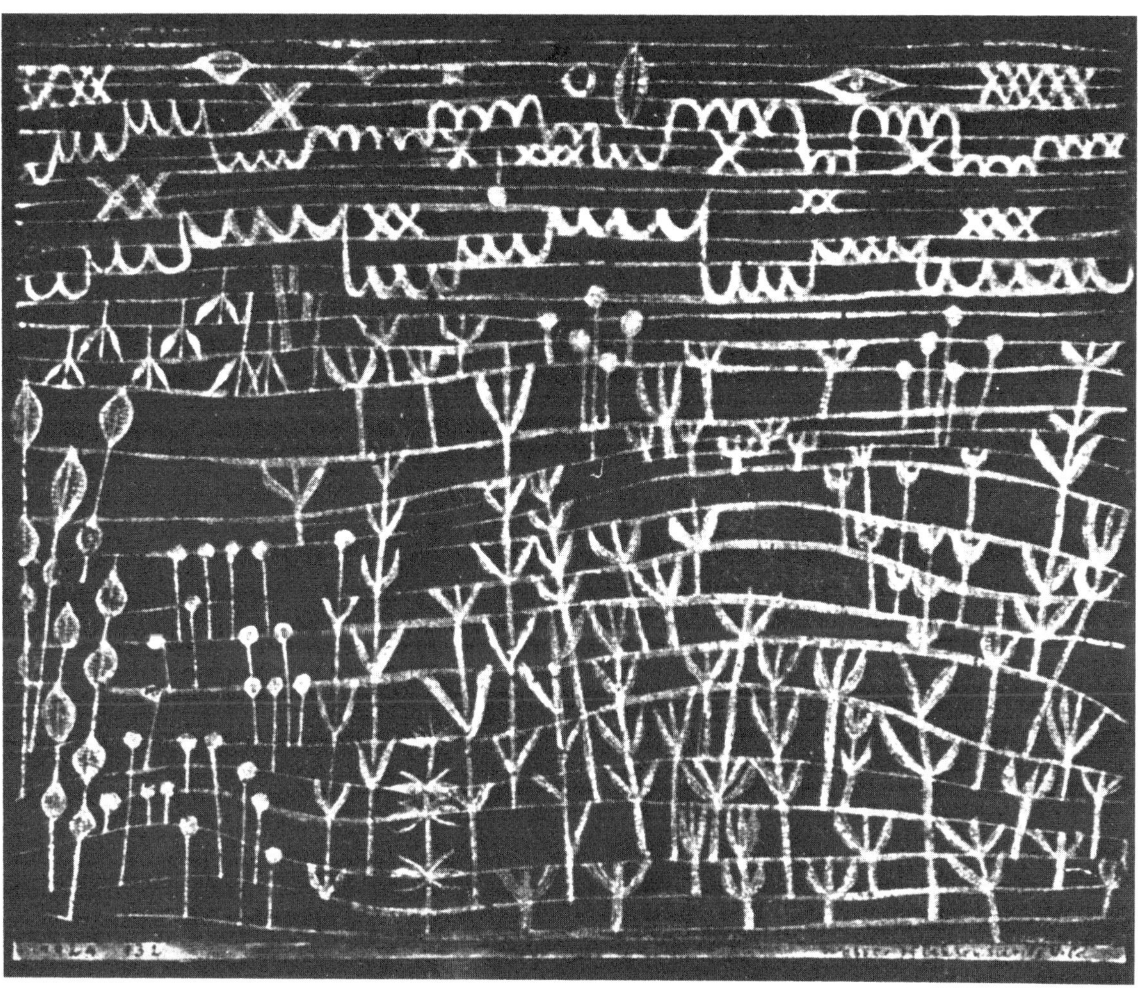

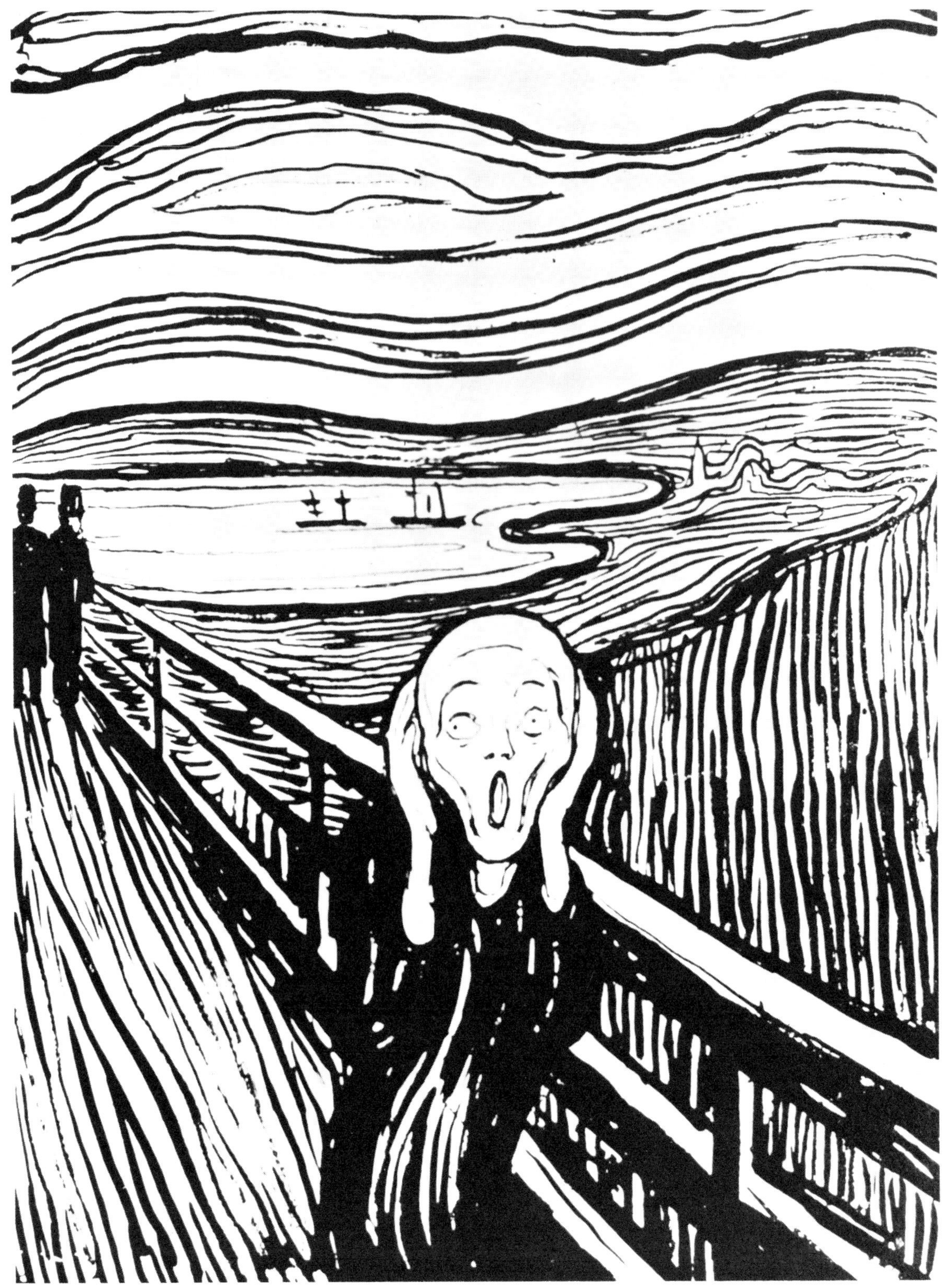

◀ *The Cry*: Edvard Munch
In this lithograph wave-like motion is expressed by the continuously parallel, swirling lines, which powerfully convey the effect of sound waves, disturbing and distorting the visual scene. Munch's use of line anticipates the sinuous curves of Art Nouveau. Art Nouveau artists, and designers in all fields including architecture, made great play with the twisting line, both as pattern and movement.

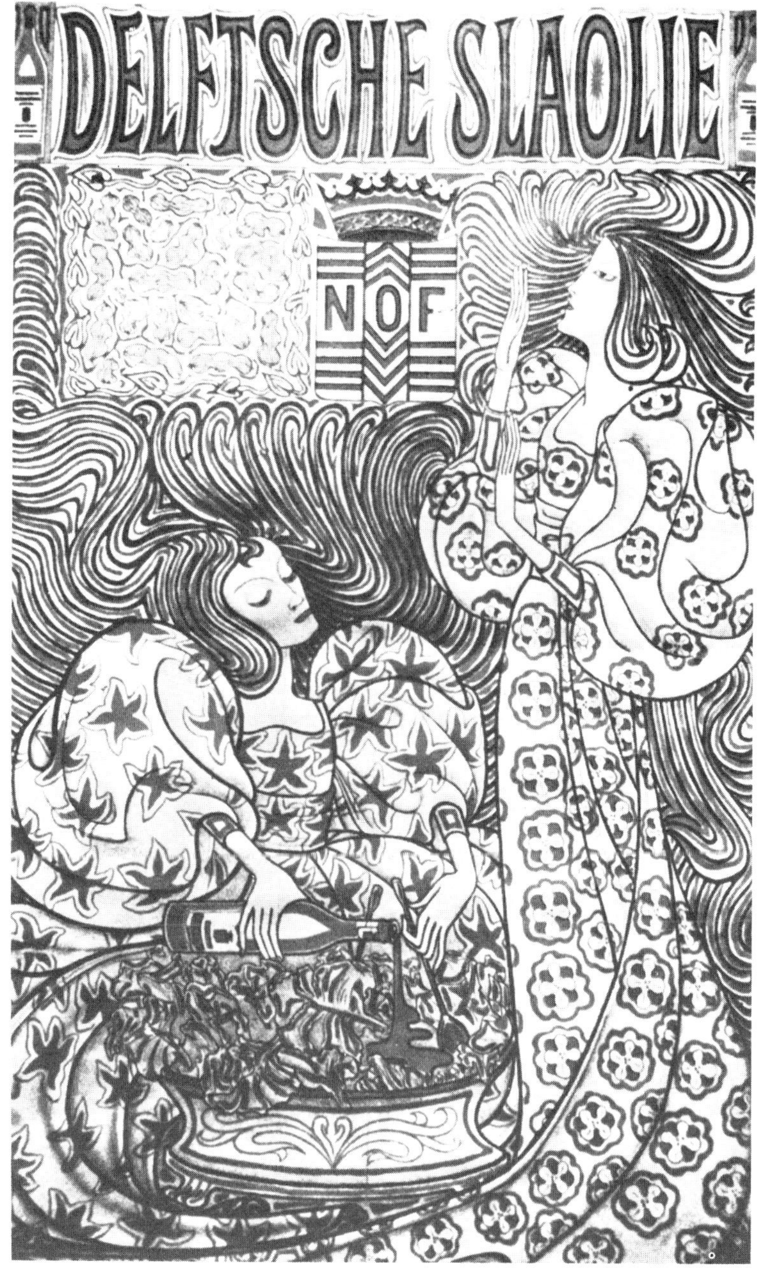

Poster for Salad Dressing: J Toorop
Although Art Nouveau was not generally popular in Holland, in Toorop's work we can see the influence of the Celtic intertwining lines, one of the characteristics of the Art Nouveau style. The wave-like movement of the floating hair occupies much of the picture space. This waving hair fetish, noticeable in much Art Nouveau work, derives largely from the Pre-Raphaelites and Symbolists.

LINE

Combing the Hair: Edgar Degas
In this figure study by Degas (whose compositions are very 'artful', i.e. full of Art) the two figures are widely separated by the movements of the arms of the left-hand figure, which establish a powerful upward thrust which is followed through by the line of the hair, acting as a link, and completing the movement through the arms of the other figure.

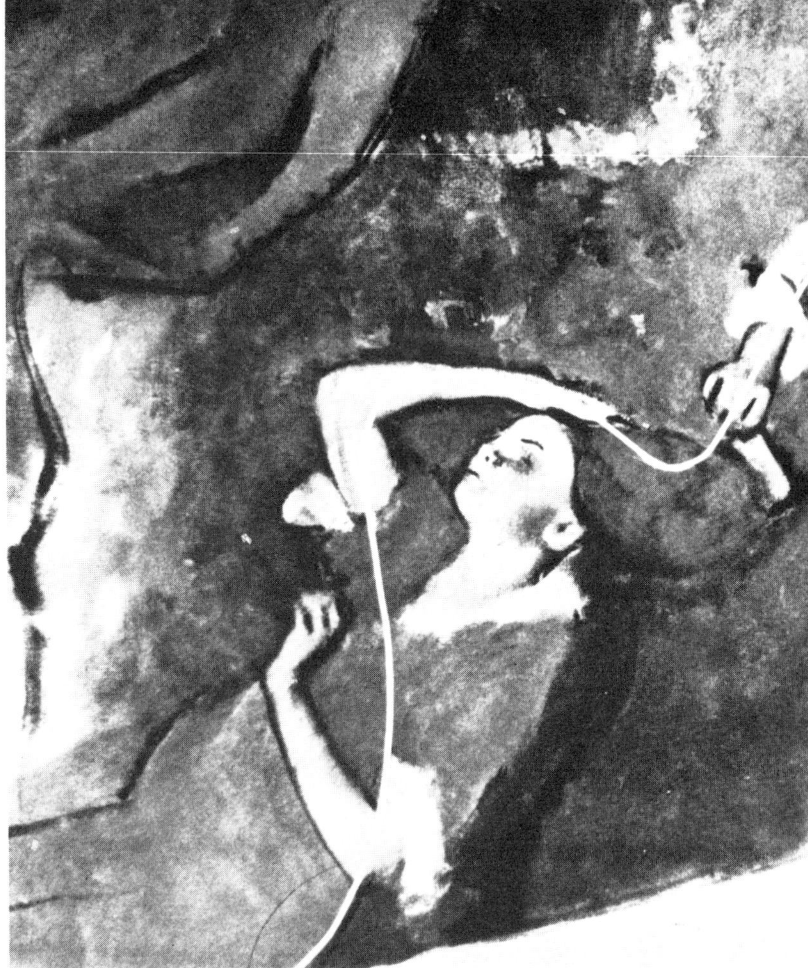

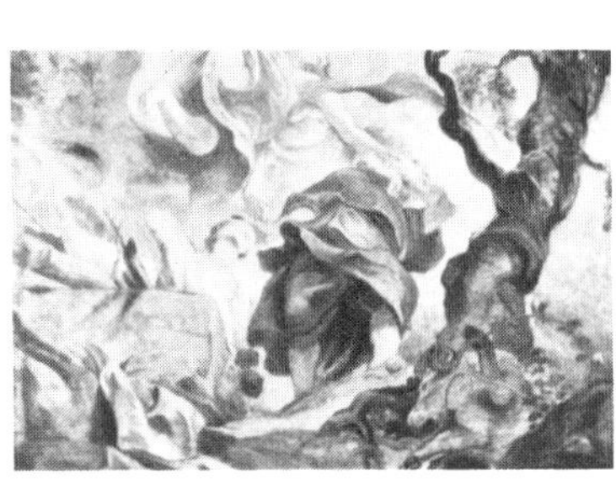

Abraham's Sacrifice: Sir Peter Paul Rubens
In the painting by Rubens the effect of movement produced by the spiralling lines is very noticeable – even the tree corkscrews out of the ground like an extension of the ram's horns.

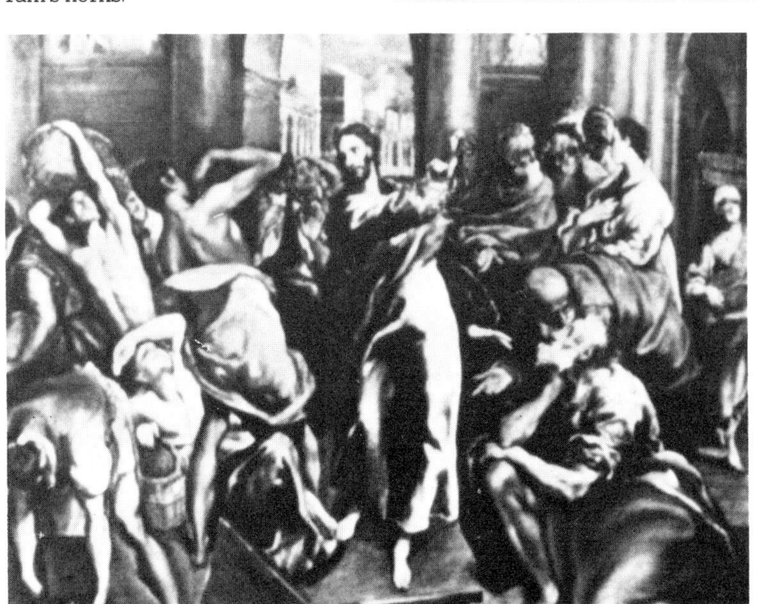

Christ Driving the Traders from the Temple: El Greco
Line as coil/recoil is well illustrated by this painting by El Greco where Christ, the central figure, coiled like a taut spring, produces an opposite reaction of recoil from the other figures in the scene. Twisting movement, as in the figure 8 seen in perspective, sometimes with the addition of the spiral, is one of the great characteristics of Baroque art. As a means of making visible these lines of movement, drapery was very widely used during this period. Drapery has the quality of being able to crystallize in space movements which have taken place only seconds before – a quality which the dancer with swirling skirts of flying draperies has always exploited to the full.

Line as force

Linear movement may take the form of the creation of visual pathways along which the eye is invited to move. Some of these visual invitations are more pressing than others, and may be so strongly emphasized as to become powerful directional thrusts. The arrow is a good example of this aspect of linear movement, expressed in the simplest terms.

These forces are not necessarily visible (as in the case of a footballer heading a football which may be in space some metres away from his head) but the upward thrust, if powerfully expressed, can extend beyond the footballer and bridge the gap between head and ball. Linear thrusts and directional forces are used to link together the various parts of the composition.

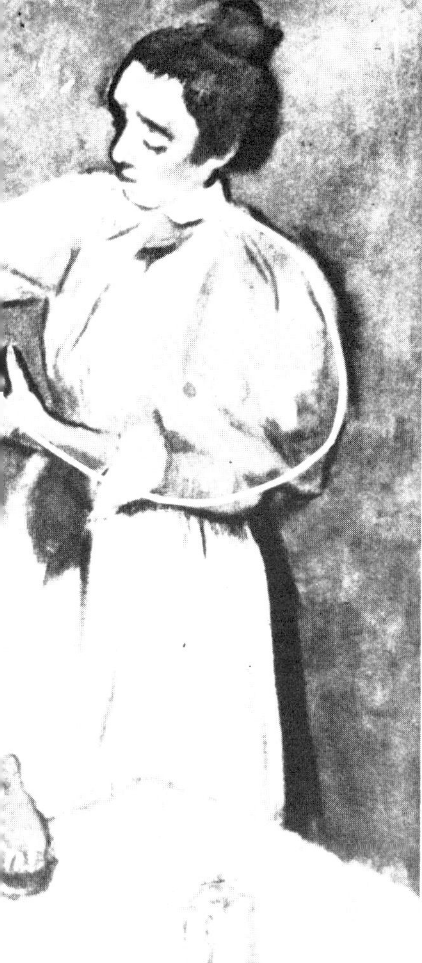

Line as coil and recoil

Just as the arrow expresses succinctly and directly the idea of a force moving in a certain direction (and can also convey the strength of that force) so the corkscrew suggests a twisting spiral movement around a central line. This capacity may be used to suggest the coil in tension or potential movement, or its opposite recoil or the release of tension.

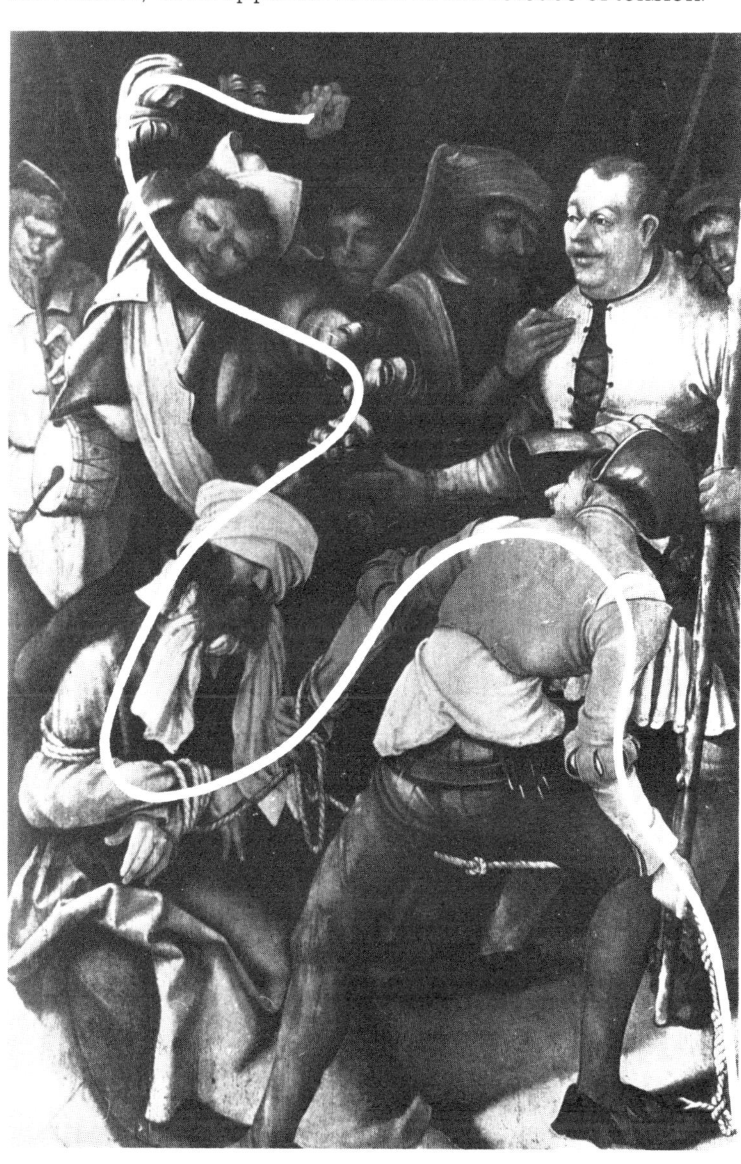

The Mocking of Christ: Grünewald
In a similar way Grünewald, in this painting, uses the rope's end to commence a movement which extends from the extreme bottom right-hand corner, through the figure of Christ, to culminate in the whip-like rhythm in the top left-hand corner. Of course there are many other complementary and contrasting lines to the main movement, e.g. the recoil of the foreground bully whose foot is planted firmly on the frame.

LINE

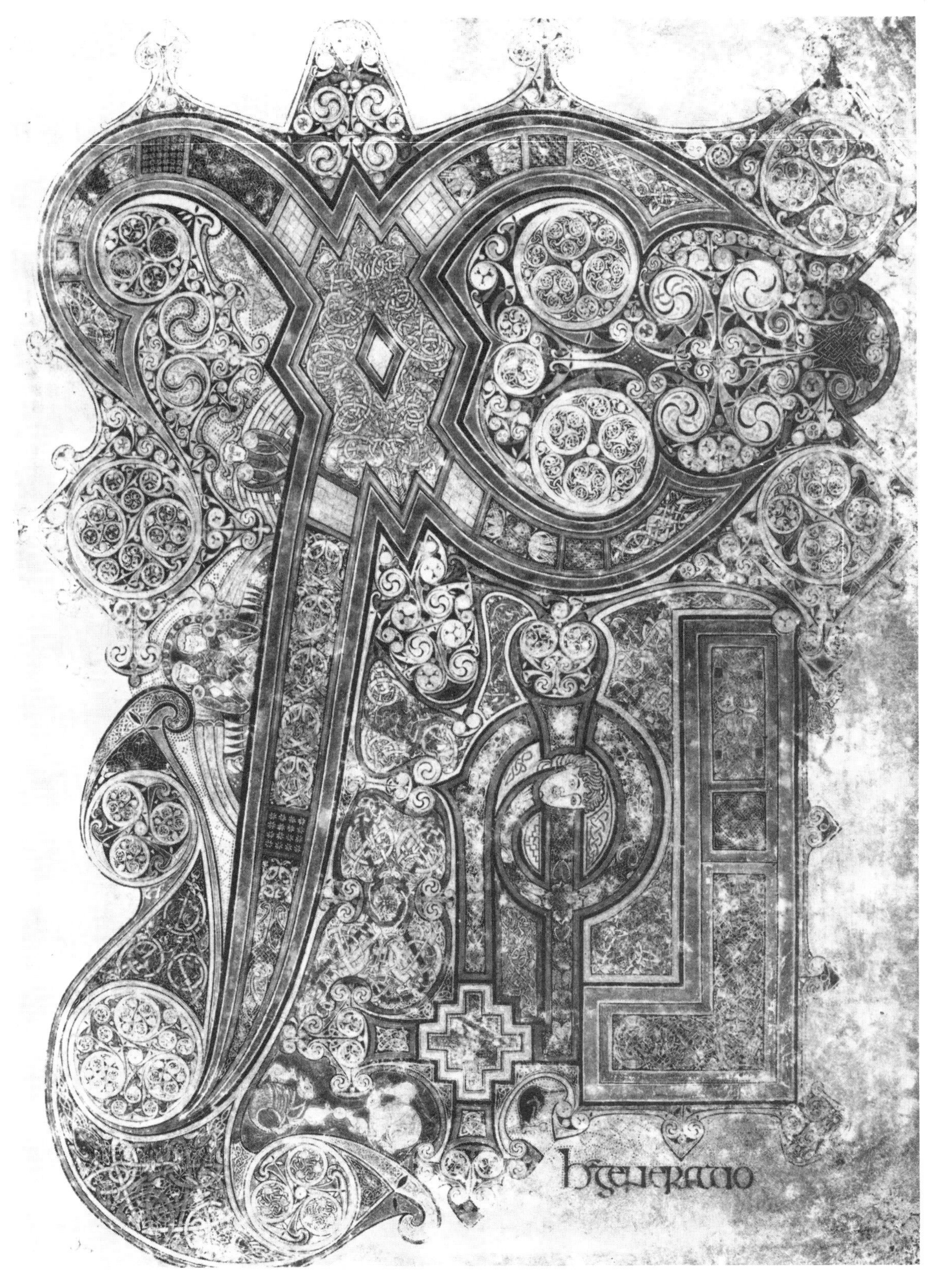

Line as pattern

The term 'pattern' implies a design made from a unit or motif arranged in such a way that the motif is repeated or echoed in the design.

From prehistoric times lines were used to create patterns. The zig-zag or chevron pattern appears on primitive designs throughout the world: there is no pattern so common or universal in its application. The motif may have derived from the use of a plaited straw or reeds as a means of making woven coverings. However, there may be a certain figurative element in this pattern, in as much as it may be connected with the representation of water, an archetypal symbol. Endless variations on this simple theme occur in many different countries.

Similarly the spiral belongs to all races, although particularly exploited by the Greeks along with another favourite motif – variously called the key, fret or meander pattern, which illustrates a most important principle, that of the double reading. Black on white may be alternatively seen as white on black – an idea of particular significance to painters, and fully exploited by the so-called 'Op' artists of the 1960s. When two black lines are drawn parallel a white line is automatically drawn between them, giving an added dimension.

Hence stripes of all kinds have a particularly strong pattern quality. By superimposing a pattern on itself, more varied, surprising and richer patterns are created, leading to the idea of interlacing – a source of endless inspiration to Islamic designers, and developed into the most intricate curvilinear complexities by Celtic artists in stone and in manuscript illumination.

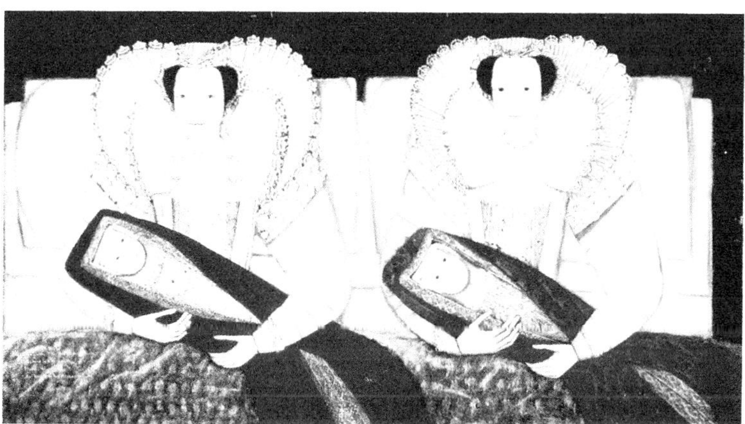

The Cholmondeley Sisters: British School, seventeenth century
The delicate tracery of linear repeat pattern (twins seem an ideal subject for repeat pattern!) suggests that of the ribs seen in the vaulted ceilings of Gothic cathedrals.

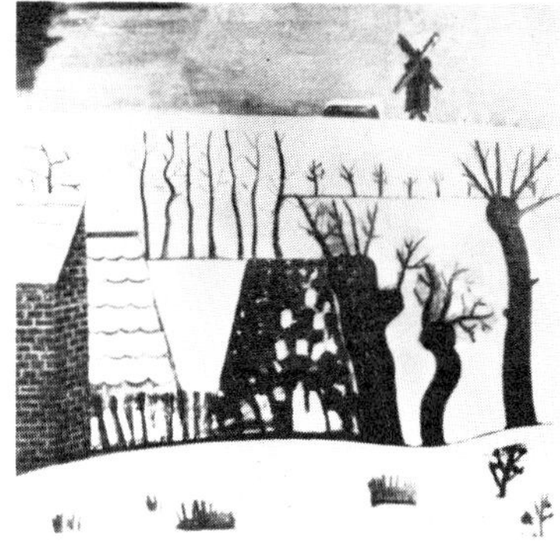

Grand Paysage d'Hiver: Jean Brusselmans
The virtual absence of colour in this winter landscape gives emphasis to the dynamic linear pattern, creating a variety of repeating and echoing lines. This is a composition in which the white and black stripes are of equal importance in conveying the sense of pattern.

The eighth-century manuscript *Book of Kells* is full of astonishingly inventive and meaningful patterns, used to enrich the page and the lives of men. The Chi Rho page is a good example, using the initial letters of the name of Christ to produce an involved interlacing of calligraphic lines weaving their intricate rhythms. The artist hides within the pattern glimpses of everyday life.

LINE

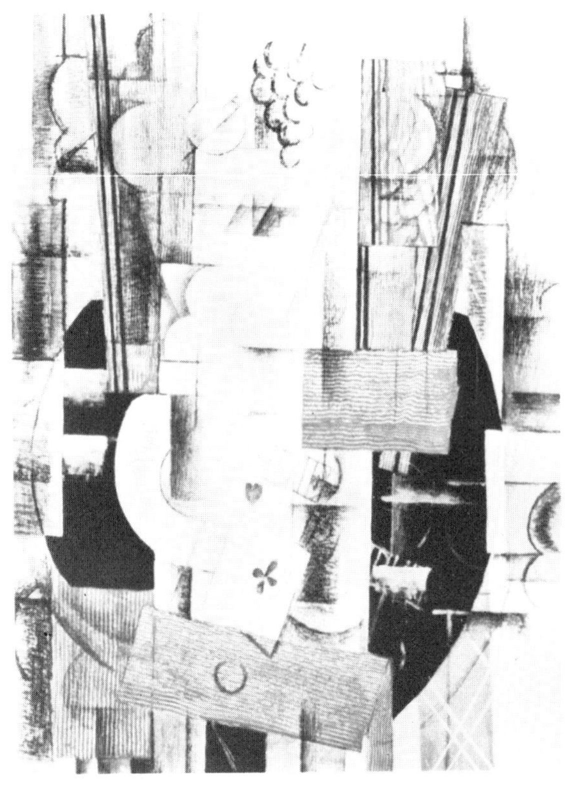

Still Life with Playing Card: Georges Braque
The Cubists, Picasso and Braque, in their 'Synthetic' phase, moved from imitating textures of things in paint and began sticking on pieces of oilcloth fabric, newspaper and printed surfaces, re-introducing the idea of collage – the name was new but the idea of sticking the real things on the painting was used much earlier – (e.g. Cavallini). But Braque in his *Composition* has imitated the texture of wood framing (his father and grandfather were house painters) using lines scraped into the paint.

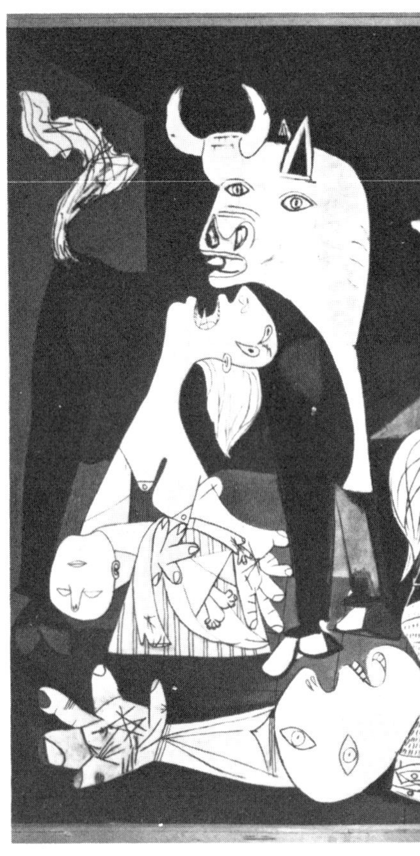

Composition in Green: Alfred Wols
Wols uses what have been called 'multi-evocative forms' inspired by the cellular structure of living organisms, fibres, frequency modulations and diffraction patterns, essentially linear in character. In this painting he uses involved irregularity of lines, partially achieved by allowing the paint to dictate its own direction (anticipating Action Painting) to produce a close-knit texture of linear fibres, reminiscent of microscopic detail. 'Quantity and measurement are no longer the central preoccupation of mathematics and science, and structure emerges as the key to our knowledge and control of the world.'

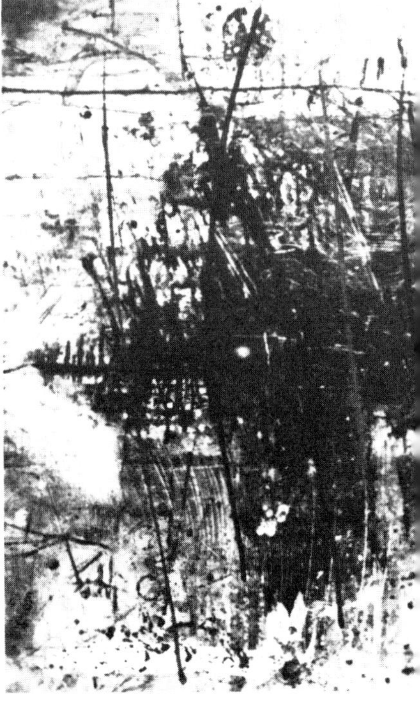

Line as texture

The word texture describes the appearance of a surface from the point of view of its tactile quality – rough, smooth, dry, wet, scaly, velvety, etc. The painter/designer uses the textured surface to enliven or enrich certain areas of the composition. He may create a physically textured surface, e.g. by the use of thick paint or palette knife, in order to reflect light; or scrape, scratch, or mix sand in with his pigment. Alternatively texture may simply be a representation or interpretation of a surface, as the surface quality of grass may be represented by using short broken lines, rather than physically sticking cuttings from the mower on to the canvas, or using grass matting.

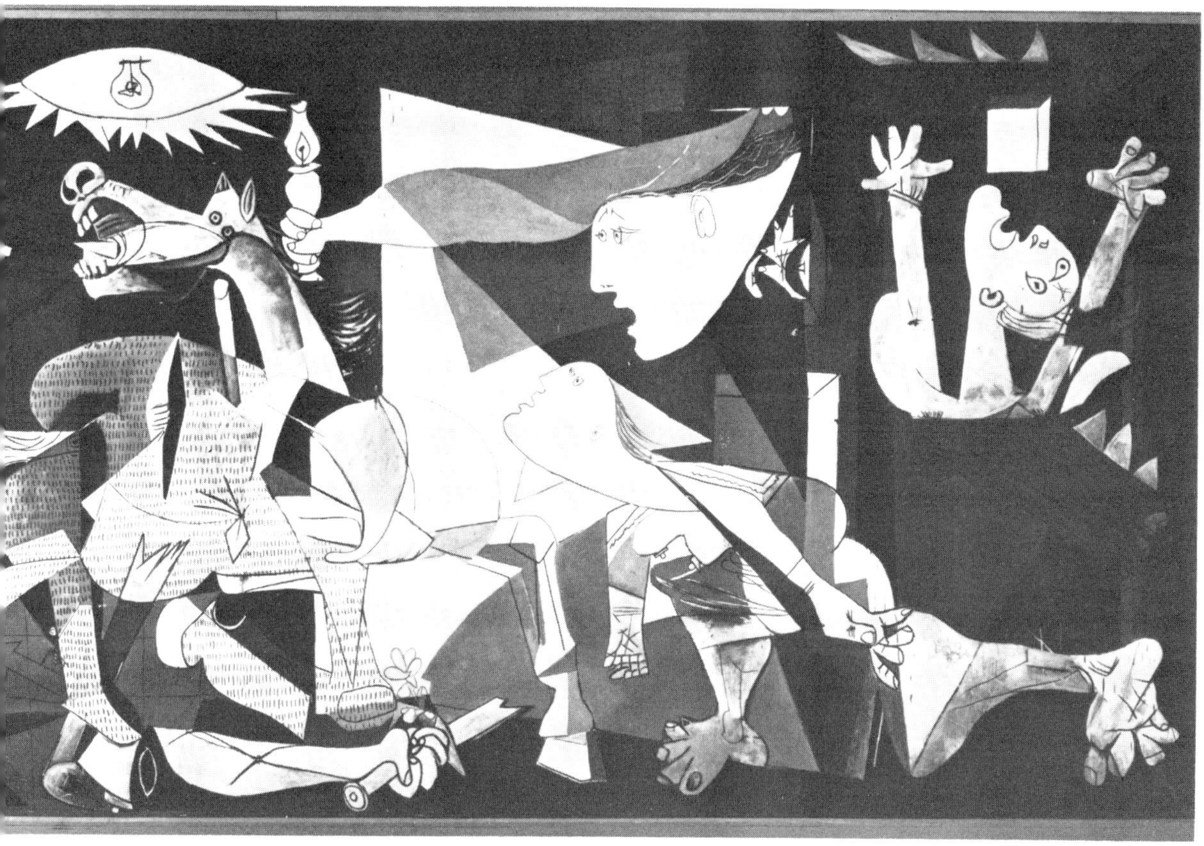

Guernica: Pablo Picasso

In the introduction to this chapter it was stated that one would not expect to find all possibilities of line exploited in one work. This is the exception. Because colour is absent, line must play a greater role than usual. Using only black and white, the colours of tragedy, drama and immediacy, Picasso protests against the bombing of the town of Guernica during the Spanish Civil War. In this painting Picasso makes use of all the means of expression of which line is capable. Lines are used to create powerfully disturbing patterns, to describe connected contours, to suggest violently opposed movements, to create linear textures; all in a strongly structured linear framework. In addition to all this, using the ability of line to express transparency and therefore simultaneity, Picasso is able to compress into one composition a whole sequence of events and viewpoints.

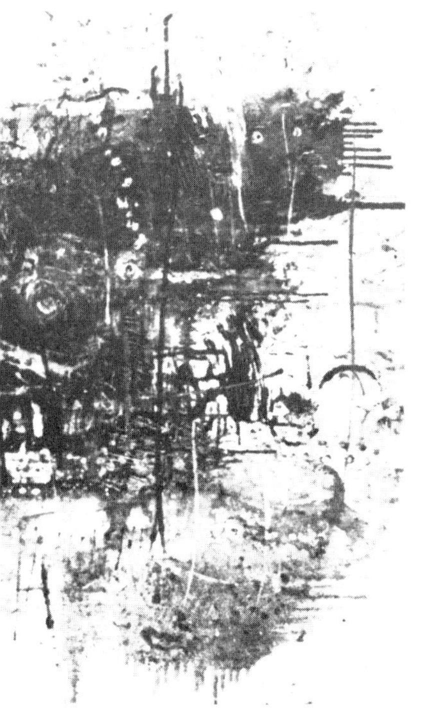

PERSPECTIVE

'Oh, what a sweet thing this perspective is.' – Paolo Uccello.

'Perspective is of such a nature that it makes what is flat appear in relief, and what is in relief appear flat.' – Leonardo da Vinci.

Throughout history artists have been concerned with the problem of how to represent three dimensions on a two-dimensional surface. At different times and in different cultures artists have used various methods to represent form and space. The two concepts are inseparable, since form is inconceivable without the space to contain it.

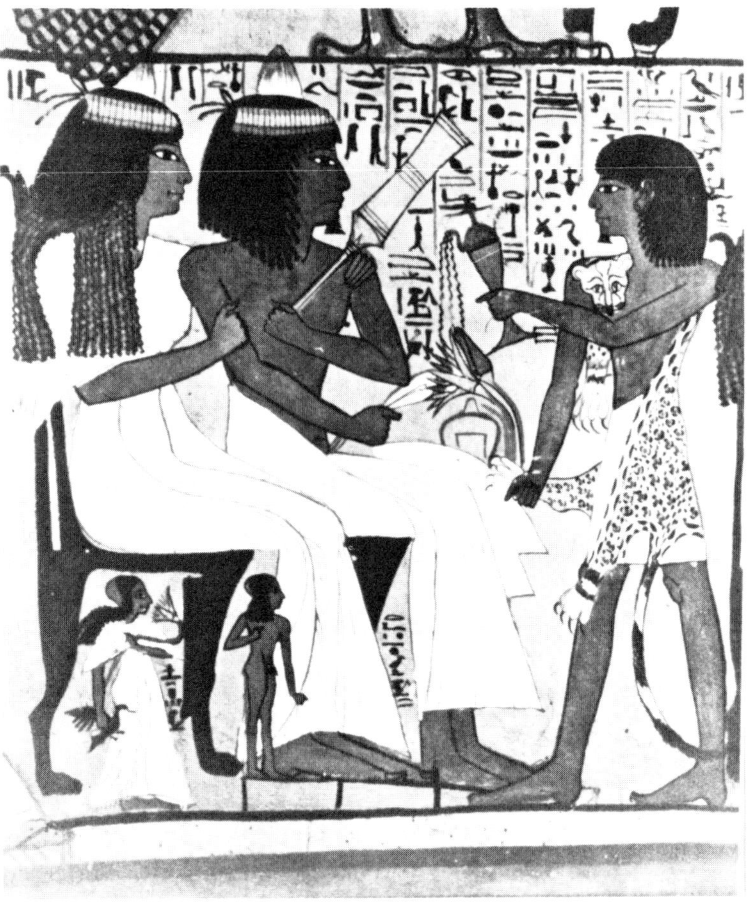

Mural from the tomb of Senejem, Egypt

In this mural painting the Pharaoh and his wife are shown seated, receiving a libation from their son acting as a funeral priest. The legs of thrones and of figures are all shown parallel to the picture plane (i.e. parallel to the surface of the painting). This is typical of all Egyptian painting, in as much as there is no attempt to create the illusion of space and depth through the use of linear perspective, but space is *represented* by one shape overlapping another – so that Senejem's shoulder is shown in front of his wife's shoulder and her hair falls in front of her gown. The size of the small figures indicates their lesser social status or importance and not diminished scale due to distance.

Mural from Casa del Frutteto, Pompeii

Although there is evidence that Greek painters of the fourth century B.C. understood foreshortening and the diverging of visual rays, the first surviving examples of the use of linear perspective are Roman mural paintings. A number were found still preserved on the walls of the houses of Pompeii buried under volcanic ash after the eruption of Vesuvius in A.D. 79. Spatially convincing, these architectural settings strongly suggest the idea of stage scenery, and were undoubtedly influenced by the theatre which was such an important feature of the ancient world. Perspective, foreshortening, and the use of light and shade all helped to create the illusion of reality, distance and forms in space.

Aspects of linear perspective in composition

The use of linear perspective is one of the means which has been employed to create the visual illusion of space, although this method has been used in comparatively few areas of the world and for comparatively short periods in the long history of art.

In the East the representation of space and distance (before Western influences made themselves felt) was achieved largely by difference of scale, and by allowing one shape to apparently overlap another. Although 'aerial perspective' (see Chapter 5), through the use of carefully graduated tones, is a prominent feature of Japanese art, the use of linear perspective is much rarer.

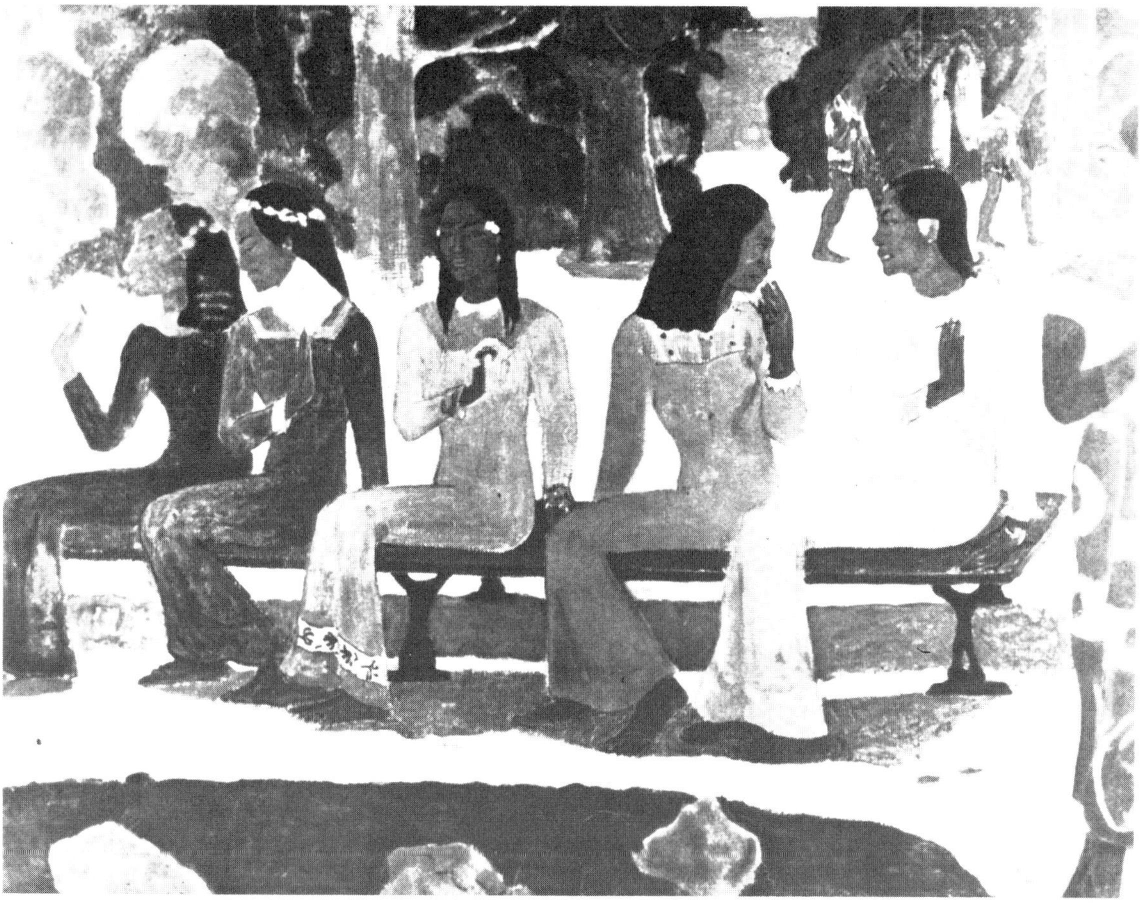

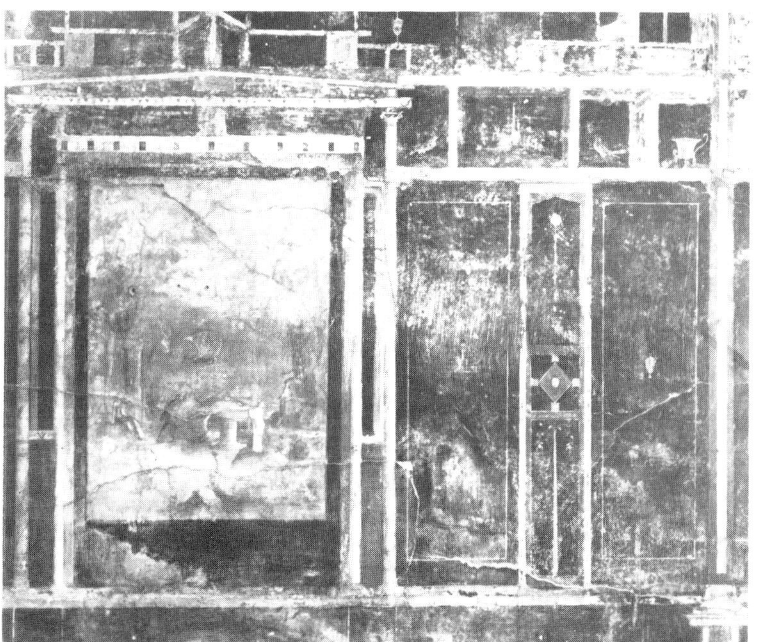

Ta Matete: Paul Gauguin
Gauguin was clearly influenced by Egyptian painting in this Tahitian scene. Apart from the curious frieze-like effect of these static figures with their formal gestures, all so reminiscent of Egyptian art, Gauguin's treatment of space is also similar. The figures are placed on a bench which is parallel to the picture plane. The thighs of the figures are made parallel to the bench, so avoiding the need for foreshortening (putting forms into perspective). Although the illusion of space in this painting is very limited since aerial and linear perspective are virtually unused, there is a tremendous sense of colour and pattern.

PERSPECTIVE

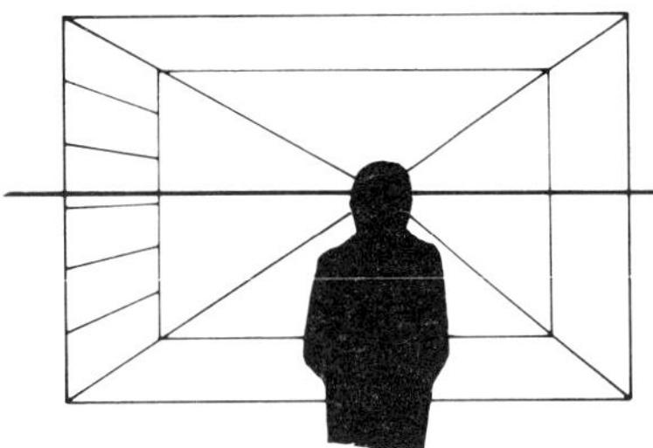

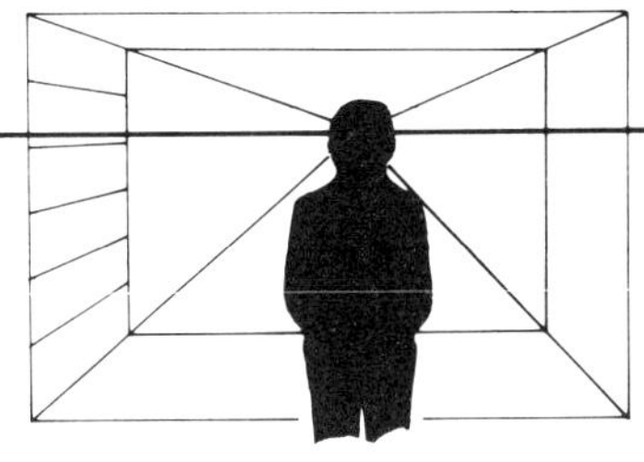

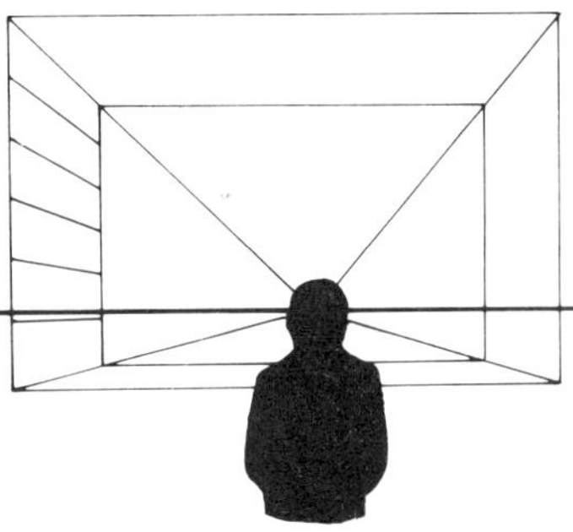

Eye levels (diagram)
Imagine a figure looking into an empty room (a). The lines of walls and floor receding into the distance all appear to converge at a point on the eye level. Lines *on* the eye level appear to be horizontal, without depth. But if one were to *actually* paint this eye level line along the walls of the room it would involve moving along one wall, along the back and returning to the front edge – a journey in depth.

If the spectator raises or lowers his eye level (b and c) thereby changing his viewpoint, the parallel lines still come to a point on his new eye level; but lines on the eye level, even though receding, always appear horizontal.

The Avenue, Middelharnis: Meindert Hobbema
In this painting by the seventeenth-century Dutch painter, the eye level is low in the picture, conveying the idea of low-lying country dominated by sky – converging lines of trees and ruts in the road lead our eye into the painting towards the distant horizon; it needs an effort to drag our eye away to see the workers busy in the orchard, in the right foreground.

The eye level or horizon line
The illusion of space created by the use of linear perspective depends on the fact that parallel lines receding from the spectator appear to meet at a point on the eye level.

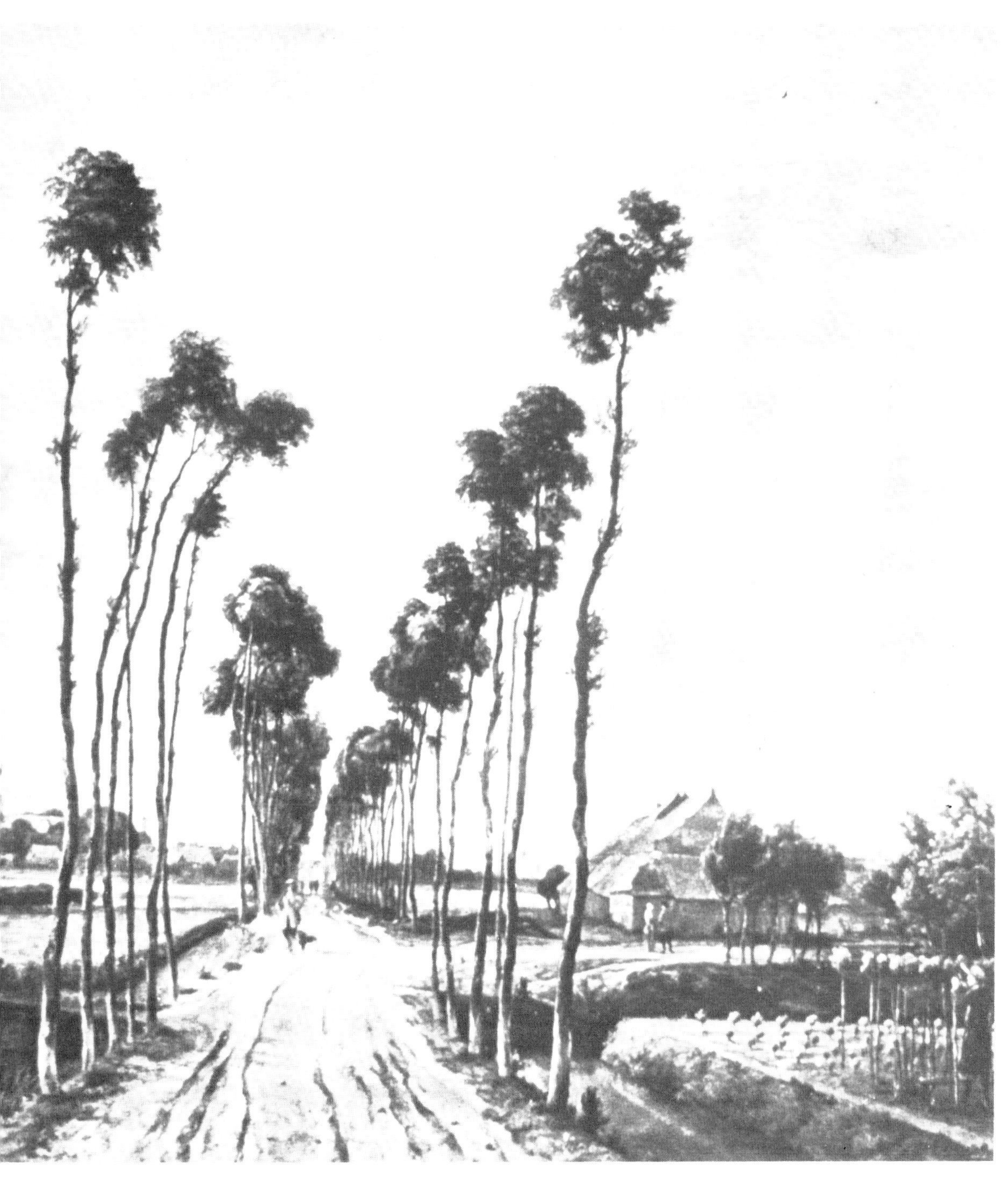

PERSPECTIVE

One, two, and three point perspective (diagram)
One-point perspective: Where all parallel lines appear to meet at one point on the eye level – or horizon line as in the previous diagrams – this is known as one-point, or parallel, perspective, and is the most commonly used system.

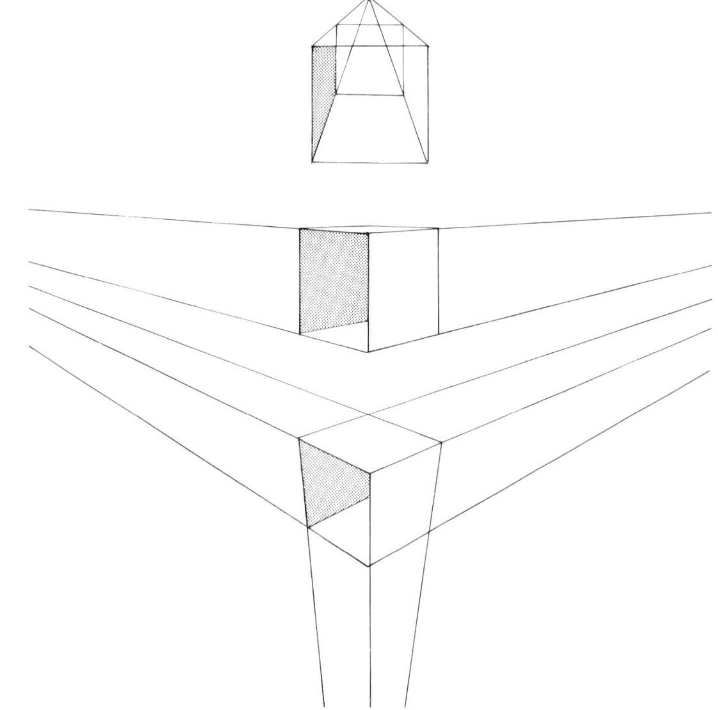

The Calumny of Apelles: Botticelli (diagram)
This allegorical painting based on a written description of a painting by the Greek master Apelles (fourth century B.C.) illustrates the perfect use of one-point perspective, since beyond the classical architecture we can glimpse the distant sea. This establishes the horizon line or eye level – so that all receding lines on, above or below the horizon appear to come to a point on this level.

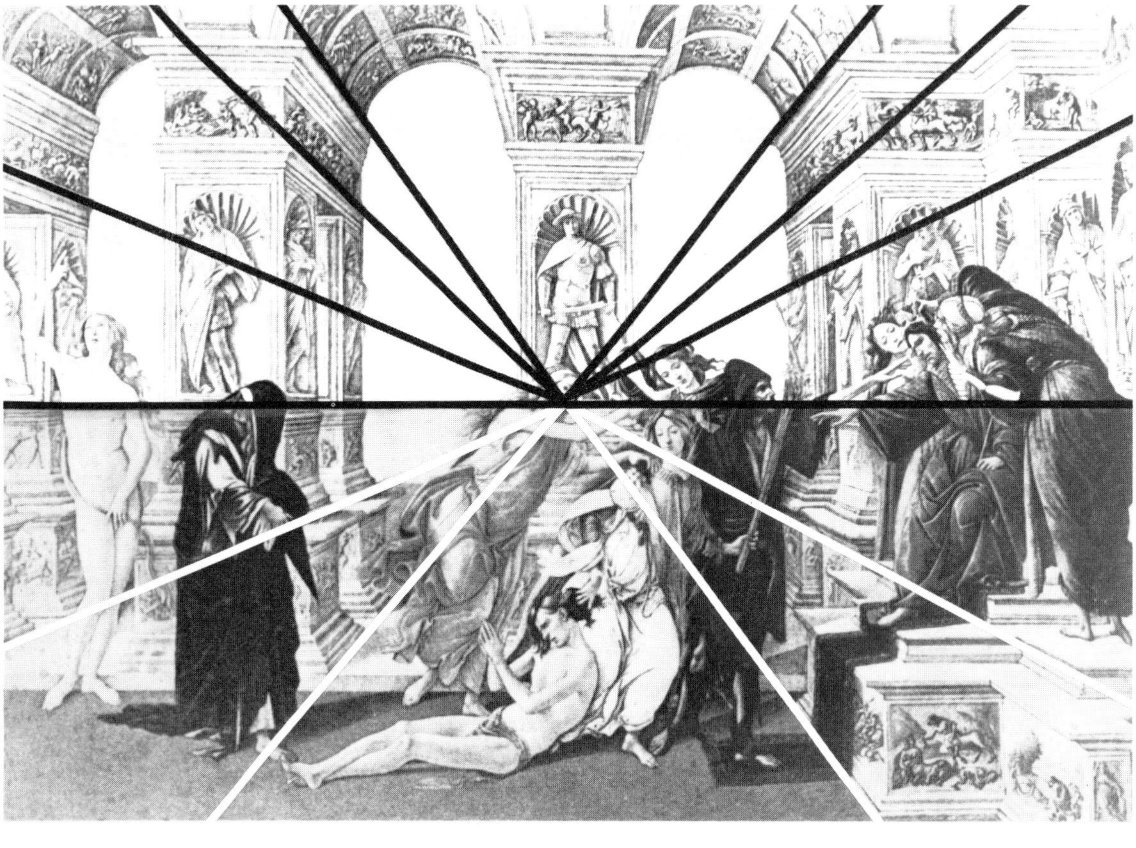

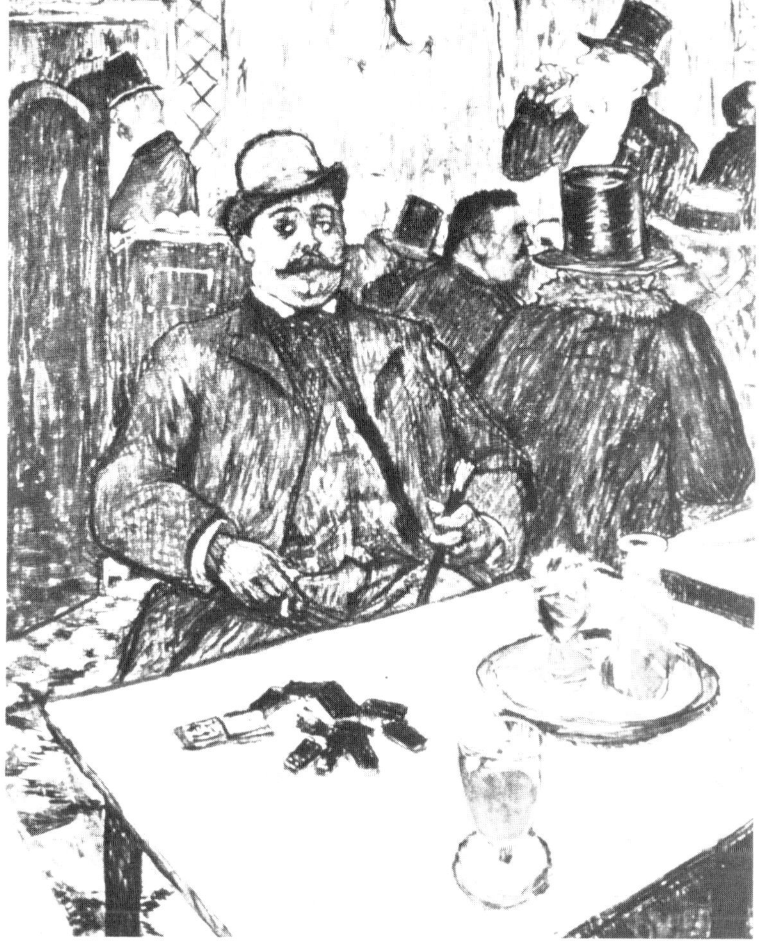

M. Boileau at the Café: Henri de Toulouse-Lautrec

Two-point perspective is involved where planes at right angles have their own 'vanishing' points, but these are still on the same eye level. Although this is not so often used in practice, this painting by Toulouse-Lautrec illustrates two-point, or angular, perspective.

Toulouse-Lautrec was a first-rate draughtsman. Like many of his contemporaries he was profoundly influenced by the Japanese prints, not only for their flat colours and silhouetted shapes but for their emphasis on the diagonal composition. Lautrec often makes use of this angular perspective to gain a carefully calculated effect of immediacy and casual composition. The apparently arbitrary cutting-off of the near corner of the table gives a sense of personal participation in this scene, by bringing the foreground so close that we can easily reach our glass of absinthe.

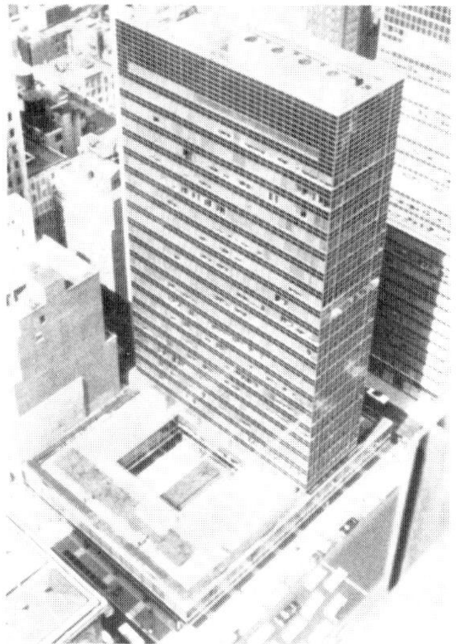

Lever House, New York
Three-point perspective. This system – described as triaxial or oblique perspective – is very rarely employed, but is occasionally used by architectural draughtsmen if an aerial view is required.

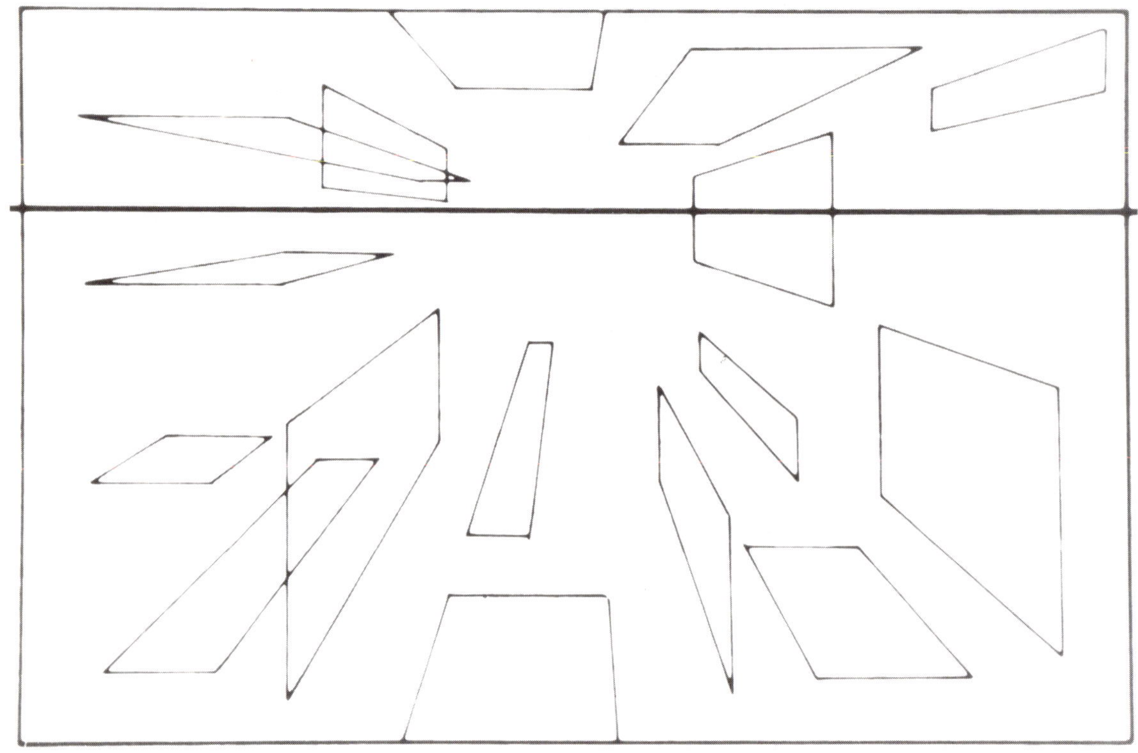

Rectangular forms and eye levels (diagram)
Transparent planes above and below the eye level, receding towards a central vanishing point, convey a powerful feeling of spatial recession.

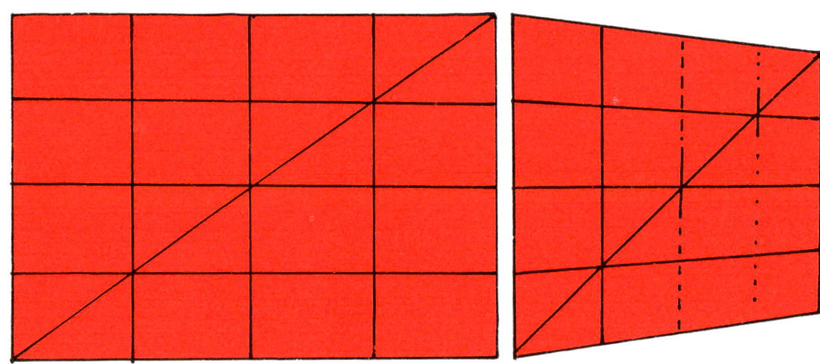

Subdivision of a rectangle (diagram)
Using the fact that rectangles of the same proportion, irrespective of their size, have common diagonals, a rectangle may be subdivided into smaller units by marking off divisions along a line parallel to the one containing the vanishing point of the plane. From these divisions lines are extended to the vanishing point, and the intersections produced by the diagonal then used to convert the columns into rows.

Uncomposed objects in Space: Paul Klee
Although the eye level (the level where plane coincides with the line) is clearly identifiable, creating the sensation that we are dealing with a logical situation, this is really the ironic joke of the dream. The introduction of the human figure flattened into two dimensions helps to convince us that the rest really is a three-dimensional world.

The rectangle in one-point perspective.

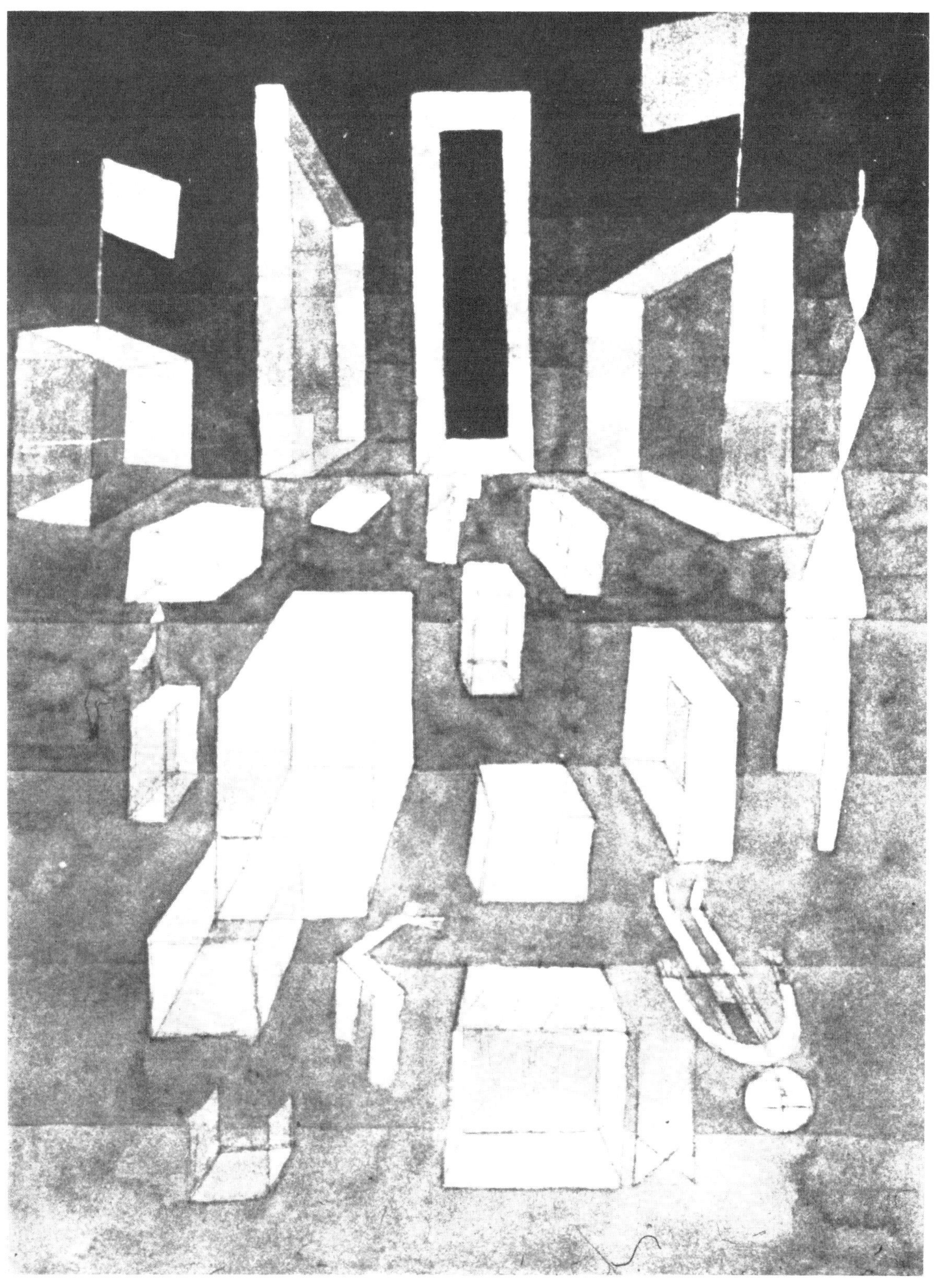

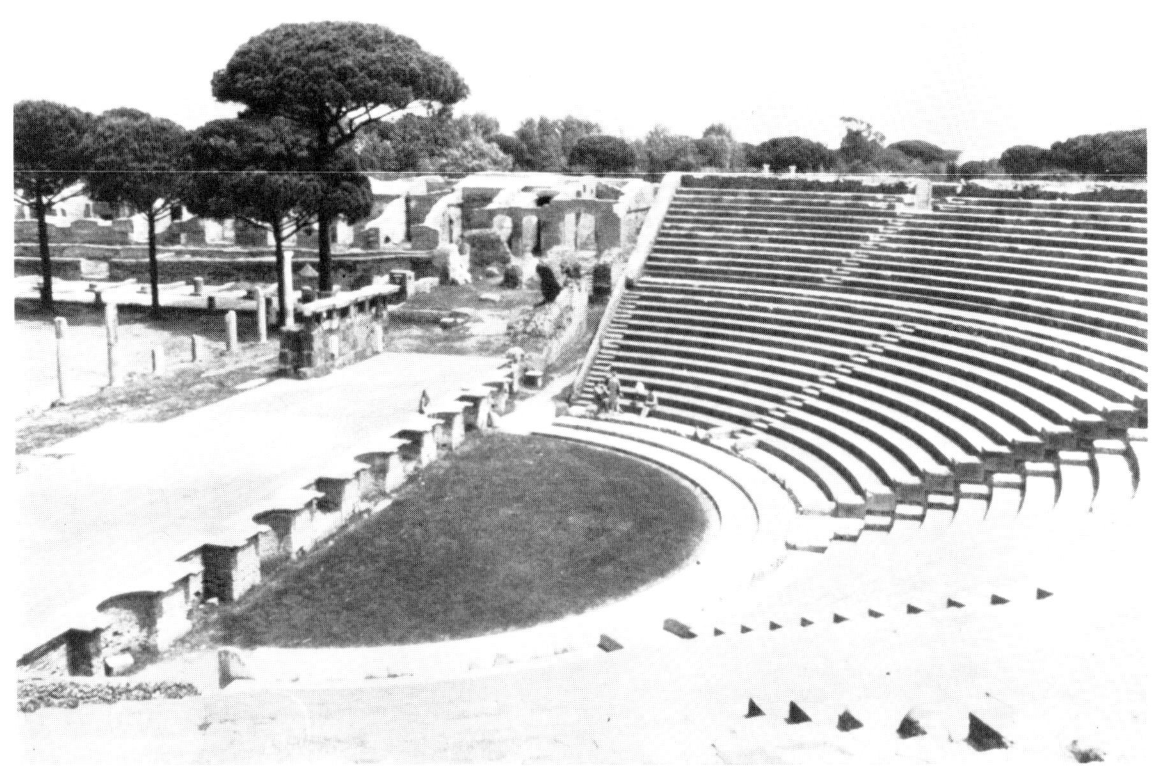

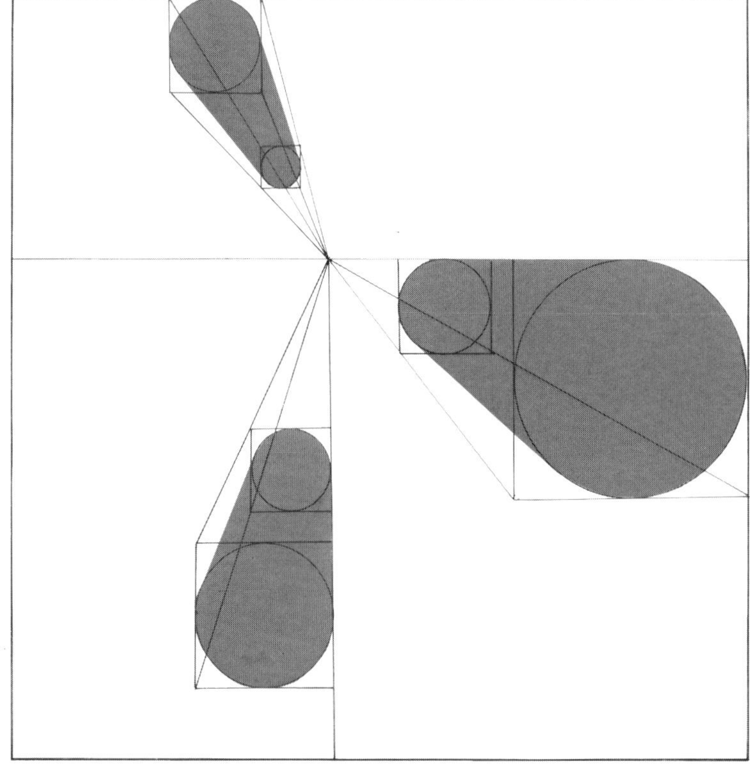

The Roman Theatre at Ostia
The photograph illustrates clearly the way in which semicircles appear more circular below the eye level and flatten as they approach nearer to eye level (in this case, the back row of the stalls).

Cylinders in perspective (diagram)
In order to describe a cylinder in perspective it is useful to use rectangular forms as a guide by inscribing a circle within the square end of the rectangular form.

The circle in perspective

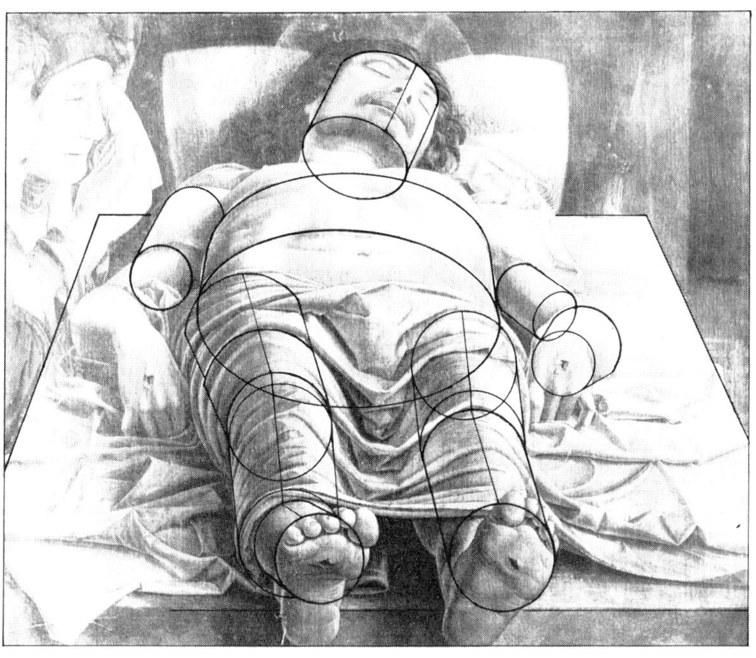

Dead Christ: Andrea Mantegna (diagram)
The use of cylinders in perspective can be clearly observed in
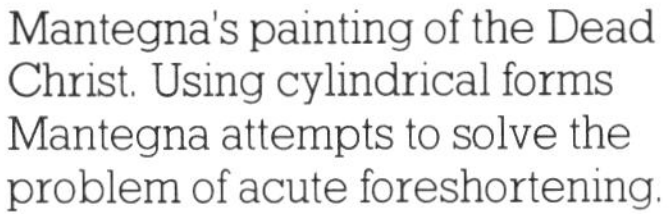
Mantegna's painting of the Dead Christ. Using cylindrical forms Mantegna attempts to solve the problem of acute foreshortening.

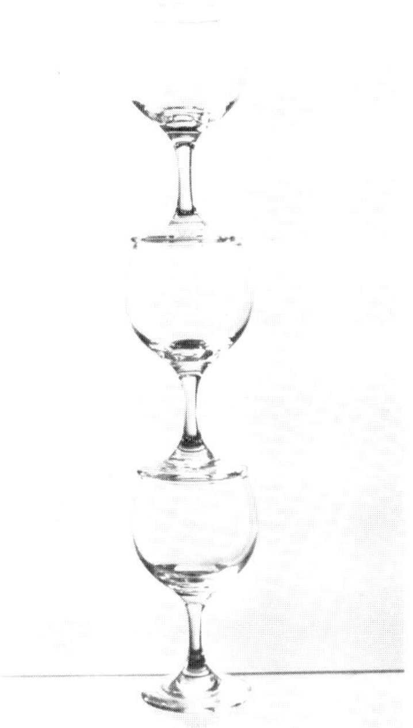

Superimposed glasses
Circles seen in perspective, whether above or below the eye level, appear to become more and more narrow ellipses as they approach the eye level, until they appear as straight lines. Above the eye level the reverse situation occurs. The photograph of wine glasses, bases balanced on rims, illustrates the appearance of a series of circles which gradually approach the eye level. If the photograph is reversed, the eye level is seen as the surface on which the glasses are placed and the ellipses tend to appear more circular as we look up towards them.

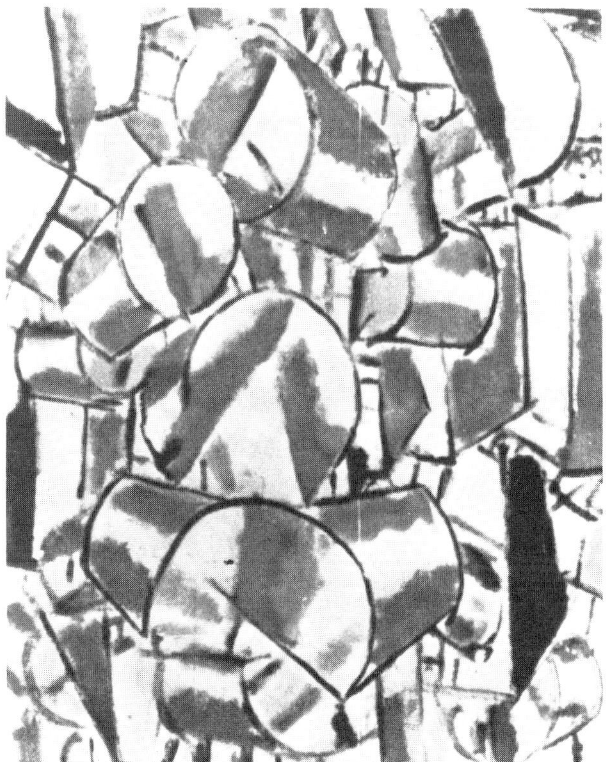

Contrast of Forms: Fernand Léger
Léger often reduced the subject matter of his paintings to cylindrical forms. He treated the human figure as an arrangement of articulated cylinders or tube-like forms (hence the label 'Tubism' applied to his work, as a development from 'Cubism'). In this painting, steely-coloured cylinders floating or rotating in space give a powerful sensation of mechanical activity, like pistons coming off an endless production line.

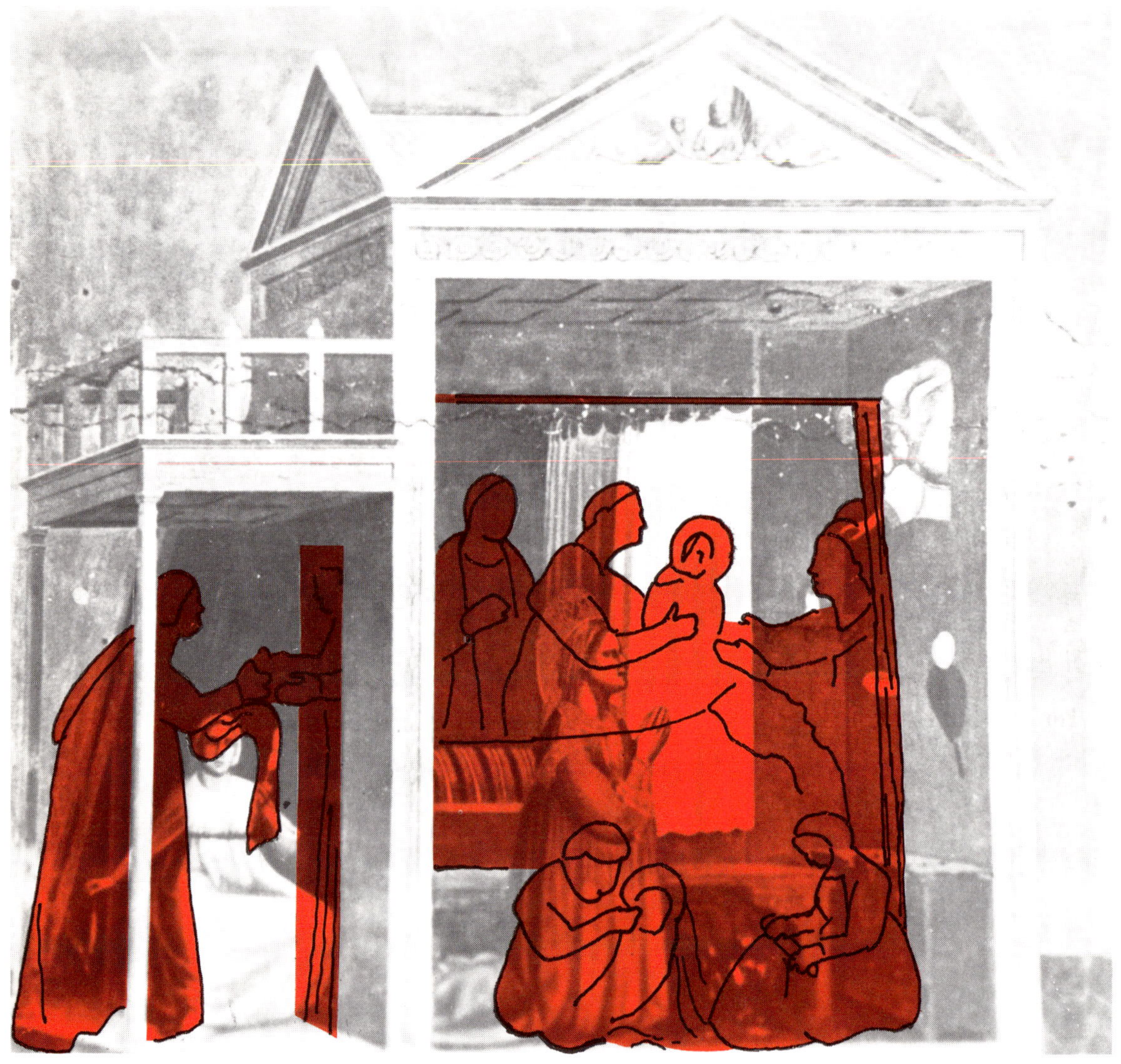

This diagram shows the position of the figures in Giotto's *The Birth of the Virgin*.

Early beginnings

During the period from the decline of the Roman Empire until the dawning of the Renaissance, the mediaeval artists, whether of painting, stained glass or sculpture, preferred to put their emphasis on the world of the spirit rather than the mundane world in which we live – a world which may be represented by rational space expressed through the use of perspective, and the everyday colours of Nature.

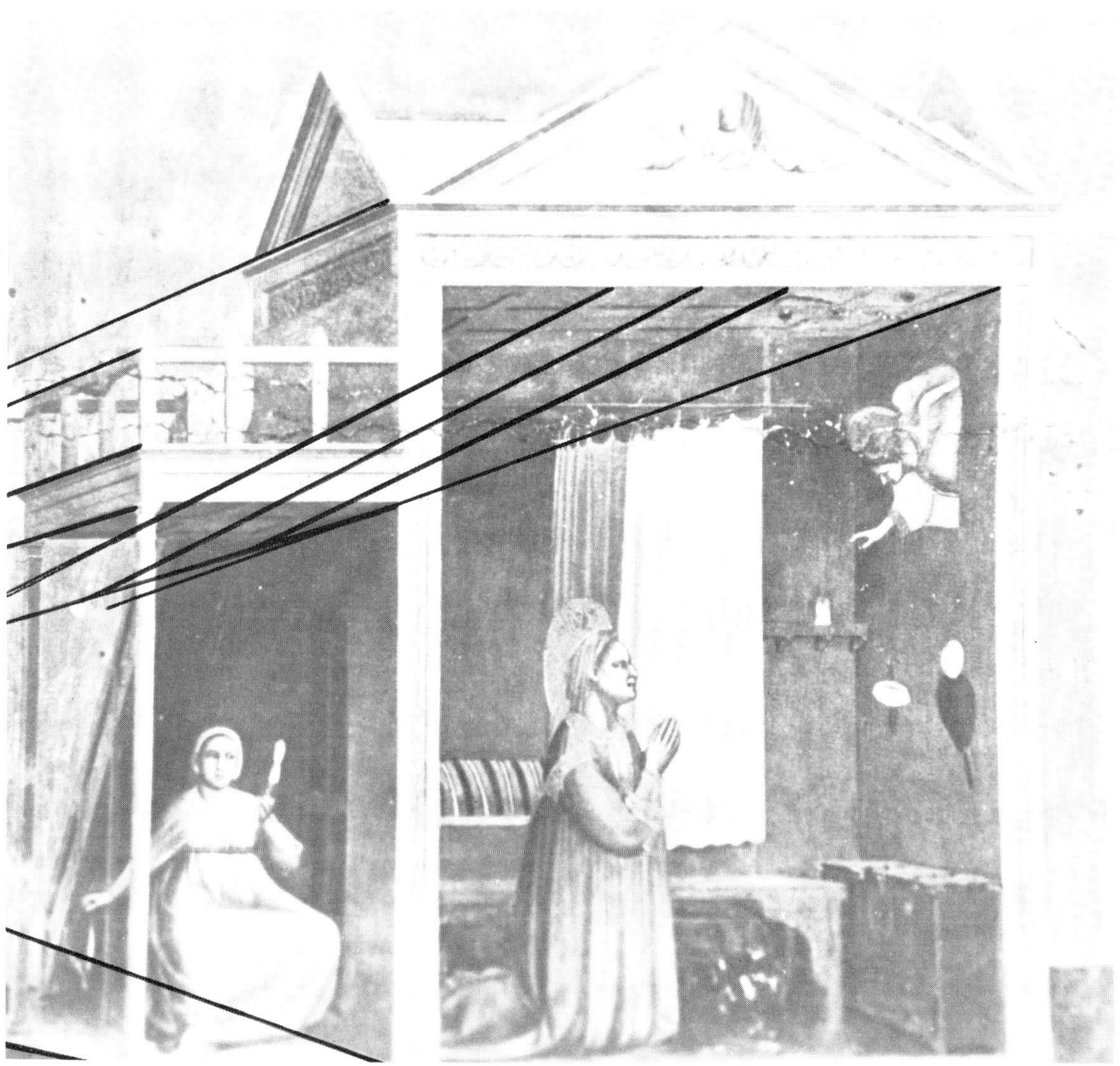

The Angel appearing to St. Anne: Giotto (diagram)

Giotto, working in Florence, was one of the first artists to re-introduce perspective as an aid to creating the realism of the every day world. His figures are given weight and space in which to move and react to their situation by appropriate gestures, pose and expression – very much like actors on a stage. These two diagrams illustrate two different frescoes from a series by Giotto, which use virtually identical 'sets' – a reasonably convincing room with one wall removed, showing a view outside as well as inside. Giotto uses this device, of the same 'set' (and the same 'props') seen in identical perspective, on other occasions in this series of frescoes from the Arena Chapel, Padua. Not only a very economical idea, but one which helps to maintain dramatic continuity of the narrative, since the 'scenery' recurs throughout.

PERSPECTIVE

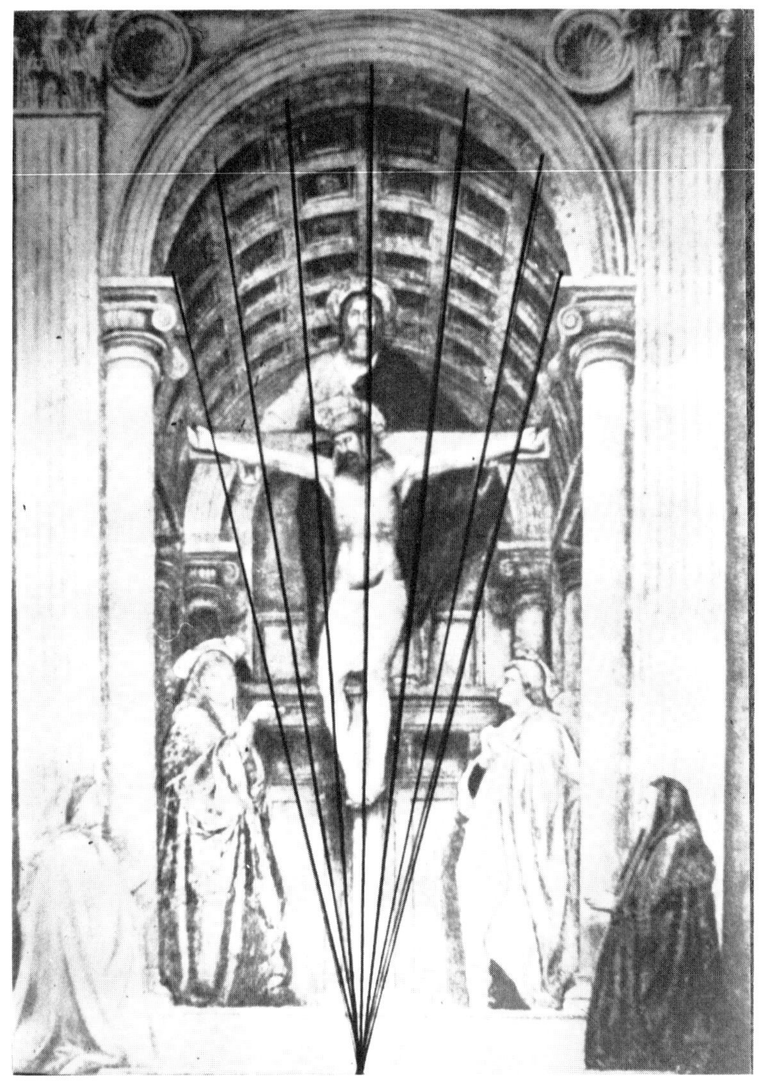

Trinity: Masaccio (diagram)
The Trinity, a fresco painted in Santa Maria Novella over the altar of St. Ignatius, shows the Virgin Mary and St. John contemplating the crucified Christ; at the sides are the donors. The very low eye level on the bottom edge of the painting (consistent with the spectator's view point) creates a powerful illusion of space, and created an equally powerful impression on the fifteenth-century artists who came to see it.

'But the most beautiful thing, apart from the figures, is the barrel-vaulted ceiling, drawn in perspective and divided into square compartments containing rosettes foreshortened and made to recede so skilfully that the surface looks as if it is indented.' Vasari (1511–1574), *Lives of the Artists*.

The Flagellation: Piero della Francesca (diagram)
The ability to use linear perspective in a consistent way developed rapidly during the Renaissance. Piero della Francesca made an extensive study of perspective and geometry. According to Vasari 'some of Piero's writings on geometry and perspective have been preserved there, and these show that he was in no way inferior in those sciences to anyone of his own or indeed of any other time. And this is illustrated by all his works which are full of perspective . . . ' This diagram illustrates the main perspective lines and shows the position of the low eye level, which helps to dissociate the foreground figures dramatically (by causing the abrupt change of scale) from the scene behind – which they so conspicuously ignore. The line of columns is drawn in such acute perspective that it virtually forms a solid wall, emphasizing the separation between these two views of life: fashion, snobbery, and cold impersonal indifference on the one hand; passion, pain, and personal involvement with human suffering on the other.

Marriage at Cana: Paolo Veronese
In this large painting (the figures are life-size!) the tables, balconies, and all the complex setting appear to have been painted with meticulous observation of the rules of perspective. The illusion of reality felt by the spectator confronted by this panoramic view is so complete that he feels himself a gatecrasher at the wedding feast.

Veronese has achieved this illusion (because of the large scale of the scene) by taking a number of vanishing points grouped together in the central area of the canvas, stretching the vanishing point as it were, so that a broader spatial effect results than that which would normally be obtained by the use of one-point classical perspective. The effect is similar to that obtained in the cinema by the use of the wide screen.

Development of one-point perspective

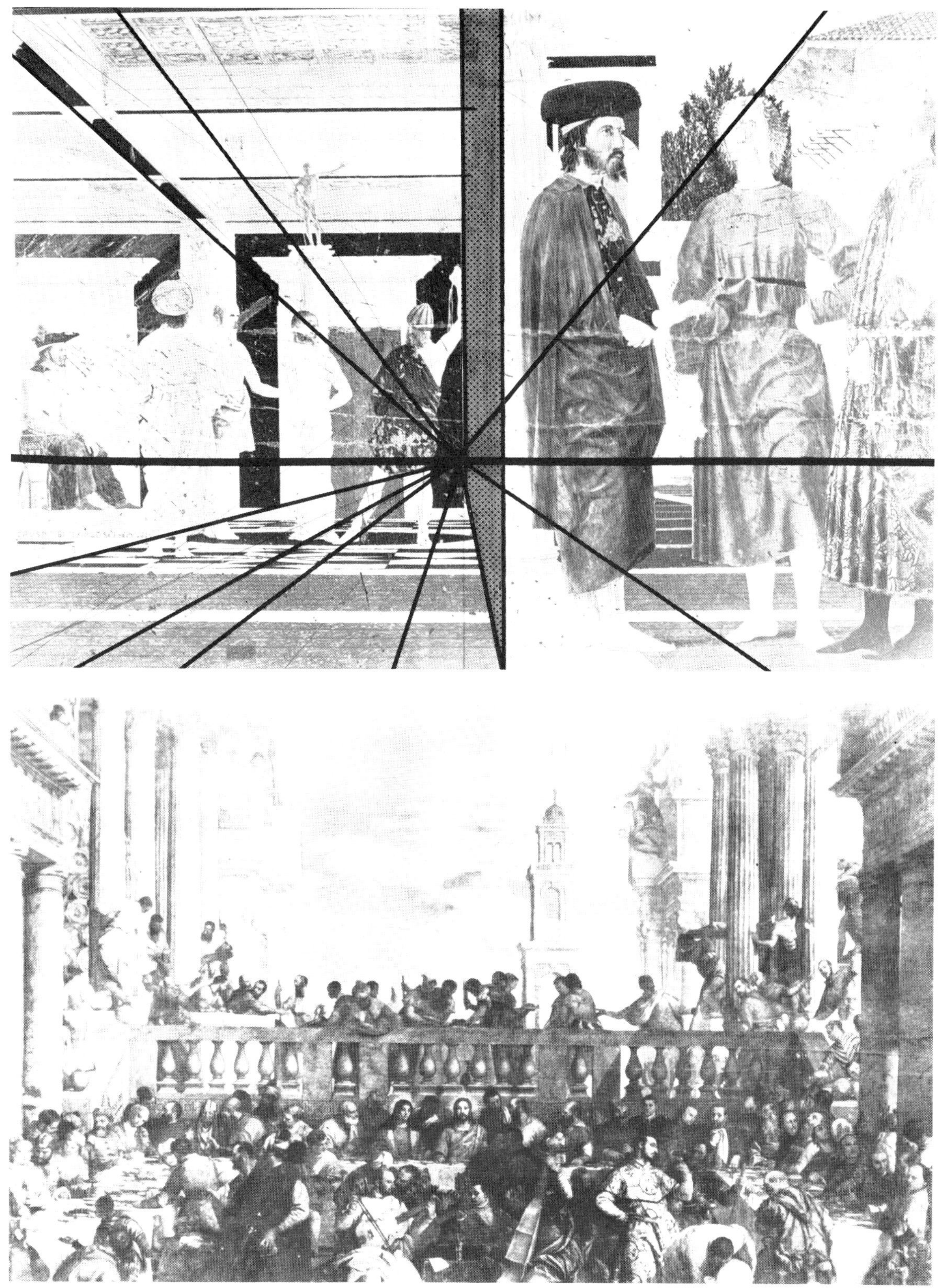

PERSPECTIVE

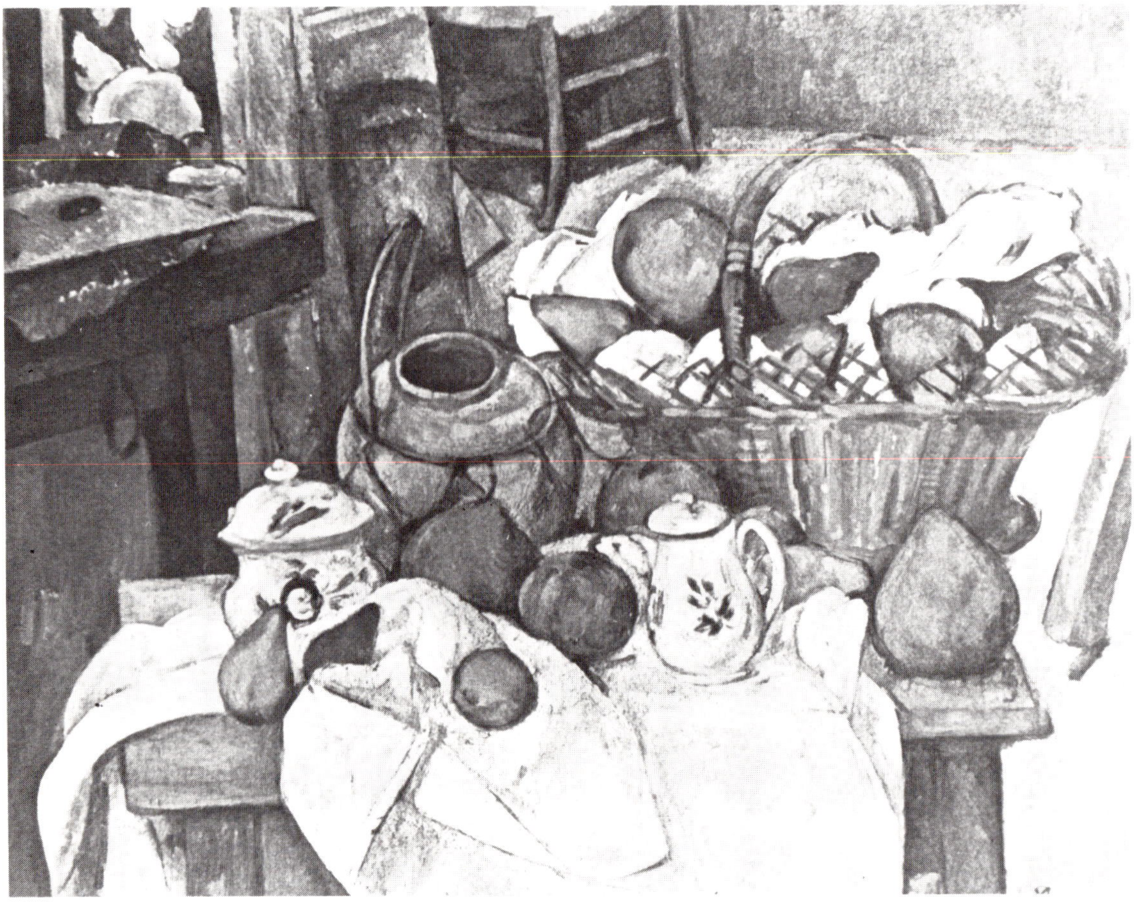

Notice the shape of the table and estimate what it would be like if the drapery were removed. It is difficult to find any evidence of perspective – wherever possible lines are parallel to the picture plane, i.e. the only lines which can be drawn which do not tend to create an illusion of spatial recession. The ellipses of jar and jug are pulled out towards the sides of the picture emphasizing the parallels to the picture plane. Colour is also used to relate foreground to background and hence to refer us again to the surface of the painting. Throughout the painting we find emphatic horizontals and verticals.

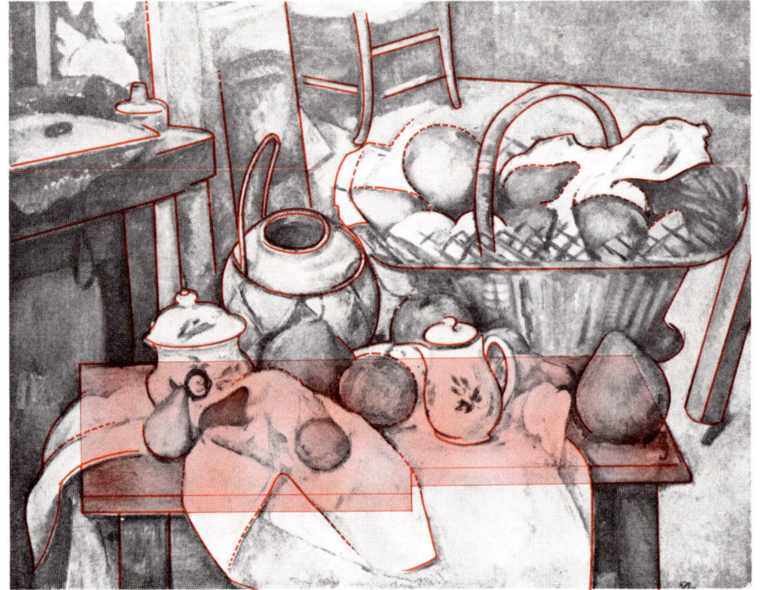

Reservoir: Pablo Picasso ▶
An analytical Cubist painting by Picasso: Picasso and Braque, in their early Cubist periods, developed aspects of Cézanne's ideas of representing space (rather than creating a spatial illusion) still further, using multiple viewpoints and tilting the subject towards the vertical. Emphasis is on change of plane rather than recession. The result is a series of planes with ambiguous relationships – front, back and sides become interchangeable.

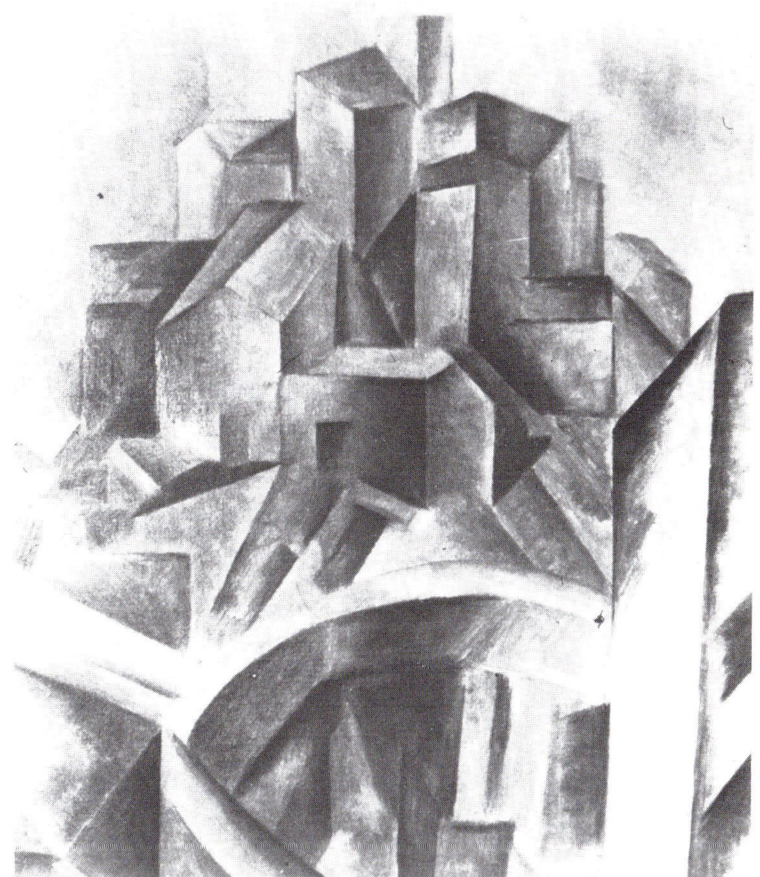

Still Life with Fruit Basket: Paul Cézanne (diagrams)
The Cubists' attitude to space was very different from that of their Expressionist counterparts, and owed a great deal to the painstaking research of Paul Cézanne. In this diagram of a still life the space occupied by the curiously-shaped table has been defined in red. Notice how the left-hand side is parallel to the picture plane. Clearly there is not space for the basket to rest on this surface, and the ginger jar would be precariously poised! In all his work Cézanne constantly (and by various means) refers us back to the picture plane. He did not try to create the illusion of space, but to *represent* space (as a low relief represents three dimensions). The ellipses of jar and basket are elongated so that they in turn remain largely parallel to the picture plane. Furthermore, in Cézanne's work he does not use a consistent single viewpoint (as in traditional perspective), but several. This idea of a multiple viewpoint was developed further by the Cubists.
The diagram (right) shows us what the shapes would have looked more like had they been drawn according to traditional perspective.

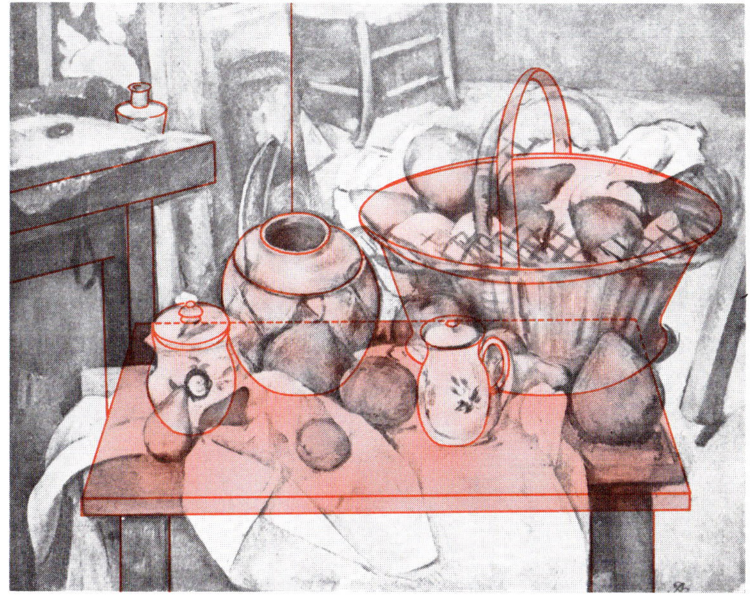

PERSPECTIVE

The Finding of St. Mark's Body: Tintoretto
In this painting we see all the devices of the Mannerists, used in masterly fashion in order to accentuate the drama of the discovery. Dramatic lighting flickers on the architecture; a spotlight plays on the contrived gestures and acute foreshortening of the figures in the foreground, and exaggerated perspective is responsible for the abrupt and disturbing change of scale.

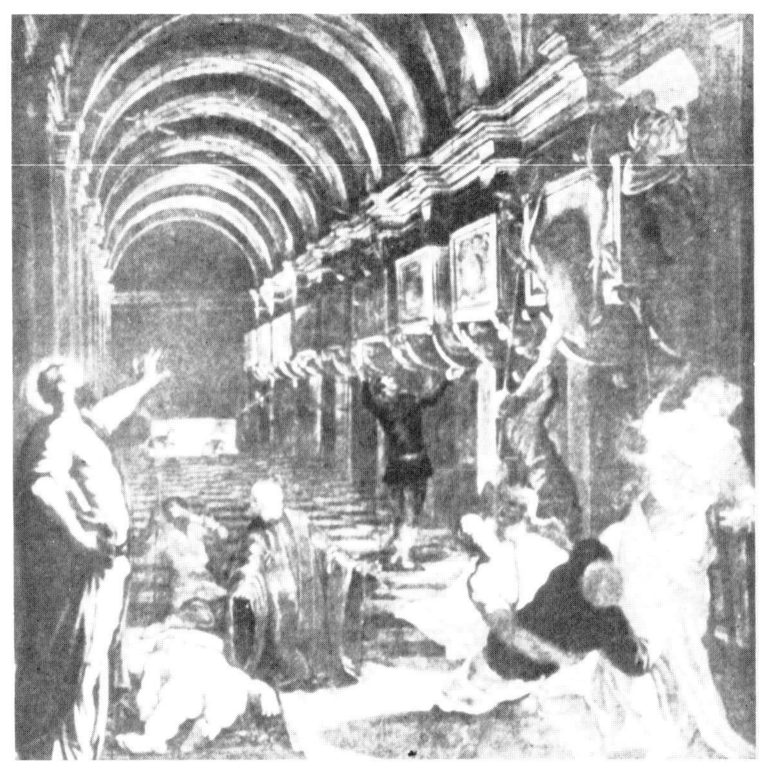

Sketch for a ceiling in the Palazzo Barberini: Pietro da Cortona
In the seventeenth century, with the Counter-reformation, there was new confidence reflected in the arts. The Baroque period saw perspective used to produce greater depths and heights than ever before. This is perspective pushed to express infinite space, rather than the finite space of the Renaissance period.

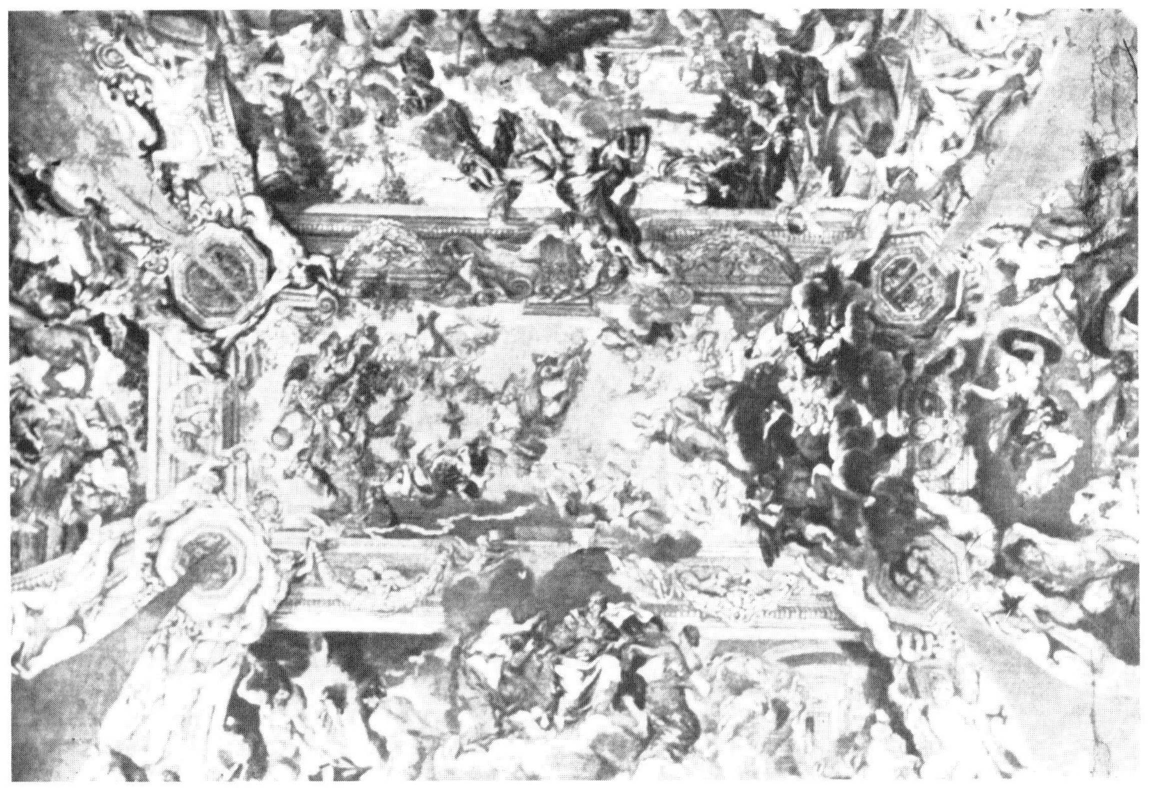

Forced perspective

The sixteenth century saw dramatic changes in the way perspective had been used by the artists of the High Renaissance. Mannerism was the new vogue and artists used forced lighting, violent foreshortening, and a forced perspective in which the parallel lines converge much more rapidly than observed in a normal situation. Of course the situation in which the Mannerists found themselves was not normal. The Reformation and the sack of Rome were only two factors disturbing the equilibrium of the Renaissance. This evidence of a disturbed state of mind, reflected in the use of forced perspective, occurs again in the work of Expressionist painters.

Bedroom at Arles: Vincent van Gogh (diagram)
The diagram shows a somewhat similar approach to perspective to that we have seen in Mannerist painting, but here the disturbance is carried further. At first sight it seems that this is a possible situation, apart from the extreme length of the bed; but analysis shows that there is no consistent vanishing point or eye level, and furthermore that it is not possible for the bed to occupy this position since the far leg, which is hidden, would have to be embedded in the wall. The Expressionists consistently distorted the representation of rational space in order to create a world which expressed their own inner turmoil.

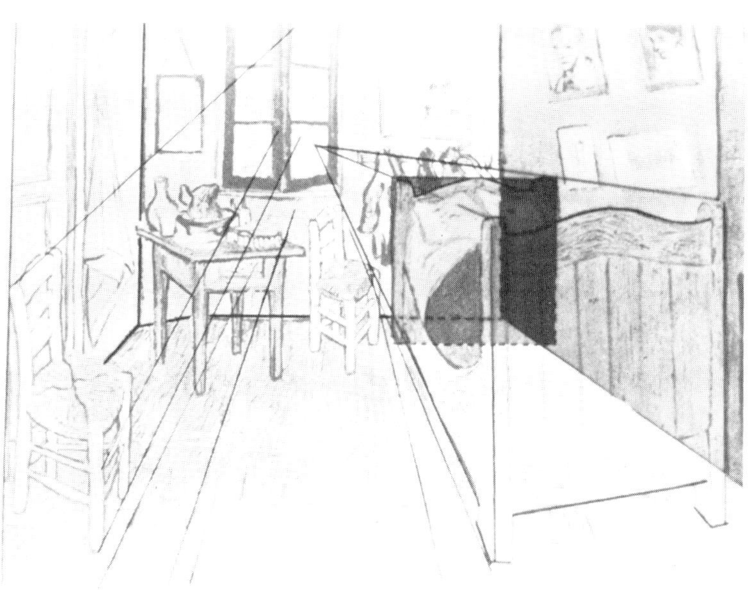

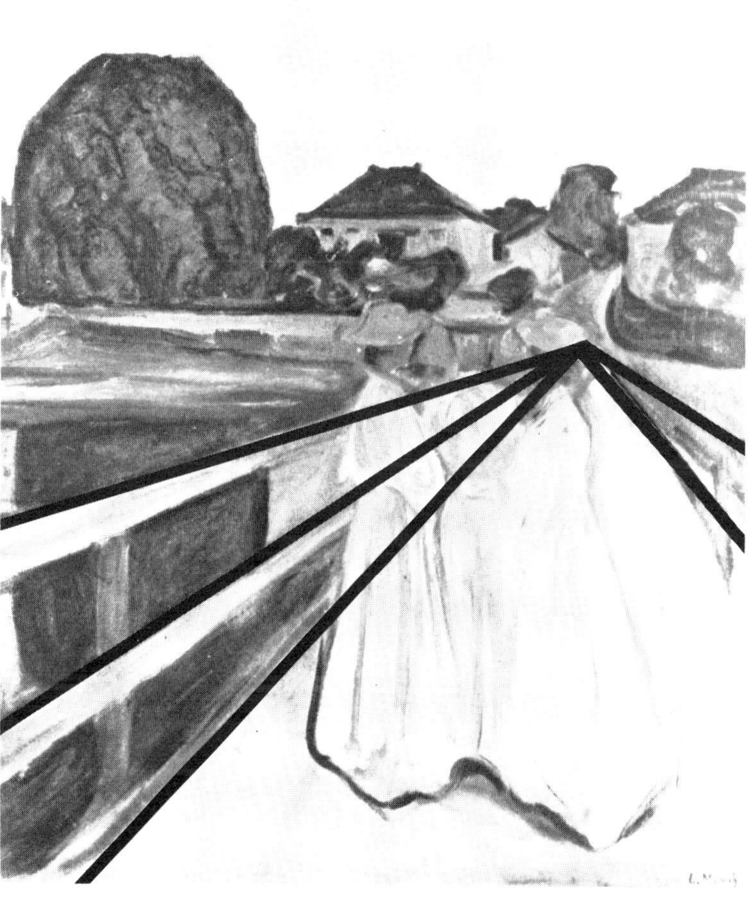

Women on a Bridge: Edvard Munch (diagram)
Another Expressionist painter, Edvard Munch, makes the perspective lines converge so rapidly that our sense of reality is challenged and infinity is brought uncomfortably close. Many other expressionist painters used perspective to express the same attitude to space – a telescoping of distance, so that our journey into the picture becomes an uncomfortable headlong rush.

Perspective of the dream

The Stockade: Paul Delvaux

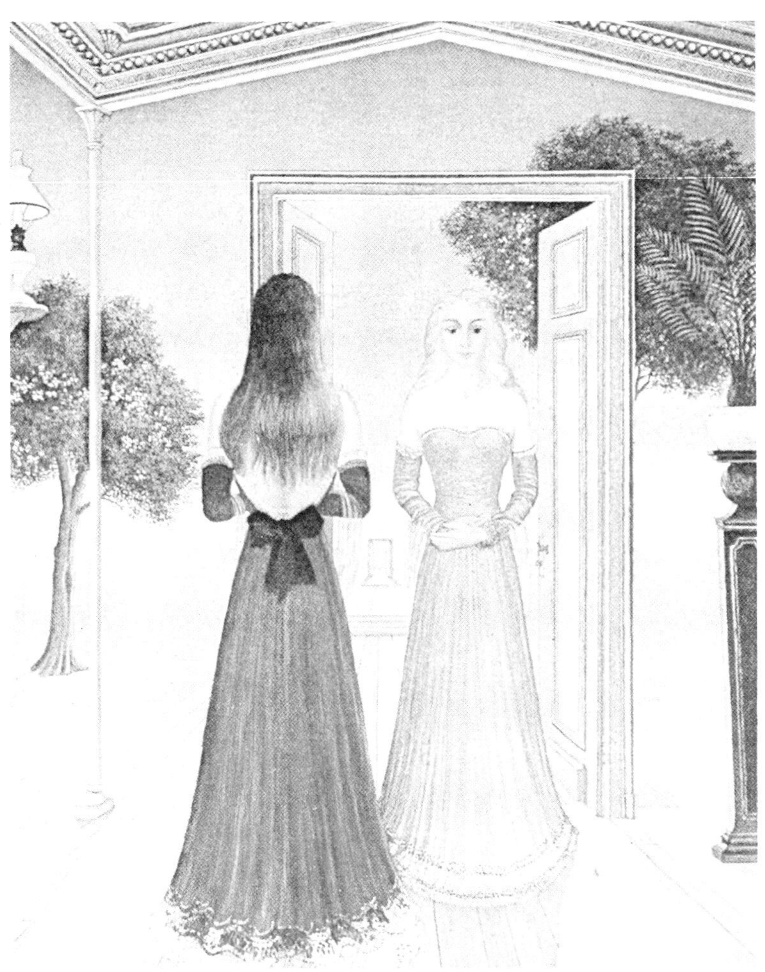

Printanière: Giorgio de Chirico

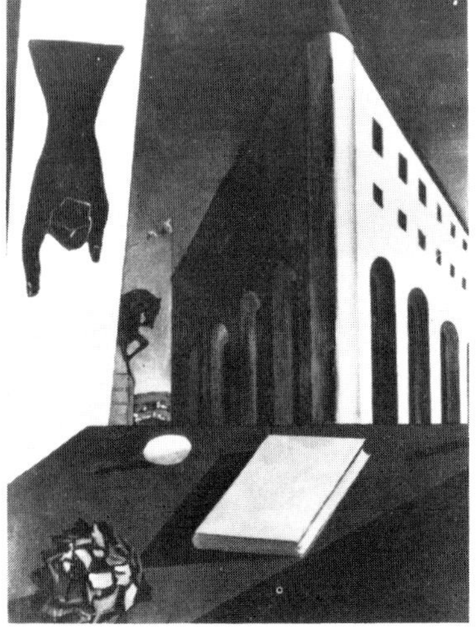

It was the Surrealists who, building on the hidden menace of de Chirico's arcades, revived the use of perspective to create spatial illusion and to convince us that the dream is reality. Vast and disturbing empty spaces become even more empty as they stretch into the far distance. Even the introduction of figures only makes the loneliness more apparent – Delvaux's elegant ladies drift slowly, soundlessly, on endless journeys to the infinity of the vanishing point, locked in their own private worlds, oblivious of time or space.

Ambiguous perspective

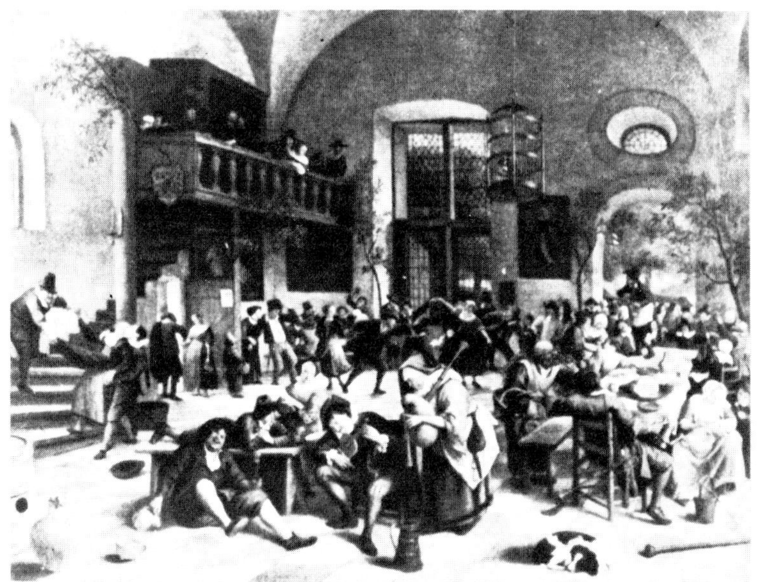

Celebration in a Tavern: Jan Steen
In this lively composition we can see many different aspects of perspective – the tiled floor of equal rectangles, the circles above and below the eye level, tables and chairs, and above this the balcony – even a spiral staircase which is quite an interesting perspective problem.

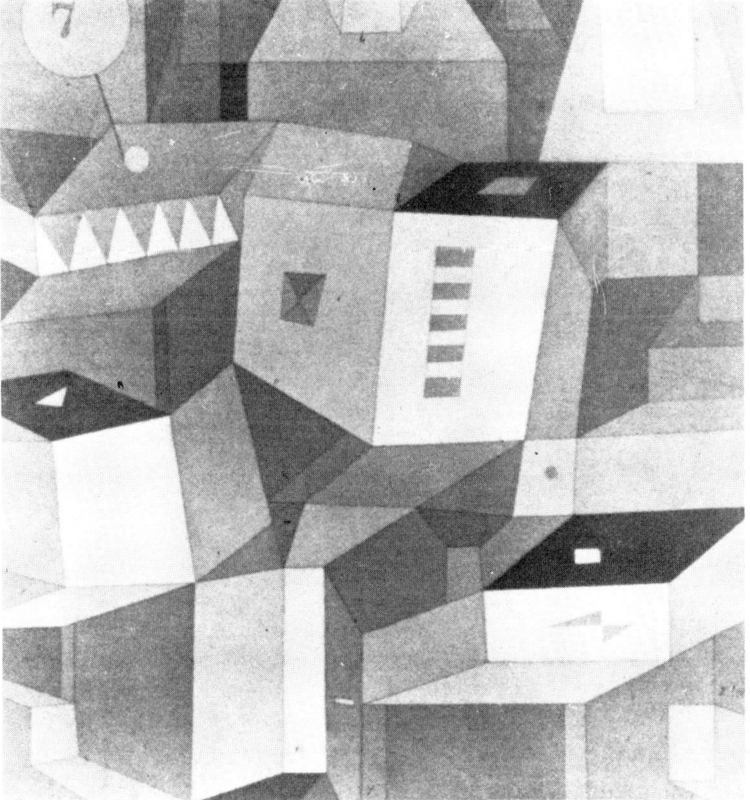

Seven o'clock over the Rooftops: Paul Klee
Klee, a master at the Bauhaus, continuously researched the possibilities and limitations of all the means of graphic expression, including the expression of space. This block-like town appears at first sight to be of simple construction, but Klee has deliberately used perspective in such an ambiguous way that it is impossible to tell which form is advancing and which receding.

GEOMETRY

'The framework of a work of art is also its most secret and deepest poetry'. J. Villon, Preface to *The Painter's Secret Geometry* by Charles Bouleau.

'As I said earlier, Piero made an intense study of painting and perspective. He acquired an intimate knowledge of Euclid, understanding better than any other geometrician the nature of the perfect curves drawn on a basis of regular bodies; and the clearest elucidation of these matters come from his pen'. Vasari, *Lives of the Artists.*

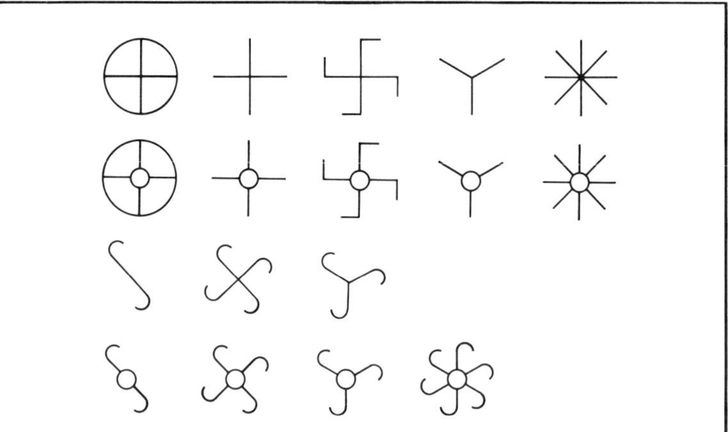

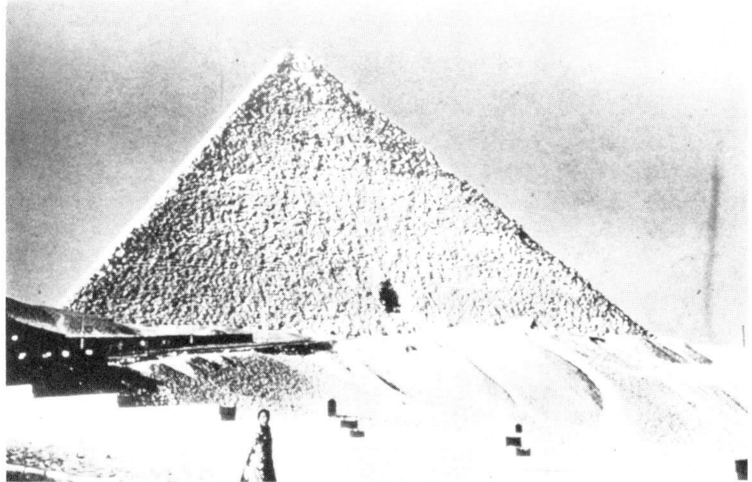

The Great Pyramid at Gizeh
In Egypt, the use of the so-called 'triangle of Osiris,' with its sides of three, four and five units, may have acquired its divine significance by virtue of the built-in right-angle. The Great Pyramid at Gizeh is an example of monumental three-dimensional geometry.

Sun wheels (diagram)
The spirals, chevrons, circles and semicircles that appear in the early art of almost all the countries of the world were probably originally pictographs representing those physical phenomena which were objects of nature worship – so-called 'sun wheels' (top diagram) appear as rock carvings, dating back to Neolithic times before the wheel was invented.

These signs gradually migrated into the art of other nations where, possibly through ignorance of their original meaning, they were copied, repeated and used to fill in simply as geometric ornament.

By 3000 B.C. the ancient civilizations of Mesopotamia and Egypt had produced surveyors, astronomers and architects whose achievements in those fields were based on accurate geometric constructions.

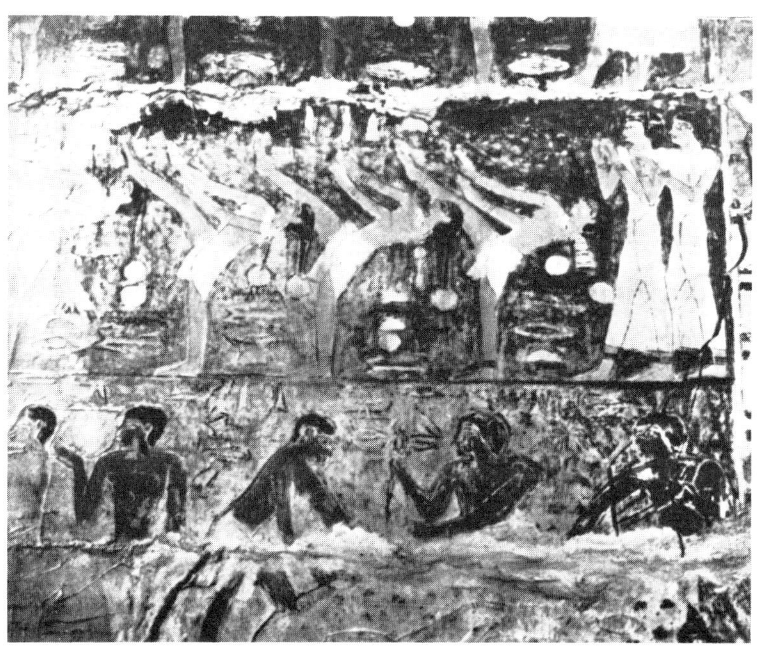

Egyptian mural painting from the Necropolis of Memphis
Systematic geometric procedure was also a feature of both Egyptian sculpture and mural painting, which were planned on a network of squares. From work which was unfinished, it is possible to see the procedure: string dipped in paint and laid across the wall was used to establish a framework of regular squares, on which the composition was constructed – which accounts for the rigid, uncompromising appearance of these works.

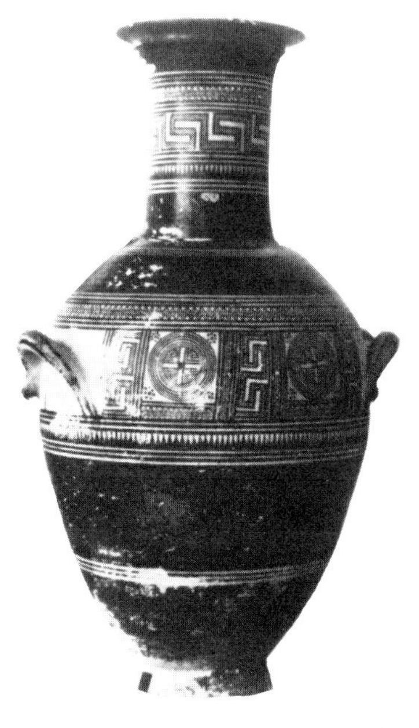

Greek amphora
Whereas the Greeks owed a great deal to Egypt and Mesopotamia, they transformed their predecessors' rigorous practice of geometry into an abstract reasoning system. During the period 900–700 B.C., Greek pottery was decorated with compass-drawn circles and abstract geometric patterns, and even human figures and animals were reduced to geometric shapes. This geometric stylization was extended to sculpture and modelling – an aspect of composition which reappeared in the twentieth century, as in the work of Léger or Le Corbusier.

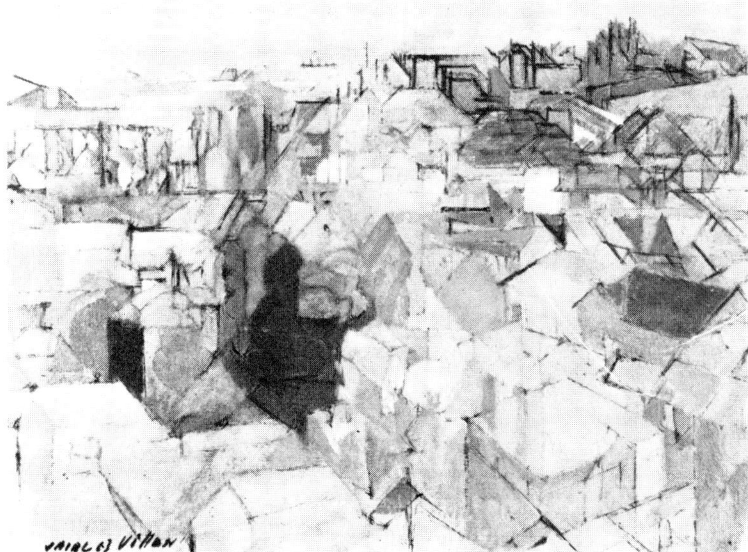

Vue de Bernay: Jacques Villon
Jacques Villon uses a geometric network of diagonals to relate roofs and buildings, and to stabilize this composition.

The diagram illustrates a simple method of dividing a line AB at the Golden Section.

1. Erect a perpendicular BD, equal to ½ AB, at B (or at A, as the construction may start from either end of the line).
2. Join AD.
3. With D as centre and DB as radius, describe an arc cutting AD at X.
4. With A as centre and AX as radius, describe an arc cutting AB at GS.

This results in a relationship where GSB : AGS :: AGS : AB, i.e. the lesser is to the greater as the greater is to the whole; and this is the proportion which has been so extensively used by artists.

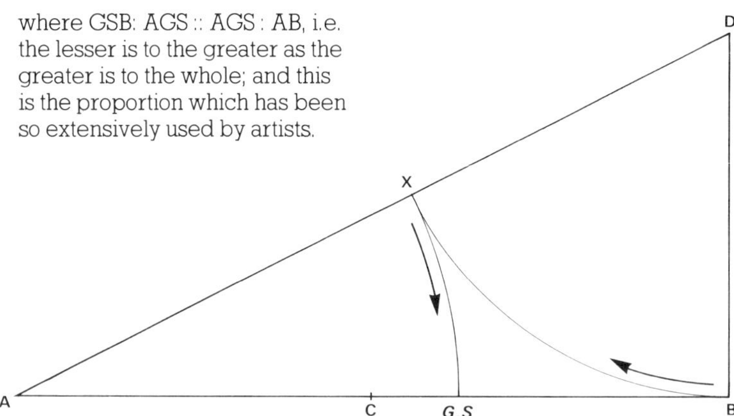

Parade: Georges Seurat (diagram)
Many artists and architects of the Renaissance looked on theories of proportion with the greatest reverence, seeing in them a rational basis for beauty. Since then other artists and architects have continued to make conscious use of the Golden Section as a means of proportioning their work – e.g. Vermeer, Rembrandt, and Seurat, and particularly Le Corbusier who based his modular system of proportion on the Fibonacci series.

Although Seurat was heavily involved in colour theory, endeavouring to find a way of conveying the effect of light by a more scientific approach, he also wished to impose a more rational system of structured composition on the snapshot effects of the Impressionists.

This painting is as carefully organized in arrangement of form as in colour. We sense some static inevitability of composition, as is found in Piero della Francesca's *The Flagellation* (see page 59) where the placing of the figure is equally governed by laws of proportion.

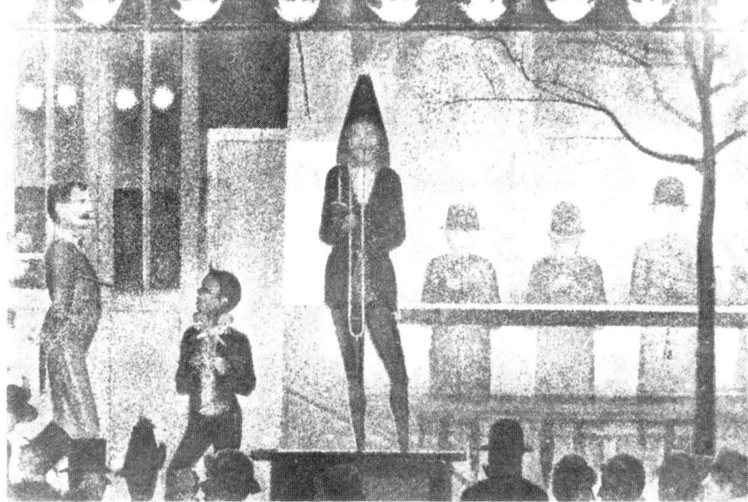

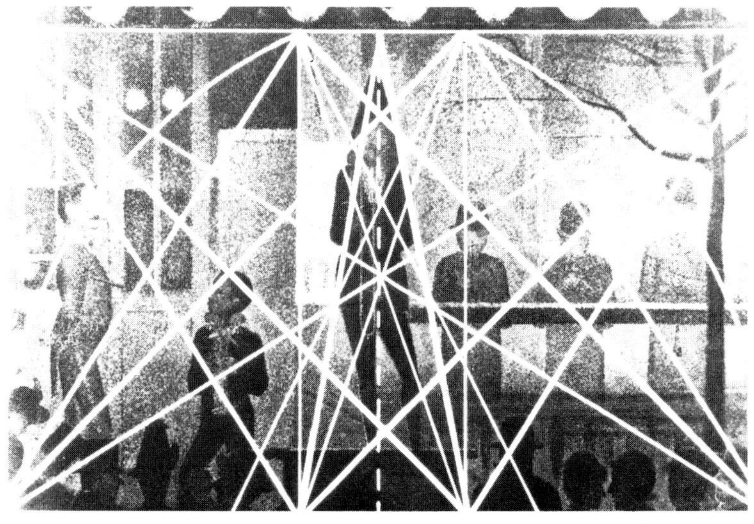

The Golden Section as the basis of geometric proportion

When one is asked to divide a line into two parts so as to create a harmonious or aesthetically satisfying relationship between them, there is a strong tendency to divide the line approximately into one-third and two-thirds, rather than half and half or one-eighth and seven-eighths. However, can the line be divided into two parts in such a way as to create an ideal relationship between these parts?

The division described by Euclid as the Golden Ratio and referred to by Renaissance writers as the Divine Proportion, which became known in the nineteenth century as the Golden Section, has for centuries been considered by artists and designers to create such an ideal relationship.

Curiously enough it is a proportion which is found frequently in Nature and is felt to be a natural division.

The Divine Proportion is described as one in which the relationship between the bigger and the smaller is the same as that between the bigger, and the bigger and the smaller added together.

The division to create this proportion can only be found by geometric means. The proportion cannot be expressed exactly in rational numbers (although the Golden Ratio has been represented numerically by Fibonacci, the medieval scholar, as a series: $\frac{1}{1}$ $\frac{2}{1}$ $\frac{3}{2}$ $\frac{5}{3}$ $\frac{8}{5}$ $\frac{13}{8}$ $\frac{21}{13}$ etc. approaching the Golden Ratio – a series whose terms in fact, become more accurate as one goes higher.

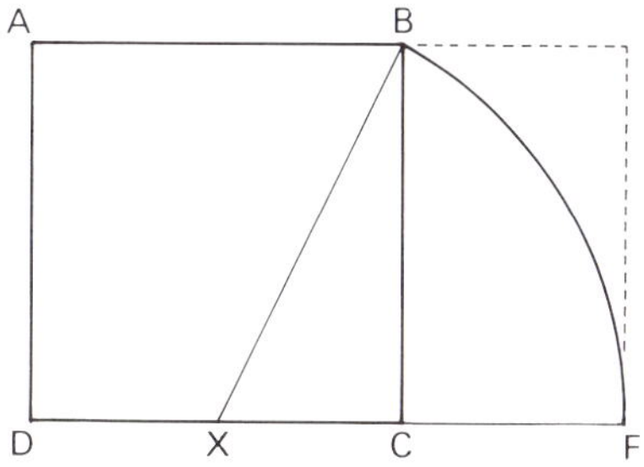

Commencing with a square ABCD, if we halve DC at X, then with X as centre and XB as radius describe an arc which cuts DC extended at F, we have a Golden Section: one in which the proportion of the short side AD to the long side DF is the same as that between the long side and the sum of the two sides.

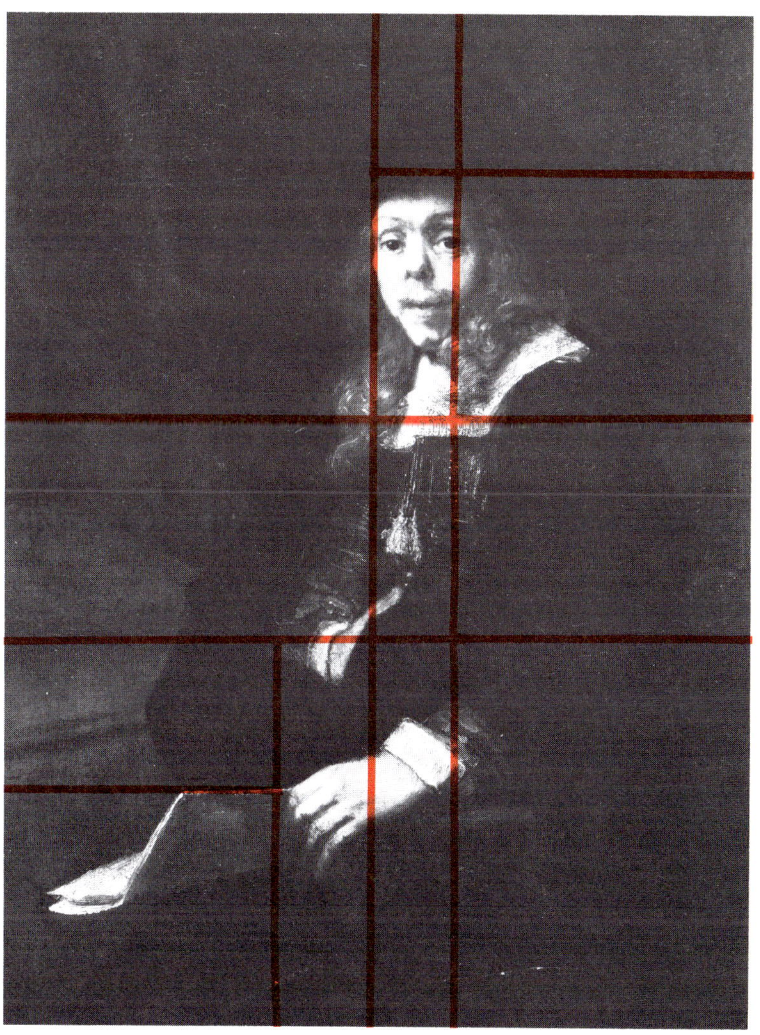

Portrait of Gerard de Lairesse: Rembrandt (diagram)
Although Rembrandt never left Holland, he was greatly influenced by Italian art. He was particularly interested in Raphael, making copies of his work, and was well aware of the renewed interest in geometry and the Renaissance artists.

By dividing this portrait of the painter Gerard de Lairesse vertically and subdividing it into four Golden Section divisions, we see how Rembrandt's placing of the salient features – face, collar, hand and book – is governed by these relationships.

GEOMETRY

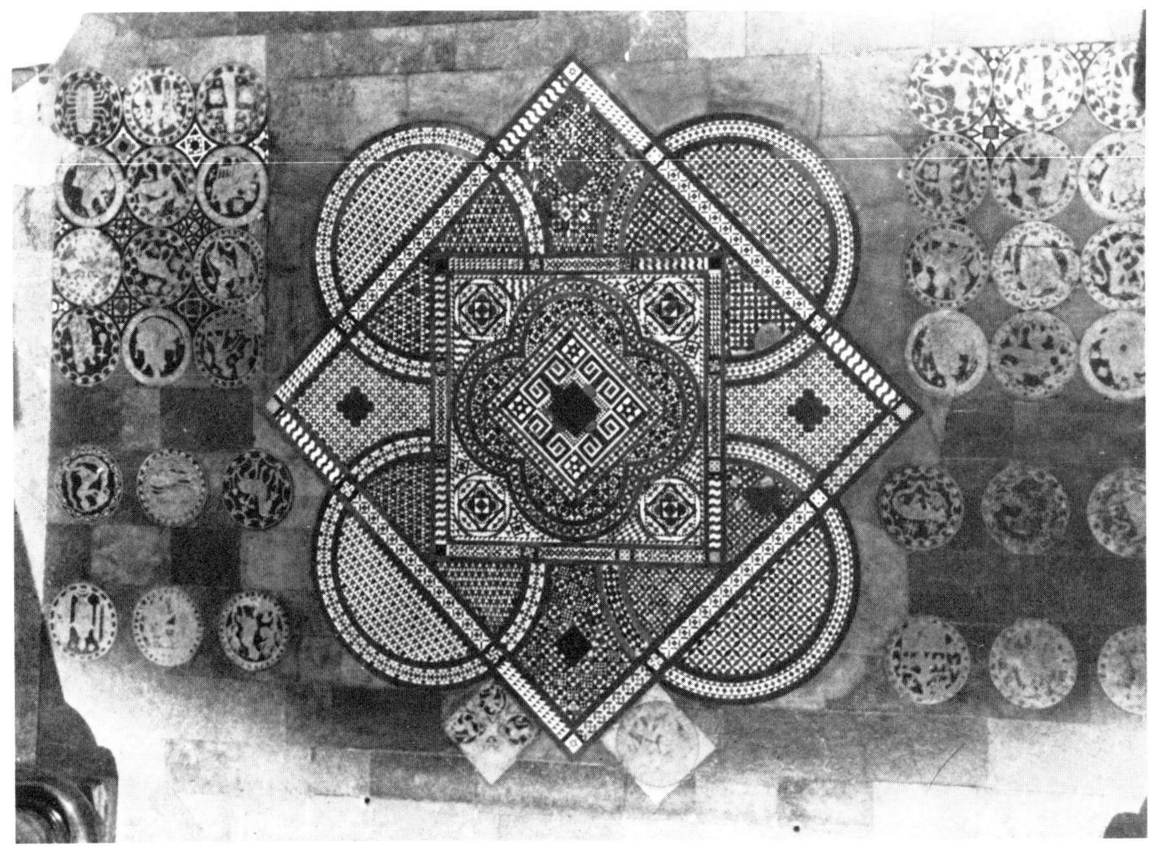

Pavement from behind the high altar, Canterbury Cathedral

This mosaic from the pavement behind the High Altar of Canterbury Cathedral incorporates not only a complex pattern but also a complex symbolism. The origins of this kind of geometric design are ancient and archetypal. The mediaeval alchemists sought the mysteries of matter, as a kind of holy quest, setting them against the heavenly spirit of Christianity, seeking a wholeness between mind and body – a search that has inspired mystics and yogi to this day.

One of the central alchemical symbols was the *quadratura circuli* – the squaring of the circle. There, two abstract figures united the world of thoughts and feeling. The rose windows of Christian churches aspired to unite the infinite with the finite through the square and the circle, an aspiration common to both Christian and Islamic symbolism.

So the complex geometry of this design from the Cathedral floor has many subconscious levels, perhaps some of which were buried in the human psyche before the advent of Christianity.

Geometry as pattern

The basis of pattern, being the repetition (or suggested repetition) of a motif, requires a framework on which one can build or organize the repeat. This framework is often the underlying (unseen but nevertheless felt) basic geometry.

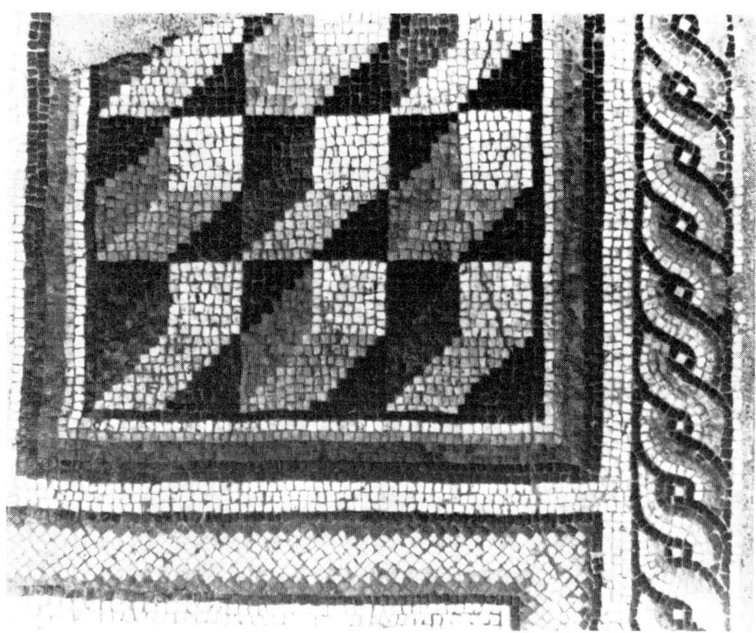

Roman mosaic floor
In this floor the geometric framework *is* the pattern, but in a number of ways. The ambiguous relationship of the planes, with their alternative readings of either three-dimensional or simply two-dimensional repeating shapes, gives added interest to this sophisticated example of geometry as pattern.

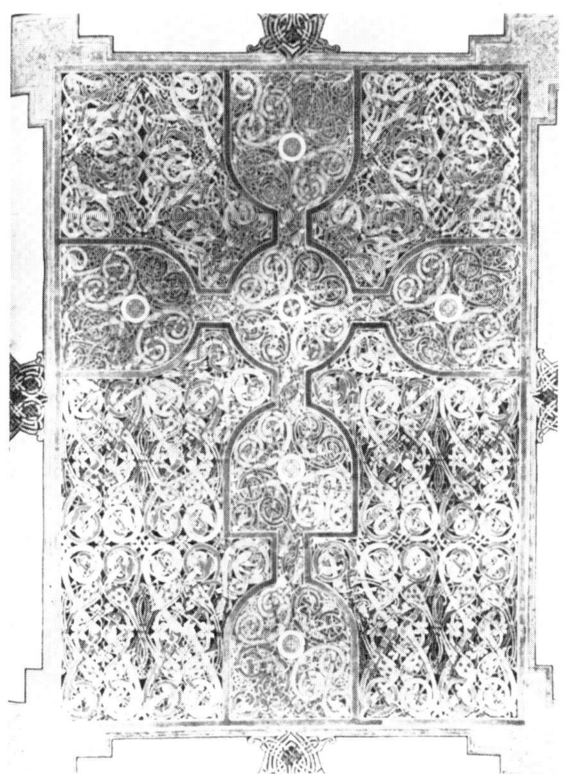

Ornamental page from the Lindisfarne Gospels
The complexity of interlacing geometric pattern was developed to a high art by the Hiberno-Saxon manuscript illuminators. Their geometric tapestry of lines was woven to the glory of God – the Great Geometrician of the Universe. Abstract beauty is achieved through geometry as the means of interrelating the parts to the whole. (This concept created a link between the Islamic world and the Ancient Egyptian/Greek world).

Note
It may be suggested that if one draws the internal geometric divisions on any painting, the lines drawn must coincide with some lines of the painting. Of course; but even if no conscious decision was made by the artist to use the internal geometry, it may be that there is a subconscious tendency to relate some of the main divisions of the painting to the natural divisions of the space. But quite clearly certain painters, including those mentioned in this section, have quite deliberately made a number of major decisions based on geometric division of the space available before commencing work: coincidence can only go so far. However, excessively complicated geometrical networks, spread all over paintings as a kind of geometric catch-all, are of little value or relevance in arriving at understanding art. Artists generally have a simple and ingenious way of organizing space.

GEOMETRY

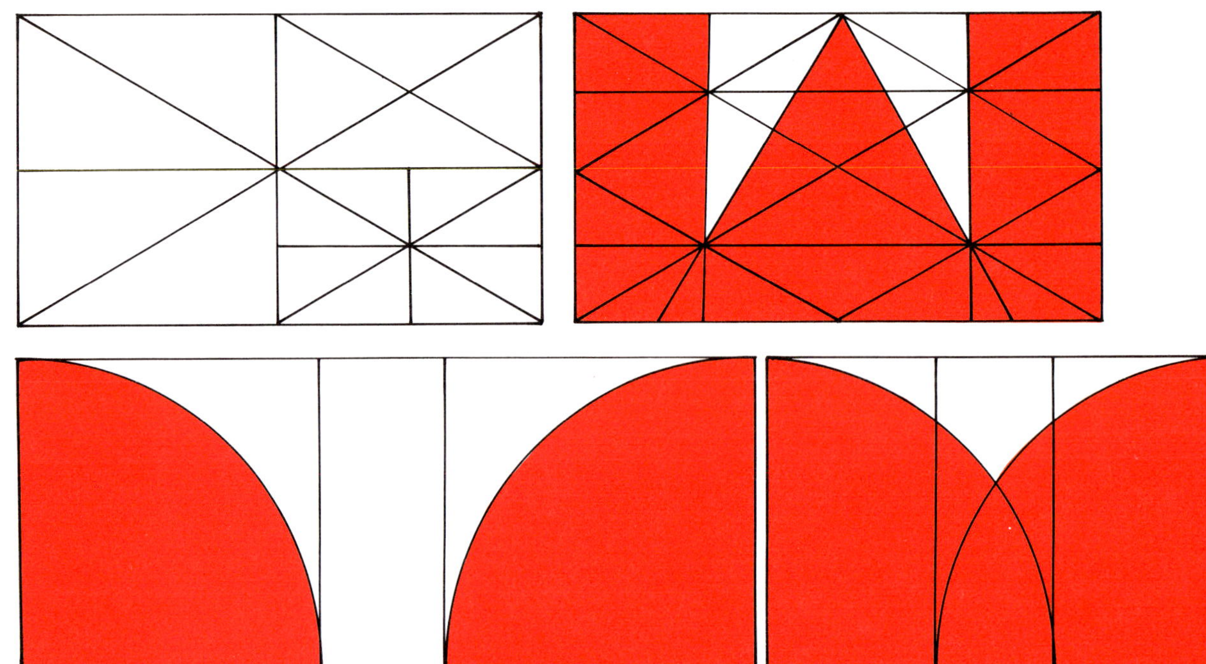

Rebatement of a rectangle (diagram)
Another simple method of constructing the painting by geometric means (a variation on the previous method) is by rotating the short sides of the rectangle on to the long side, thus producing either a separate rectangle between, or a rectangle caused by overlapping.

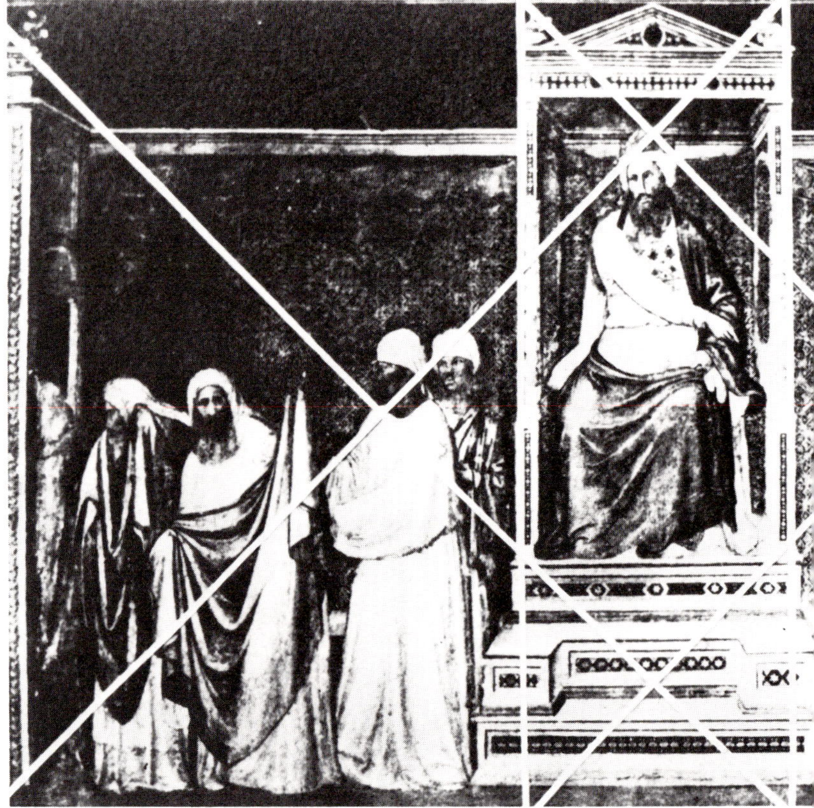

The Trial by Fire: Giotto (diagram)
A simple and immaculate example of this kind of rebatement division is provided in this painting by Giotto. The sides of the throne are arrived at by rebating the sides of the painting, and the position of the back wall screen by the intersecting of the diagonals of the overlapping rectangles.

Geometry as construction

The rectangle is the most commonly-used shape in design. Concealed within this shape (as we saw in the section on the point) are natural divisions and proportions which can be used by the artist armed only with a straight-edge, by which means it is possible to create innumerable relationships of shape, all related to the original rectangle. This is the geometric basis of much of the work of the Renaissance and of the neo-Classical painters following in their footsteps (see Note on page 71).

The diagrams (above left) illustrate the progressive division of a rectangle based on the internal geometry.

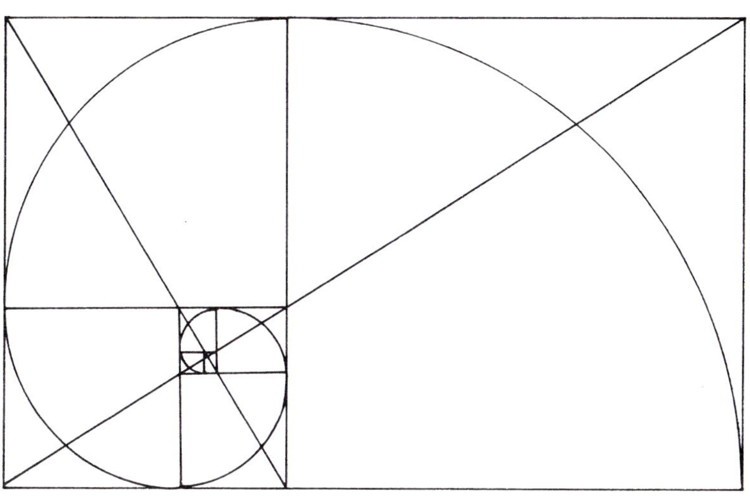

Rectangle of the whirling squares (diagram)
If we construct a golden section rectangle as described on page 69, and then subtract a square from this rectangle, we are left with another golden section rectangle. We may continue to subtract successive squares, and always have a golden section rectangle as remainder, decreasing in constant ratio to infinity. By using a compass to draw segments of circles in these squares we arrive at a spiral.

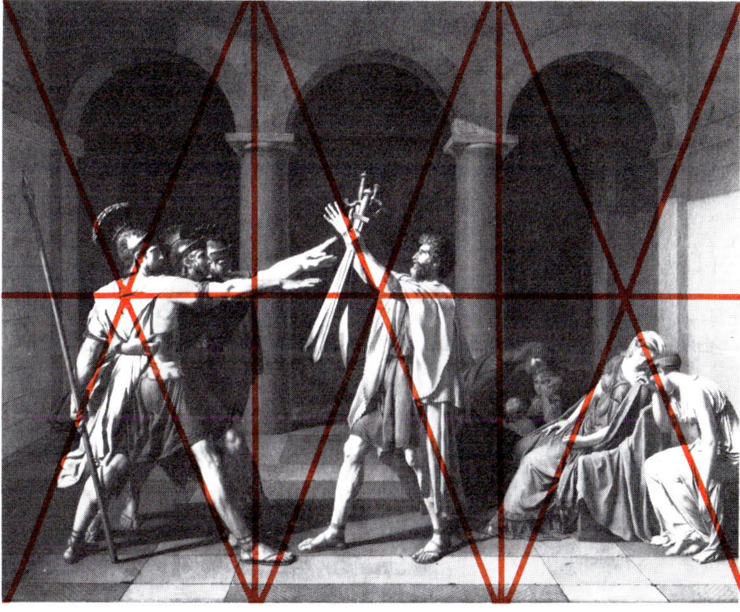

Oath of the Horatii: David (diagram)
Like all classical and neo-Classical painters, David places his figures and classical background parallel to the picture plane. All is arranged with the greatest care to contribute to that feeling of law and order which we associate with Classicism. A simple basic geometry based on the division of the painting with three equal parts, corresponding to the architecture, helps us to understand the main distribution of the figures and the directional thrusts.

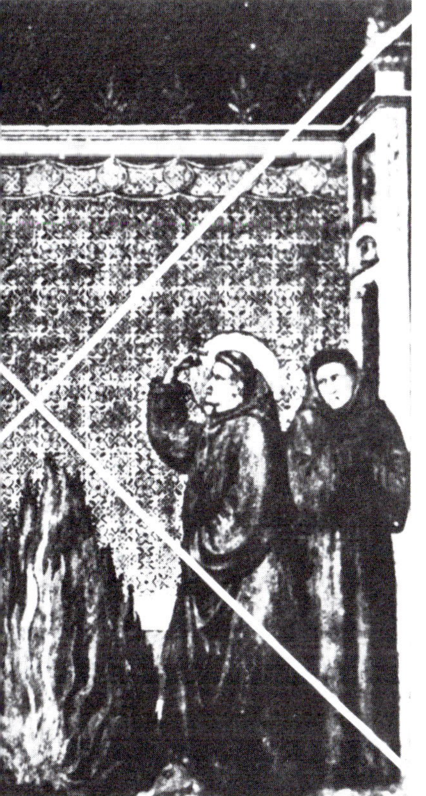

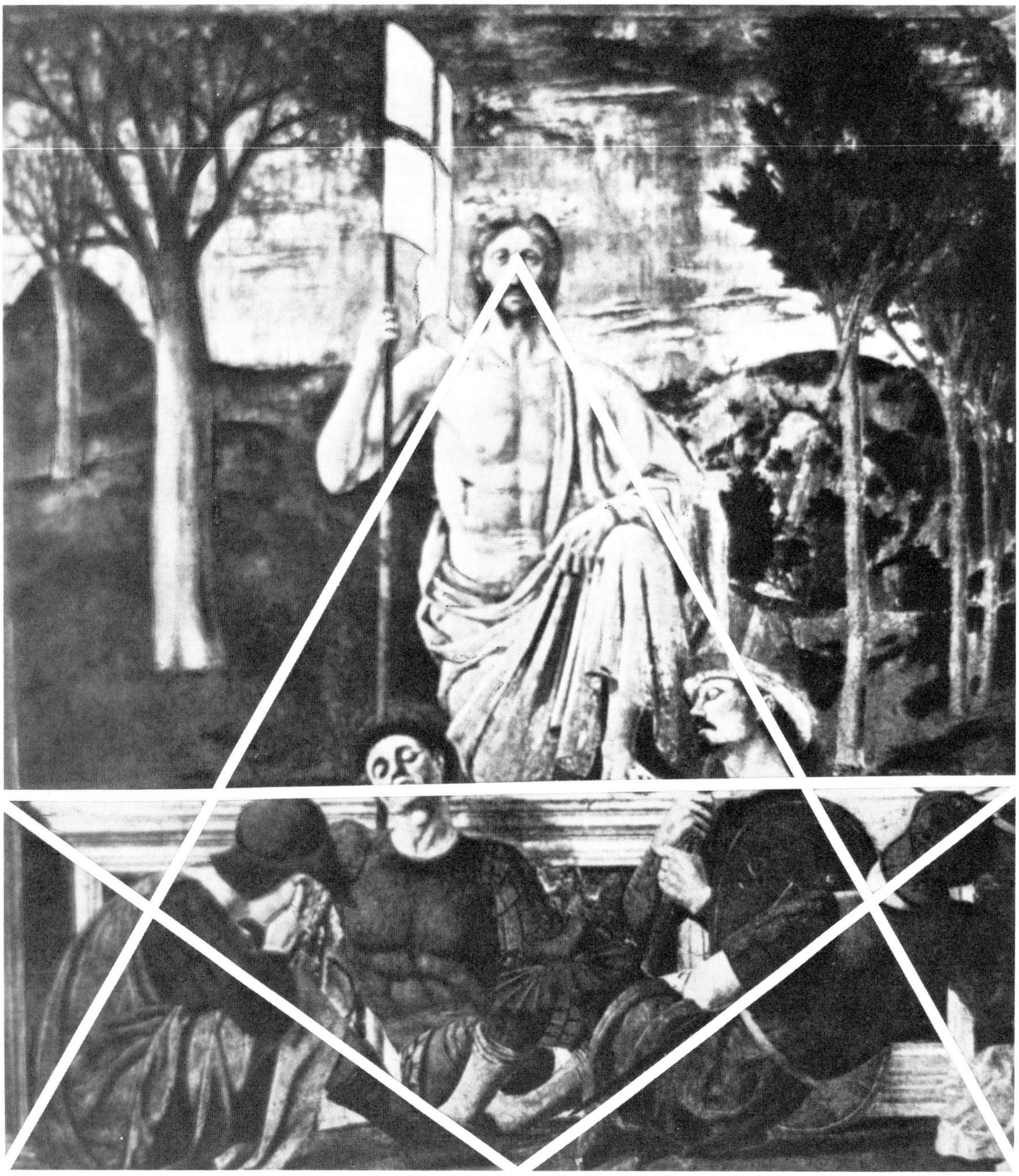

The triangle as the basis of composition

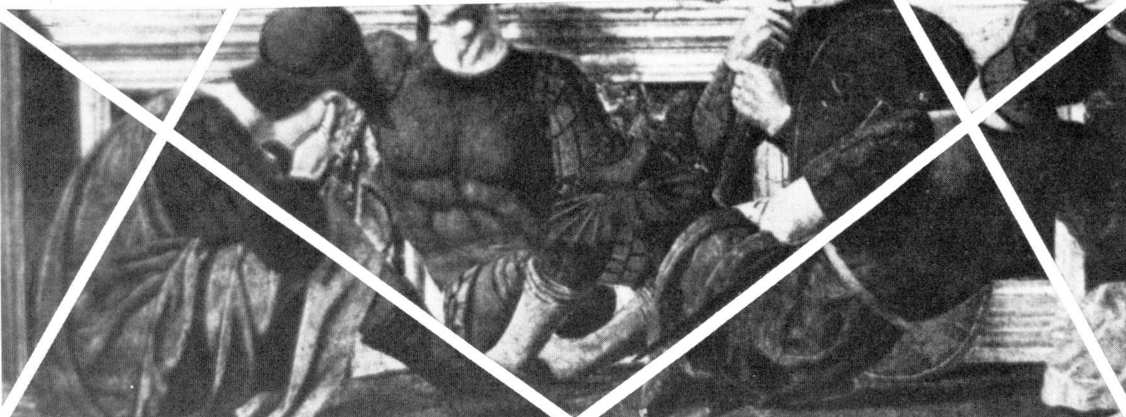

The Resurrection: Piero della Francesca (diagram)

The triangle, as a basic element of composition, was commonly used during the Renaissance. In this painting by Piero della Francesca, taking the top of the tomb as base line and constructing an equilateral triangle, we find Christ's head as its apex, completely central in the composition.

Completing an inverted isosceles triangle below the top of the tomb, we notice (by association) the cleverly-contrived way in which Piero has exactly balanced one sleeping soldier against another; so that this whole painting is one of immaculate balance on each side of Christ, the central axis.

The circle

'As the geometer his mind applies
to square the circle, nor for all his wit
finds the right formula, howe'er he tries. . .'

Dante, *Paradiso* xxxiii 9, 133–35, translated by Barbara Reynolds.

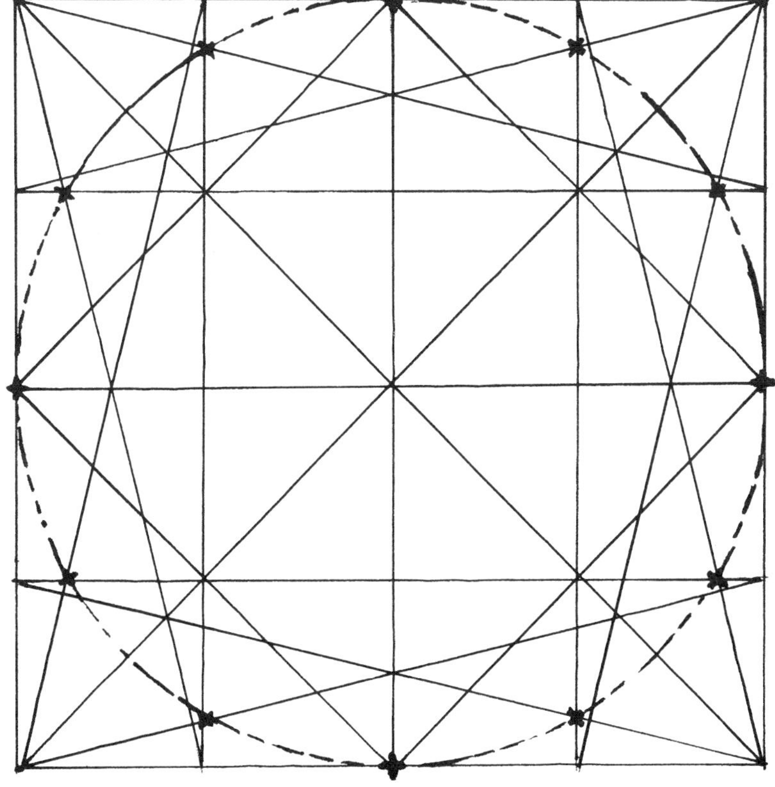

The geometry of the circle (diagram)

The basic geometry of the circle can be appreciated best by considering the method by which artists construct the circle from the square.

By subdividing the square as shown, twelve points are found which enable one to construct the circle as shown or equally well in perspective.

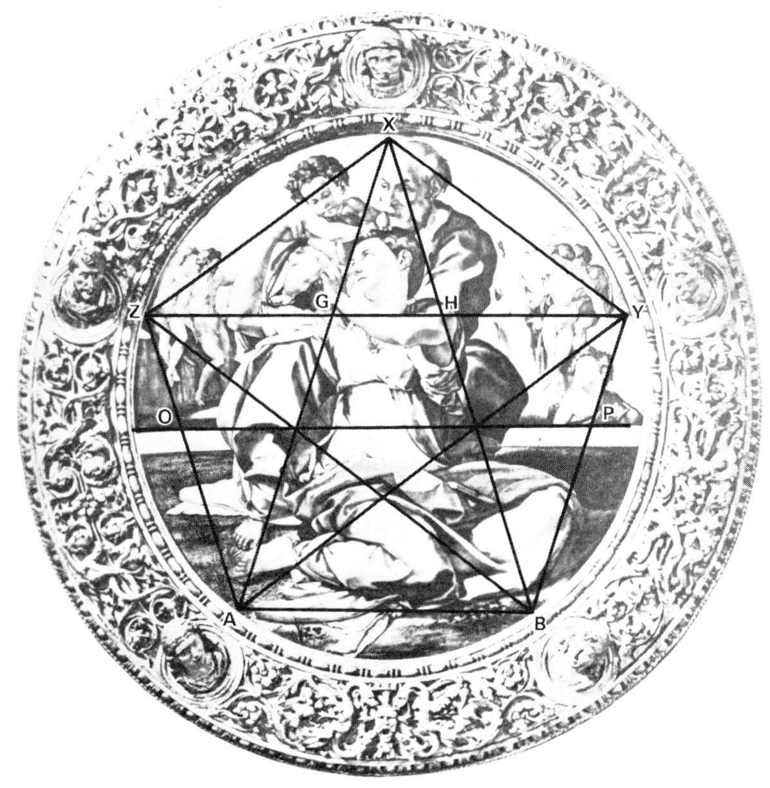

The Holy Family: Michelangelo (diagram)

When a pentagon ABY X Z is inscribed in a circle, the diagonals produce an inscribed pentagonal star. The series of proportions produced are *all* those of the Golden Section.

e.g. $\frac{AX}{AG} = \frac{AG}{GX} = \frac{GX}{GH}$ etc.

Michelangelo used this system of the inscribed pentagon to govern the composition of this circular painting which is still in its original frame. The placing of the modelled heads on the five corners of the pentagon are clear pointers to the geometry of the construction.

Notice how the placing of the horizontal feature dividing foreground from background is placed on a line passing through intersection O/P.

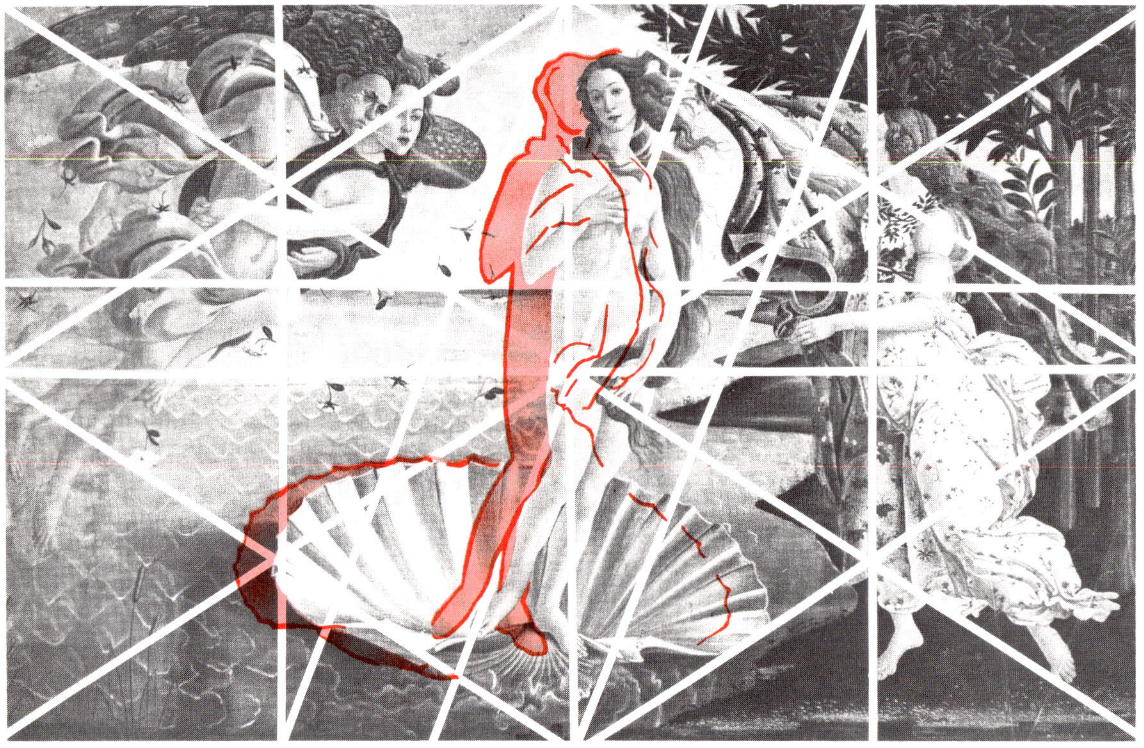

The Birth of Venus: Botticelli (diagram)
The Birth of Venus by Botticelli is of particular interest in its geometry since analysis shows the position of Venus to have been moved off-centre by a degree which precisely conveys that suggestion of movement from a central starting point consistent with the idea of zephyrs blowing the shell towards the shore. Any further displacement towards the awaiting nymph would suggest too fast a movement for that dreamy drifting so characteristic of Botticelli, and so consistent with the subject.

Geometry as movement

Geometry, like the newly awakened interest in perspective, was one of the mainsprings of Renaissance painting.

The Parable of the Blind: Pieter Breughel (diagram)

This painting by Breughel illustrates the words from the Gospel of St. Matthew 'If the blind lead the blind, both shall fall into the ditch'. Basically six figures are arranged as four and two in a descending diagonal. The axes of each of these figures is clearly related (is it coincidence that these axial directions seem to pass through the sightless eyes of the blind?). Commencing with the verticality of figure 1 (notice the emphasis on the vertical folds of the cloak) the others follow a gradually accelerating angle of deflection from this vertical until reaching the gap between figures 4 and 5 there is a dramatic pause, before numbers 5 and 6 lurch into a greater degree of deflection than before, with number 6 ending as near horizontal. The degree of movement starts gradually and gathers momentum.

While the geometric structure chosen by Breughel on which to base his figures suggests tottering movement, he contrasts this with the strongly-based triangle of home and church – clearly a visual reference to the true meaning of the parable, that those who are blind to religion and the values of home and hearth must fall into the abyss.

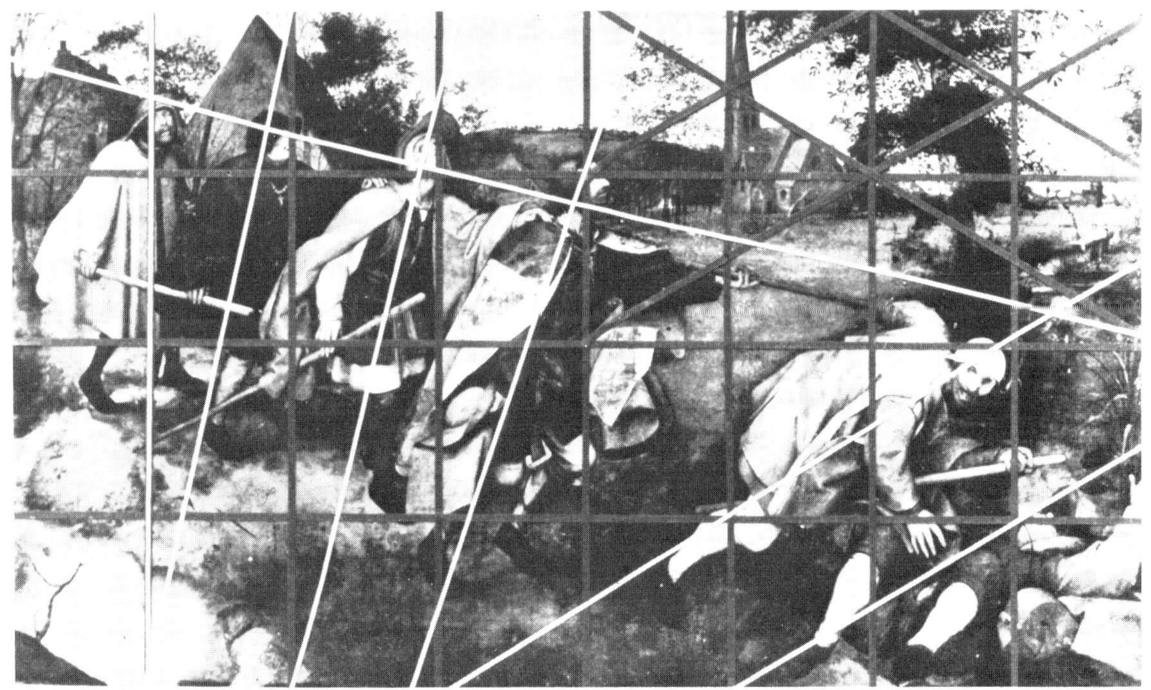

GEOMETRY

Geometry as shape and form

In 1917 Gris wrote to Kahnweiler saying 'I would like to continue the tradition of painting with plastic means while bringing to it a new aesthetic based on the intellect.'

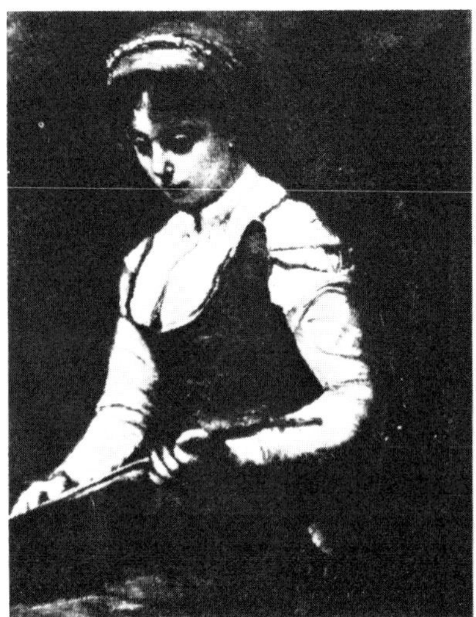

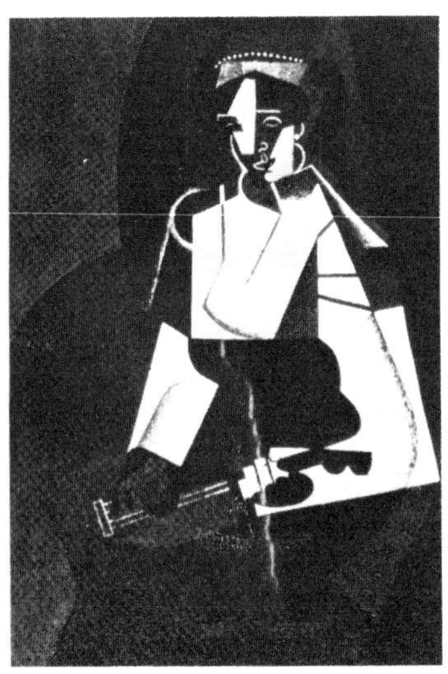

Girl with a Mandolin: Camille Corot, analysed by Juan Gris
This analysis of a Corot by Gris takes the tradition of painting and imposes a new aesthetic based on pure geometry. Where lines can be interpreted as straight, they are ruled. Subtle shifting curves of the original become taut and geometrically disciplined.

This preoccupation with finding geometric equivalents for shapes has been of major importance to many artists from the beginning of the century. The immediate origins of their inspiration are to be found in that 'Primitive of a New Art', Cézanne.

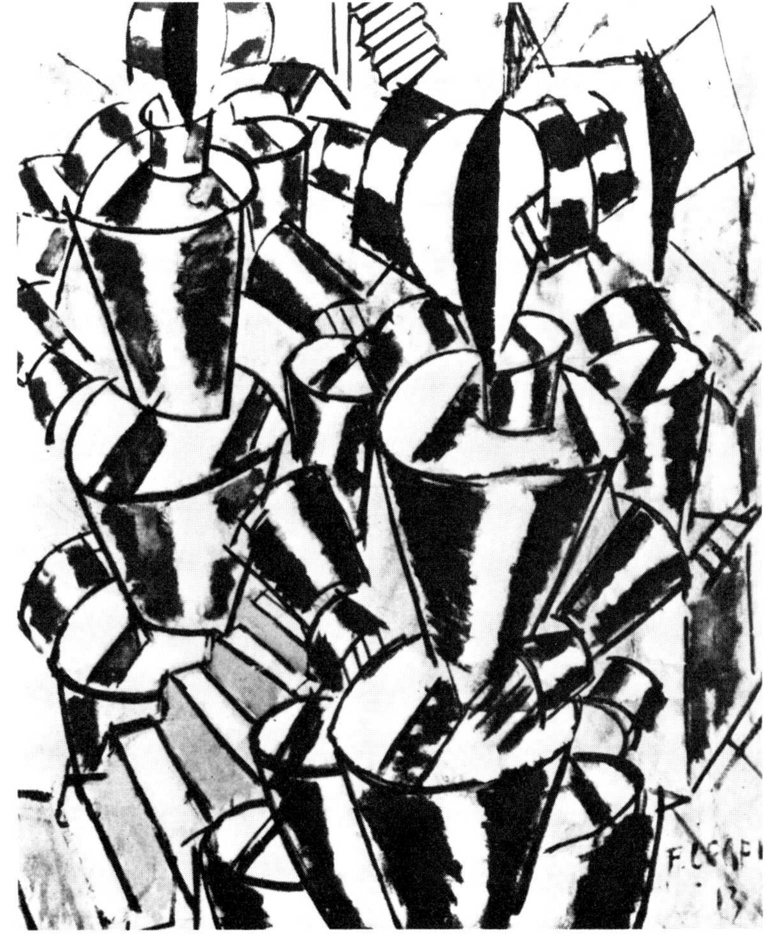

Staircase: Fernand Léger
Many twentieth century artists have clearly considered very carefully Cézanne's words: 'Treat Nature by the cylinder, the sphere and the cone, everything in proper perspective so that each side of an object is directed towards a central point.'

Léger seems to have taken Cézanne's words very much to heart – in many of his paintings, figures (and landscapes) have been reduced to that basic solid geometry advocated by Cézanne.

Geometry as Subject

As early as 1914 Kasimir Malevich had produced a painting of a black square on a white ground, and by 1918 a white square on a white ground! Surely this is the ultimate example of the 'primacy of pure sensation in the visual arts', Malevich's own definition of the new art of Suprematism which he had invented.

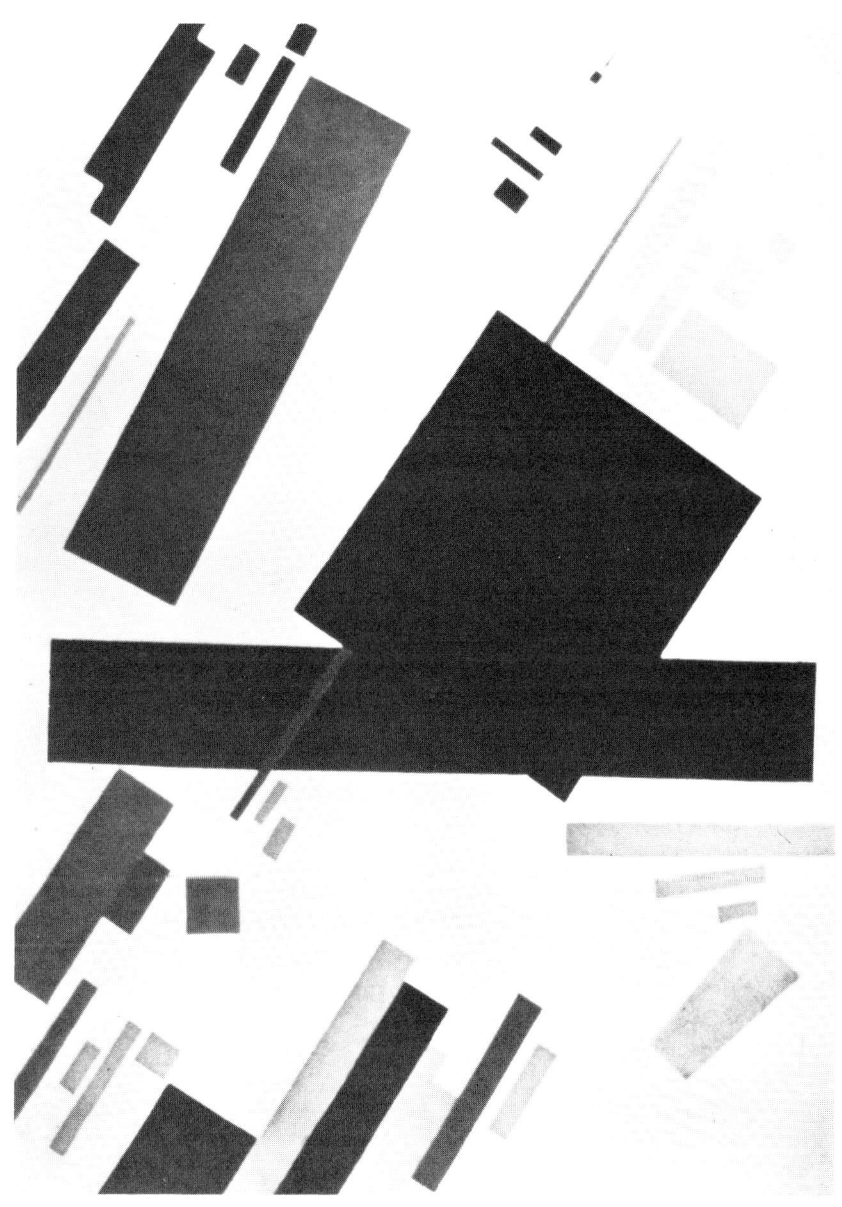

Suprematist Composition: Kasimir Malevich

Malevich's paintings are concerned only with the relationship between one geometric shape and another. It is a purely visual art, dealing with tensions and proportions.

This new art, which 'fights against the forms of yesterday and the aesthetics of yesterday' and with its mission 'to free the development of art from the imitative forms of the past' was to have a profound effect on art, architecture and artefacts of this century – initially on the artists of De Stijl.

TONE

Tone is the convention used in drawing and painting to simulate the effect of lighting by creating shadow and the modelling of surfaces, and consequently creating the illusion of form. Tone thus enables us to represent *form* and this is one of its main functions.

Tone as form

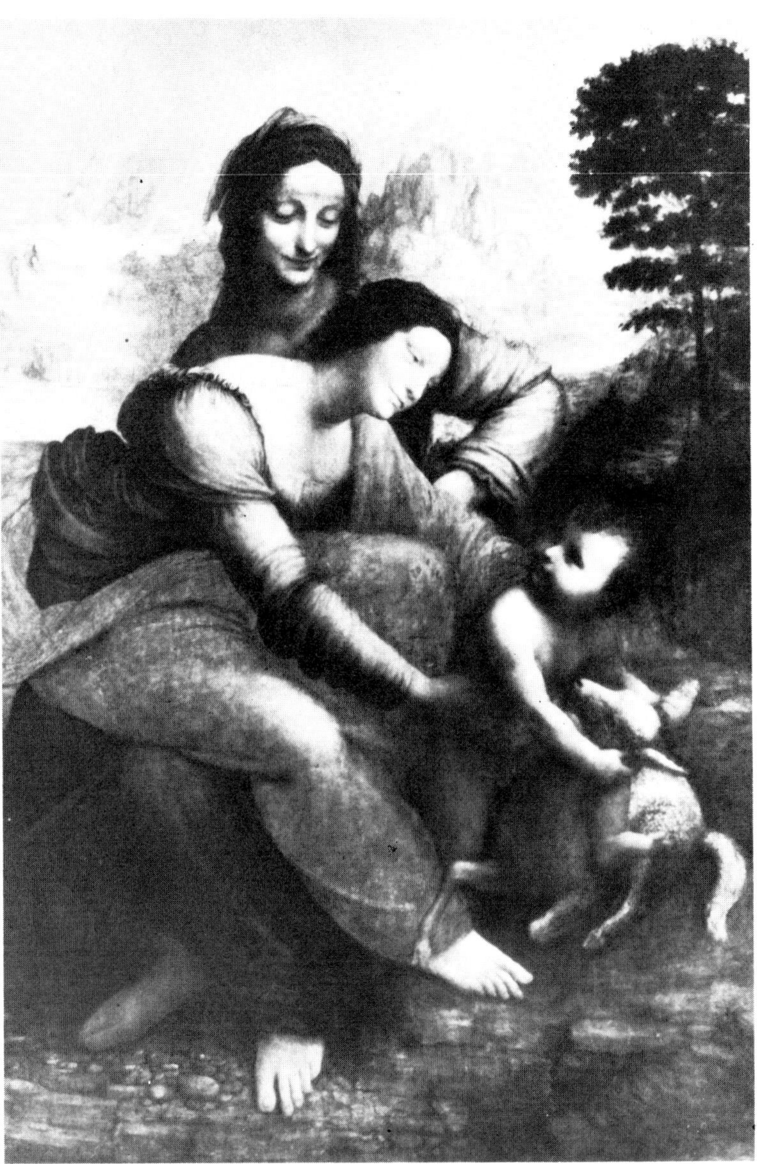

Virgin and Child with St. Anne: Leonardo da Vinci
Florentine painters of the Renaissance tended to give more importance to tone and more reponsibility to line than their Venetian contemporaries, who were generally more concerned with colour. This painting by Leonardo da Vinci, although printed in monochrome, shows the form of the figures very clearly – both the forms underlying the drapery and the drapery itself are given a feeling of solidity by the skilful use of tone. Leonardo's use of tone ranges from rich velvety darks to the most delicate nuances suggesting soft reflections of light. His treatment of the tones in the distant scene is particularly subtle.

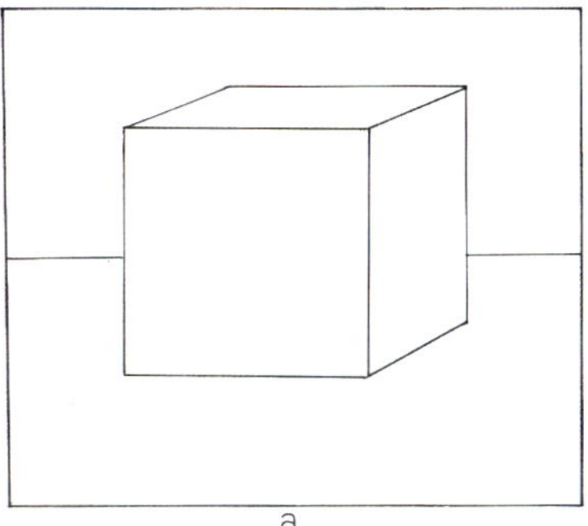

a

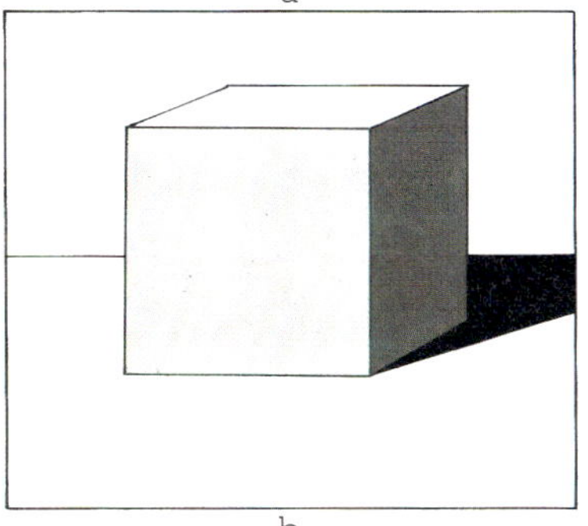

b

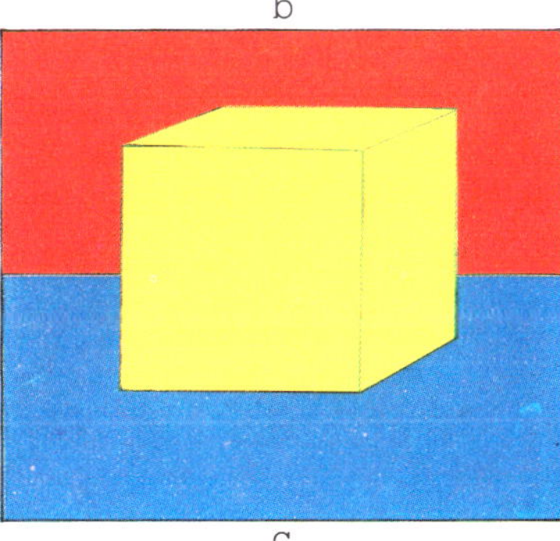

c

Tone values (diagrams)
When an object is drawn in line only (a) the information conveyed in terms of form is limited and may be confusing. In order to express the three-dimensional quality of the form it is necessary to add tone (b). Although the illusion of form is more powerful, the object is described as a white form against a white background. The addition of colour to diagram b conveys a different sensory impression but adds little to the sense of form (c). The introduction of colour, however, raises a new problem since the word 'tone' is used not only to express the idea of shadow but also to express the relative value of colours.

Colours are said to possess a 'tone value' according to whether they are light or dark: a light colour has a light tone value, and vice versa. Colours may be different in hue but of the same value. This ability to see colour in terms of their corresponding tone values is an essential part of the painter's talent and training. When we photograph diagram c in monochrome (d) we can get an idea of the tone values of the colours – the cube has a light value, the background and floor are darker tones of approximately equal value. But for a complete realization of the cube in three dimensions and colour we need to combine all these diagrams (e).

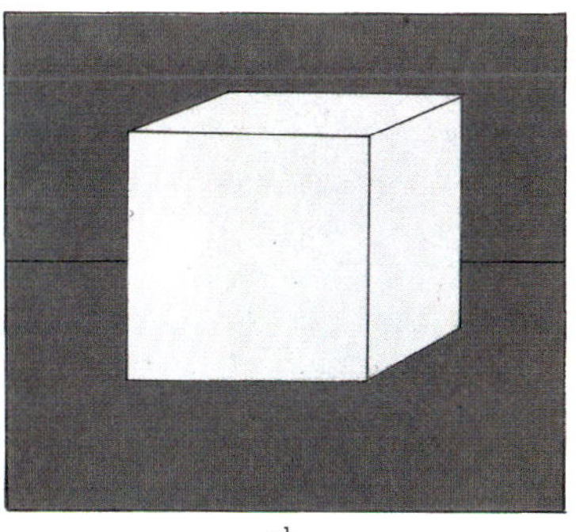

d

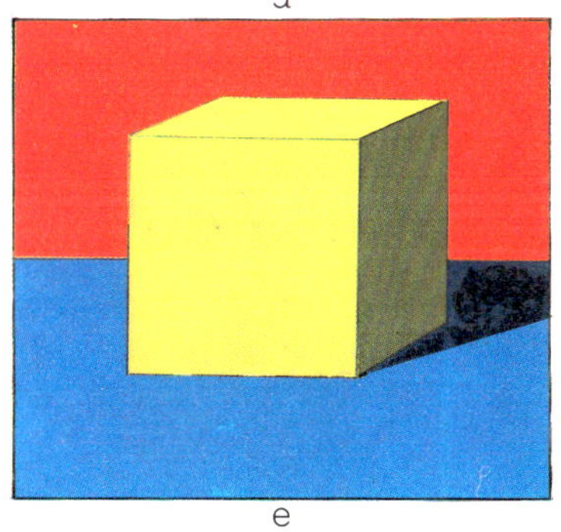

e

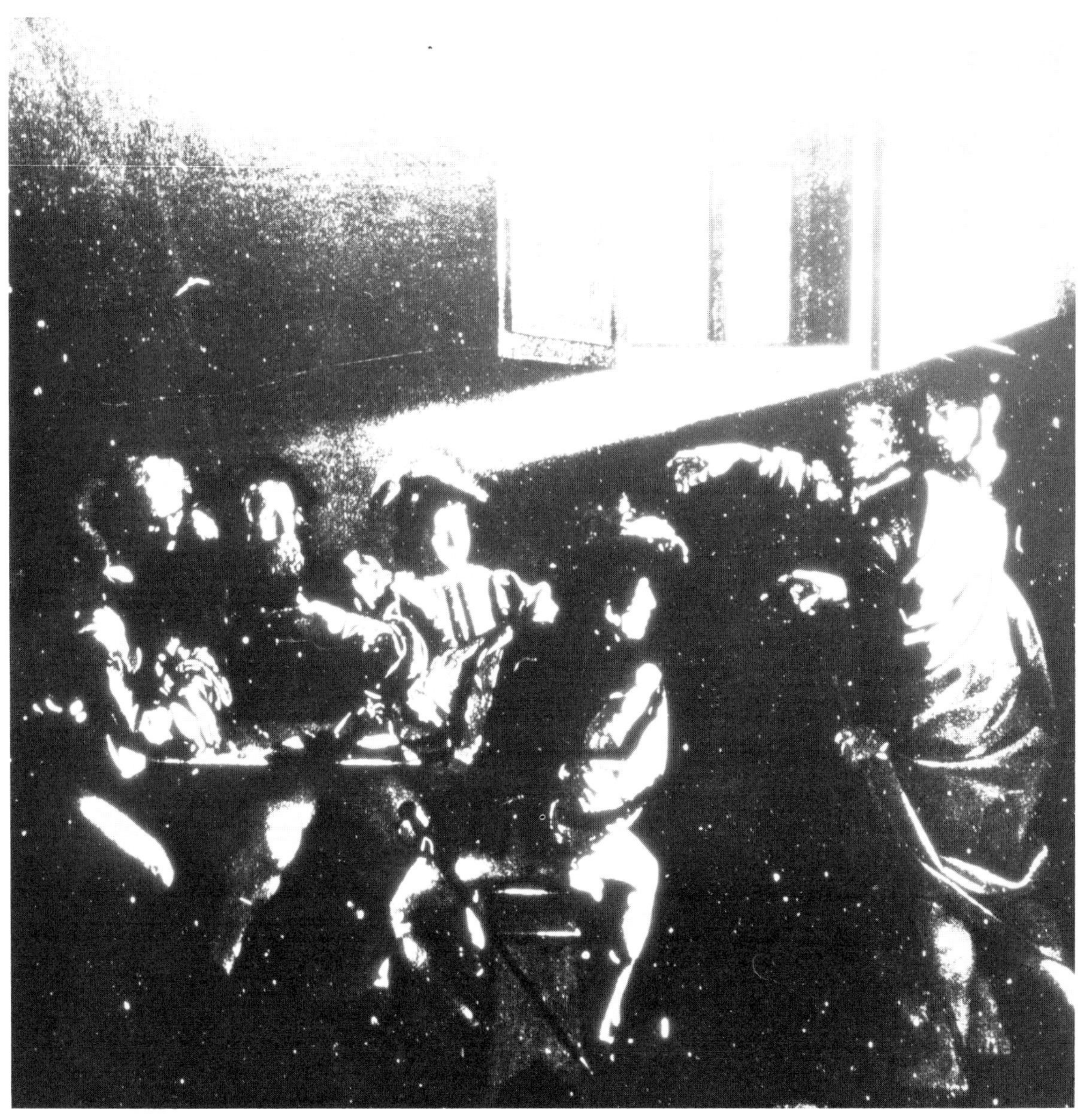

The Calling of St. Matthew:
Caravaggio (diagram)

In this diagram dramatic and powerful gesture contributes to the feeling of tension, but it is the use of chiaroscuro which accentuates the sense of drama in this significant moment. There is a very abrupt transition between the light/dark areas (further exaggerated in this diagram) and this creates the harsh spotlight effect. Significant parts of the scene are suddenly revealed while other parts are cast into deep shadow.

Tone as lighting

By increasing the contrast between dark and light tones, a device known as chiaroscuro (literally light/dark), the effect of strong lighting is achieved, resulting in a corresponding increase in the sense of drama. This exaggeration of light and shade was used by Rembrandt, and particularly by the Tenebrist painter Caravaggio.

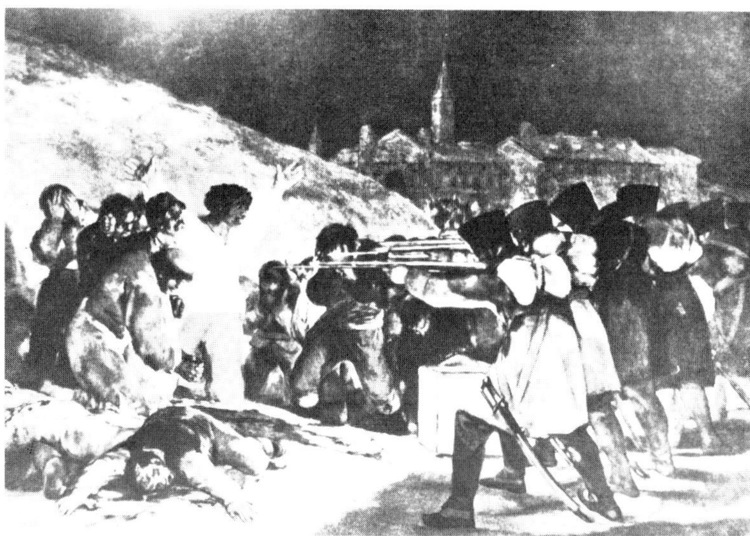

Executions of the third of May 1808: Francisco Goya
A victim is crucified, in the glare from a spot lamp–shadows leap to life as the dead slump to earth.

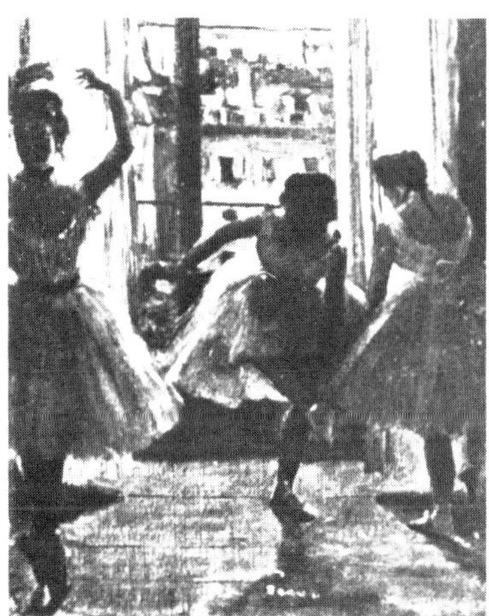

Ballerinas practising in front of a Window: Edgar Degas
Some artists have been particularly interested in painting against the light, including Claude, Turner (particularly influenced by Claude) and Degas. Notice the rich dark tones of flesh when seen against the light; Degas used the same kind of effect in paintings of racehorses – perhaps he saw in them the same kind of nervous energy and disciplined bodies.

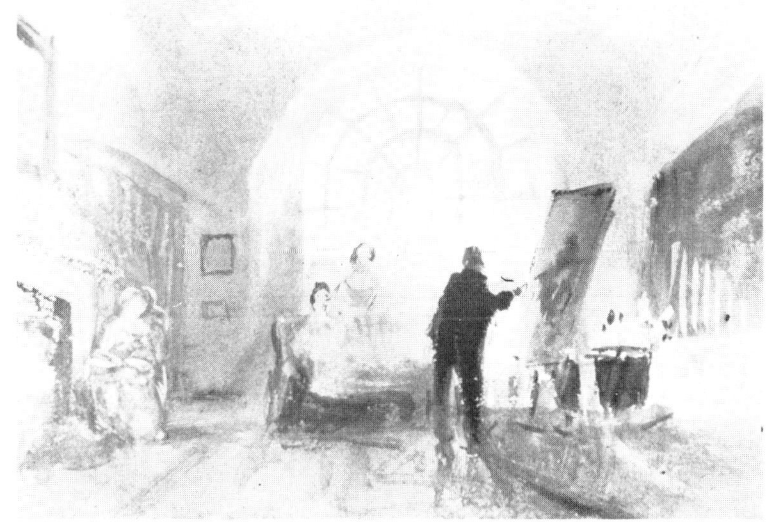

Interior at Petworth: J. M. W. Turner
To achieve this effect of light flooding the interior and dissolving rather than revealing forms, Turner used a blue ground as middle tone.

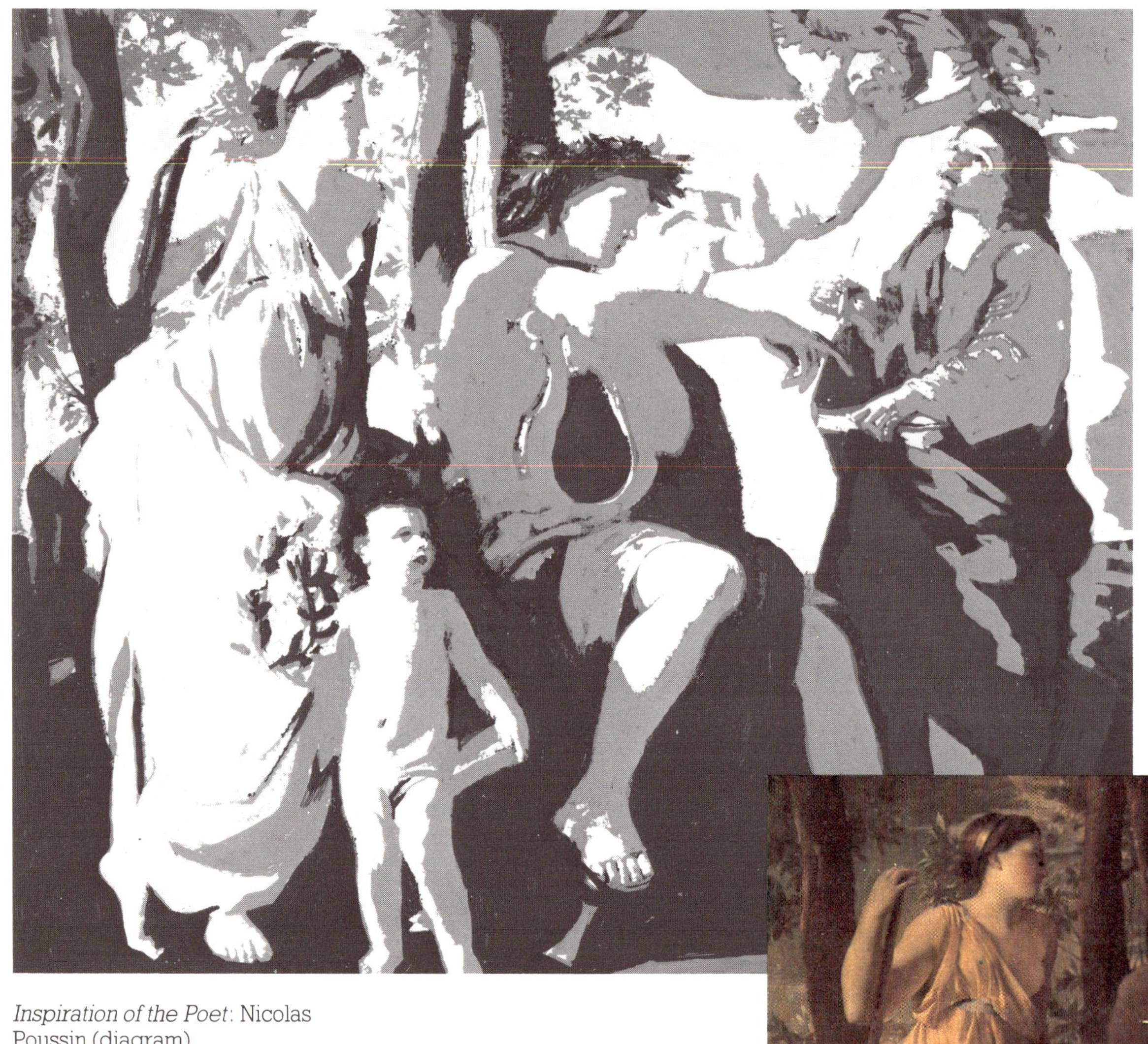

Inspiration of the Poet: Nicolas Poussin (diagram)
In this simplified tonal analysis, Poussin's tones have been reduced to three only: light, half-tone, and shadow tones, interpreted here as white, grey and black. Interpreting the *colours* of the original as tones in this way makes it much easier to see the flow of tone linking one form with another, and to understand how artists think in terms of light and dark shapes, rather than in terms of the physical boundaries of objects.

Seeing the painting in full colour and comparing it with the diagram we can appreciate how Poussin's tonal scheme is basically very simple, and this contributes to that sense of order and clarity conveyed by classical work.

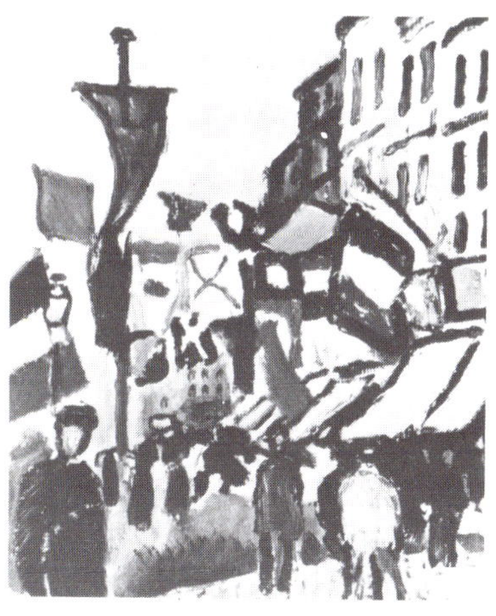

Fourteenth of July at Le Havre: Raoul Dufy
Dufy simplifies shapes and colours so that the painting is virtually in three tones, corresponding to the tone values of the white, red, blue of the flags.

Stained glass window in the chapel of St. James, St. Gall, Switzerland
In the same way this stained glass conveys a strong sense of *pattern* by the simple tone values of the primary colours yellow, red and blue.

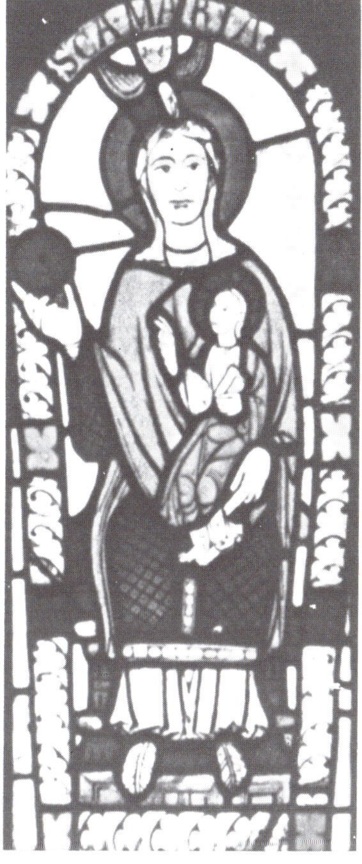

Lazarus: 12th-century fresco from Sant Climent de Taull
Here the tonal simplicity–it is carried out in three tones–is largely responsible for the strong sense of pattern

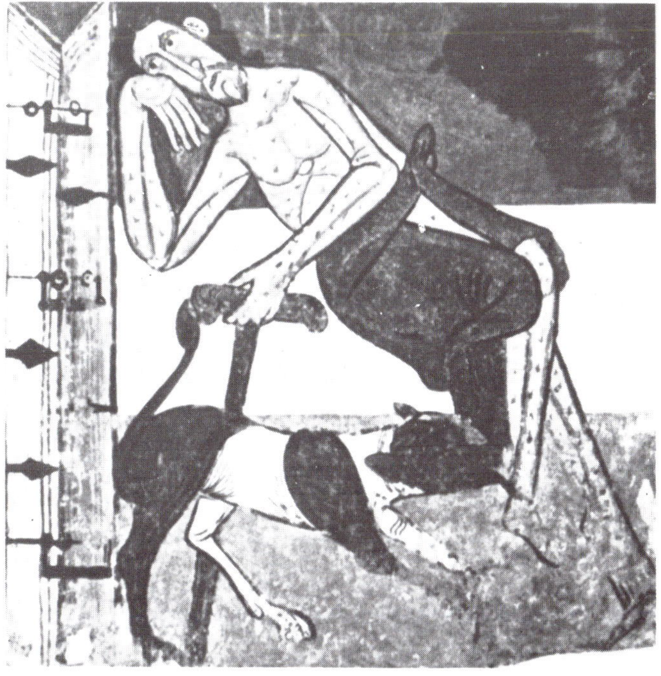

TONE

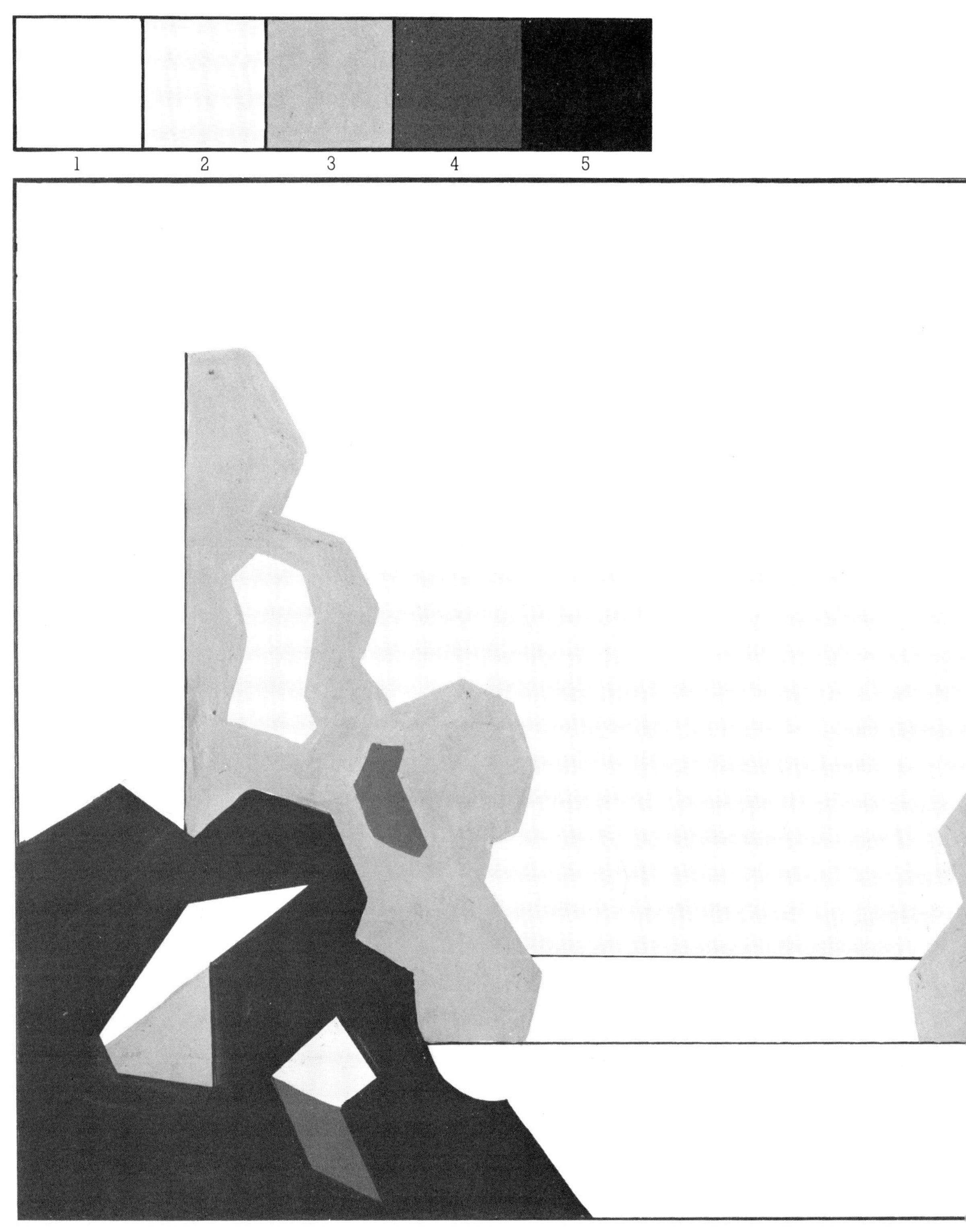

Schematic landscape (diagram)
In this diagram we have a tonal scale divided into five equal intervals. The schematic landscape is divided into three planes: foreground, middle distance and distance. The foreground uses tones from the extremes of the scale – 1 – 3 – 5; the middle distance uses 2 – 3 – 4; and the distance 3 only. This gradual closing up of the tonal intervals, or narrowing of the tonal scale, has the effect of flattening the distant forms by diminishing the contrast and hence creates a sense of distance. This feeling for intervals of tone (like an understanding and appreciation of the tone values of colours) is an essential part of the painter's equipment.

Tone as distance (aerial perspective)

In addition to creating a sense of form and drama, tone is used to represent aerial perspective.

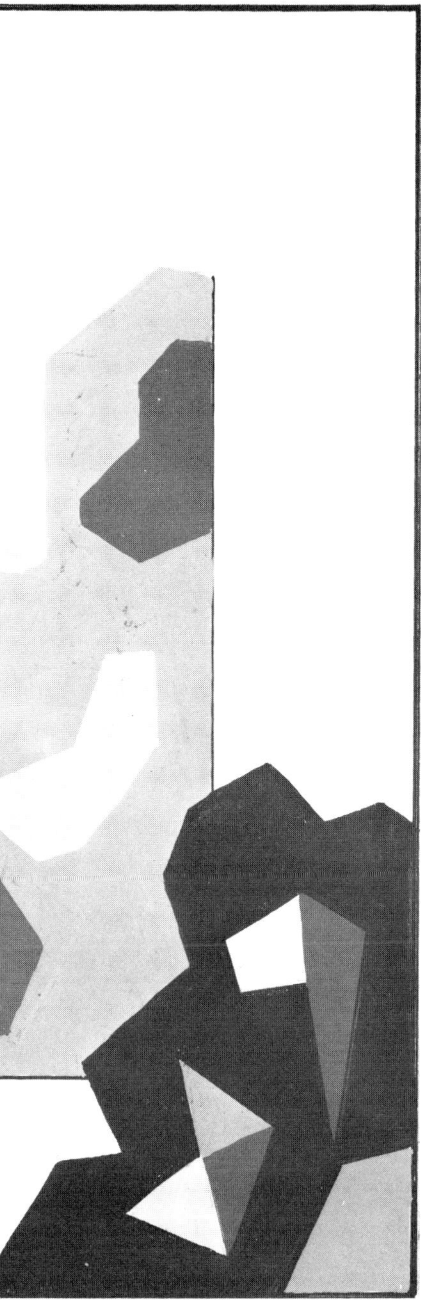

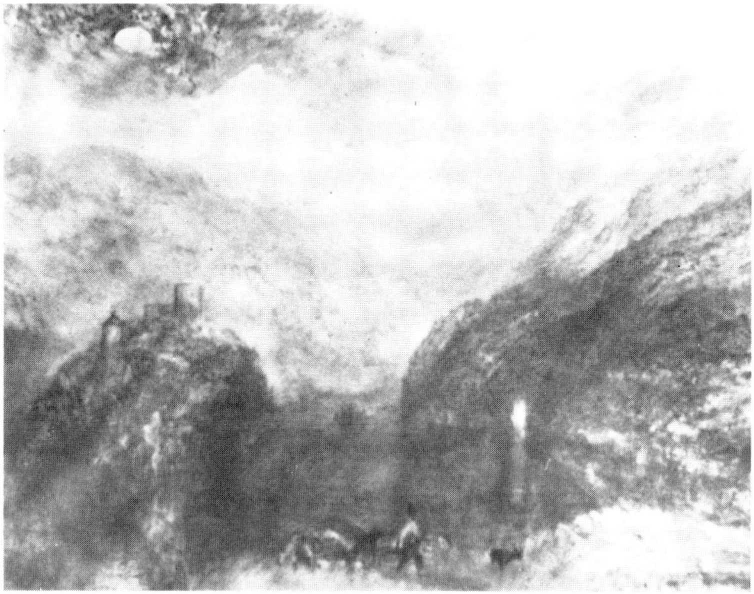

Lake at Brienz: J. M. W. Turner
Turner, like many landscape painters, makes full use of aerial perspective to convey vast and misty distances. He carefully selects his tonal intervals, systematically reducing the contrast between them as he leads our eyes into the distance.

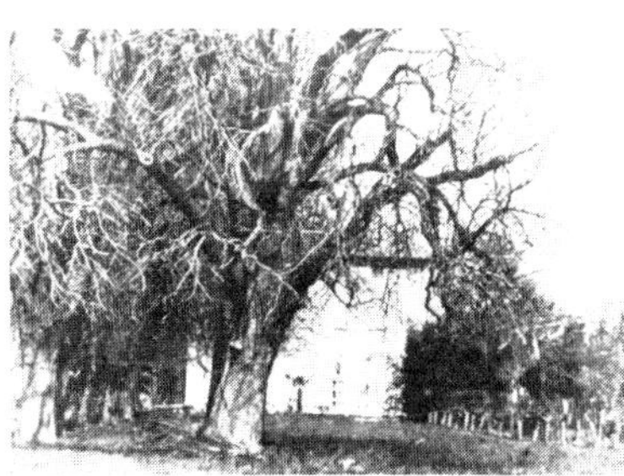

Tonal selection

A photograph generally consists of a multiplicity of tones. The camera records slight changes from light to dark over the whole surface. The result is often a virtually meaningless jumble, without that sense of balance and coherent organization that distinguishes painting from photography.

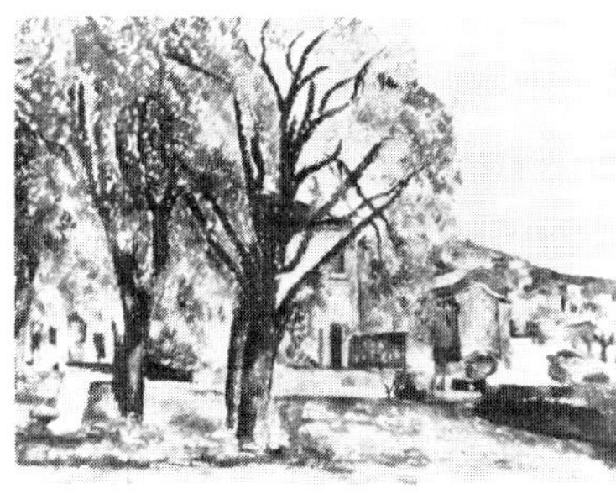

Chestnut Trees and Farm Buildings at the Jas de Bouffan: Paul Cézanne
In this monochrome reproduction of Cézanne's painting of the same scene, we can see how he has selected only a few of the multiplicity of tones, and used these with a sense of the precise interval separating one from another. The painter simplifies the available tone and colour information, selects what he needs, and then organizes these in a coherent way.

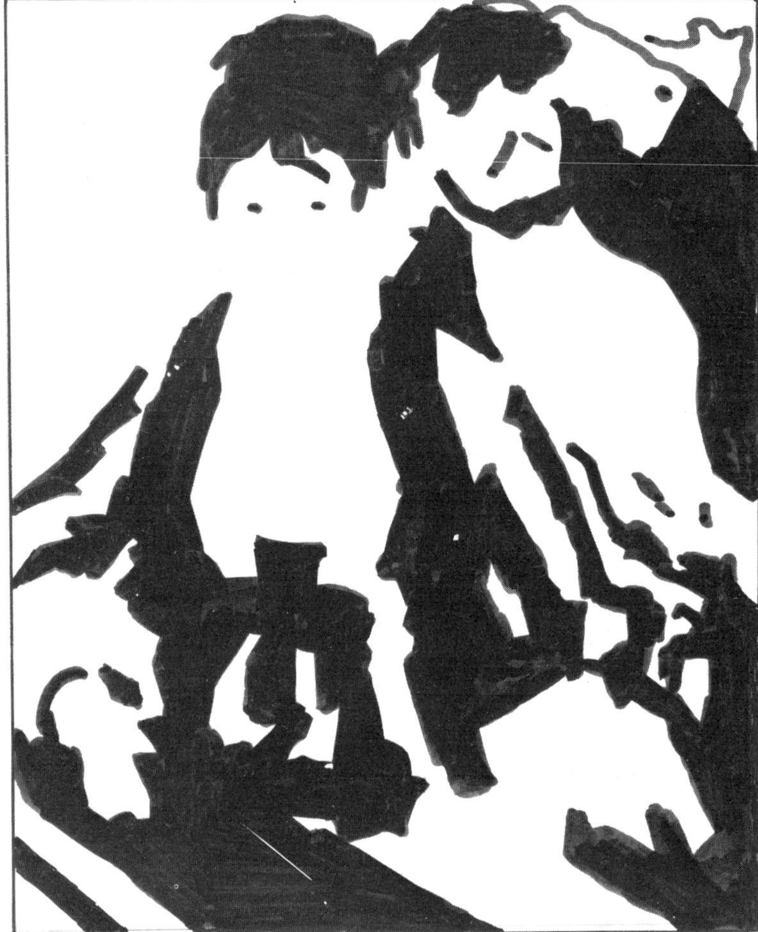

La Loge: Pierre Renoir (diagram)
In this two-tone analysis of a painting by Renoir of two figures in a box at the theatre, variations of tone have been omitted so that the pattern value of the black and white evening clothes, opera glasses, etc., is brought out more clearly.

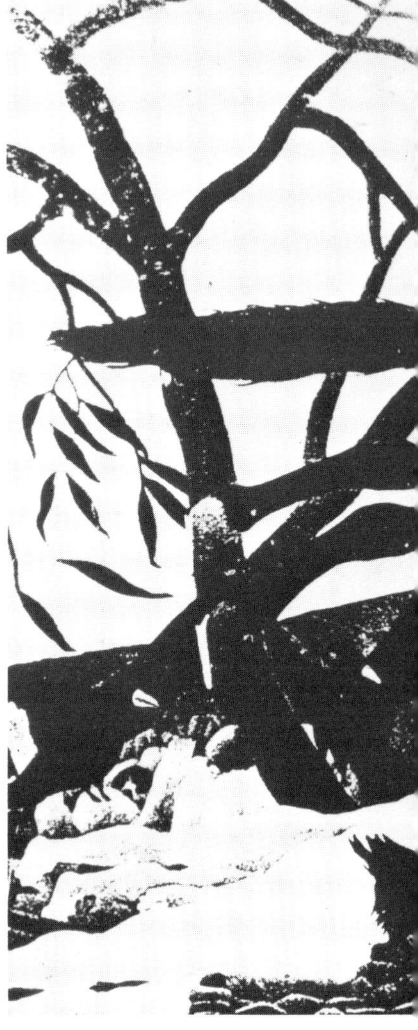

War: 'le Douanier' Rousseau (diagram)
In this analysis of the light/dark values of a painting by Rousseau the legs of the black horse and dark branches of the trees create a strong pattern, in which the negative shapes play an important role.

Tone as pattern
The tones of a painting or design are largely responsible for creating the feeling of pattern, and strong tonal patterns result from strong tonal contrasts.

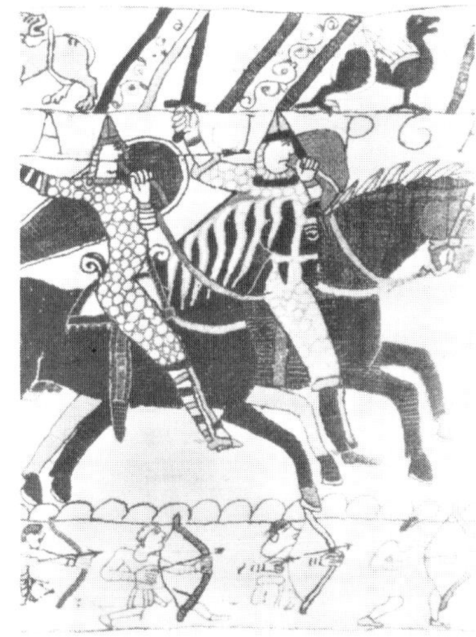

The Bayeux Tapestry (detail)
The whole of this so-called tapestry is a design, making extensive use of the positive and negative value of light and dark shapes. The designer obviously understood that when one draws two parallel black lines (positive) one has created a white line (negative) between them, e.g. the horse's mane.

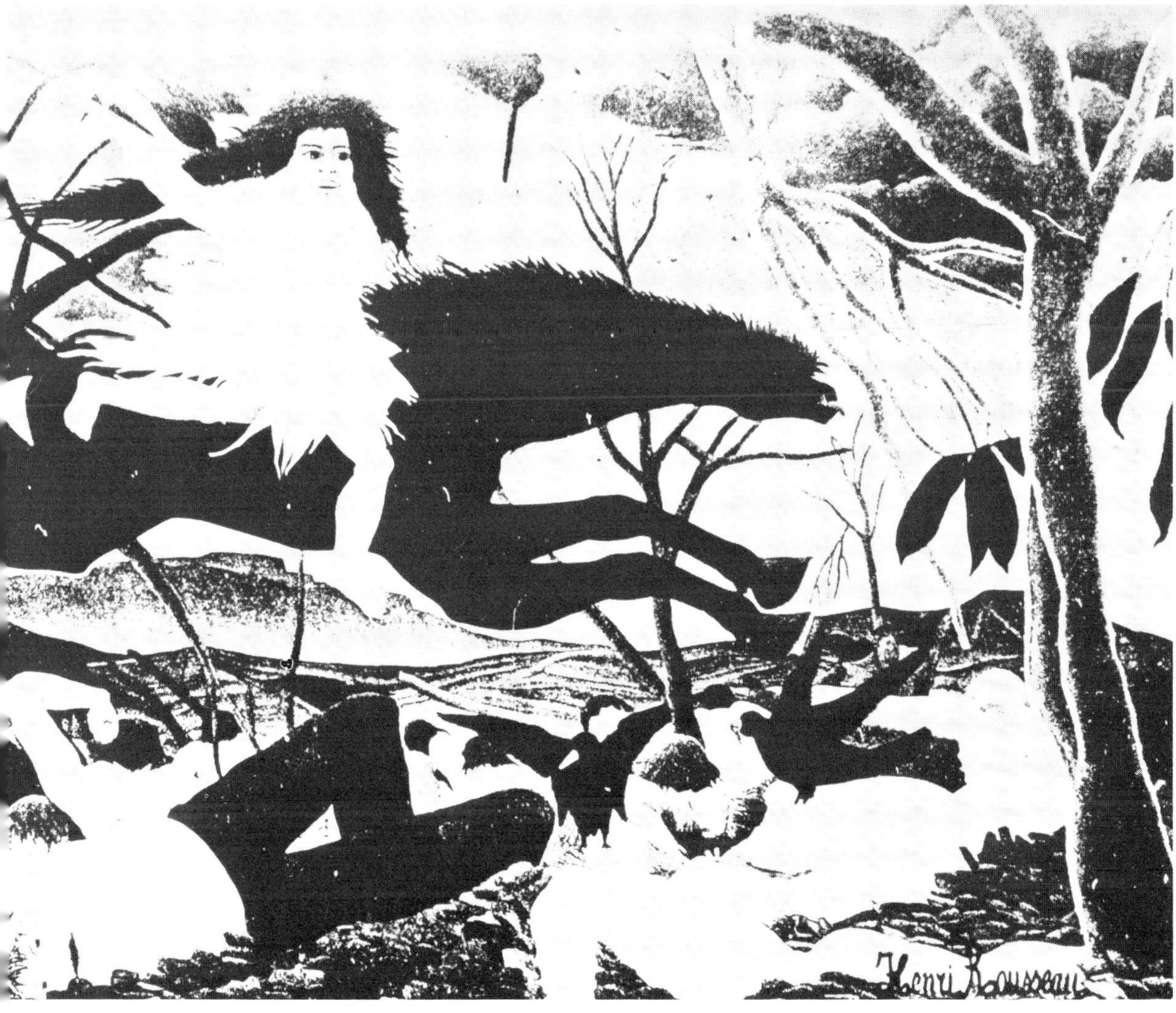

TONE

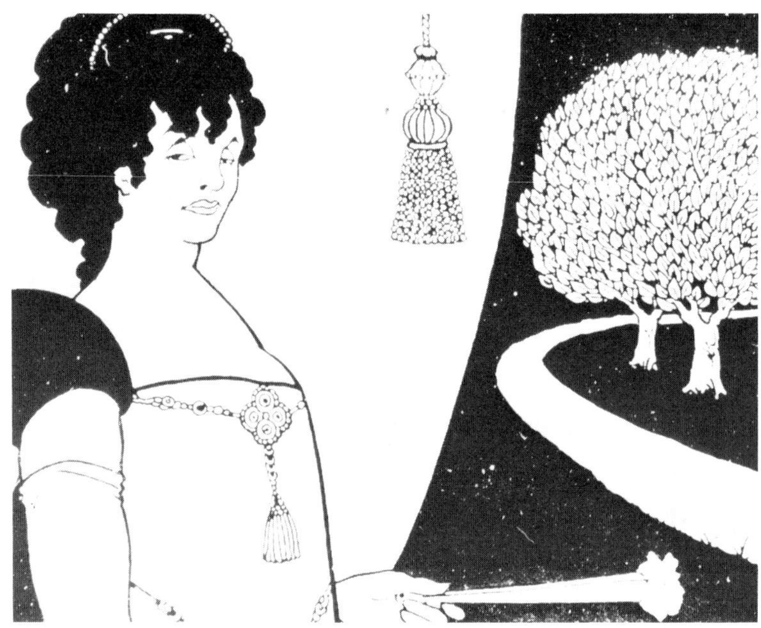

Madame Réjane: Aubrey Beardsley
By comparing these two versions we can appreciate clearly the way in which Beardsley considered the positive and negative aspects of the shapes.

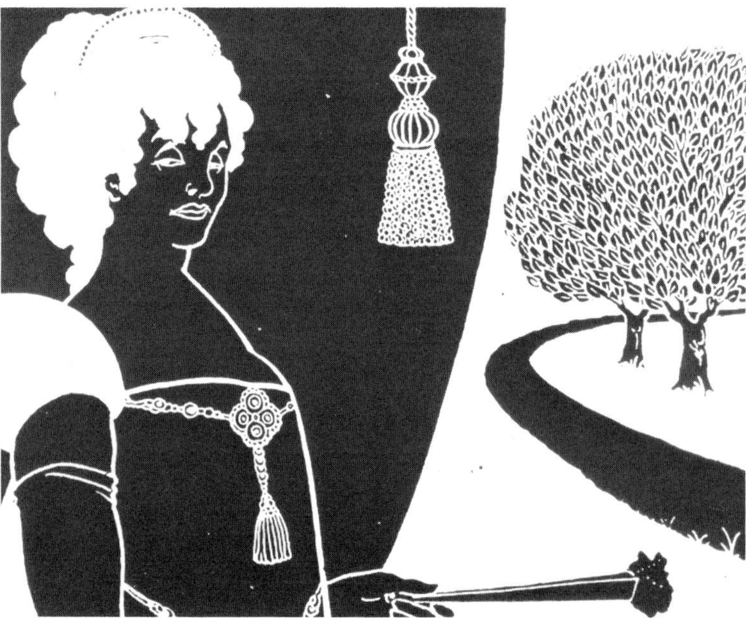

Aubrey Beardsley was a great black and white illustrator. In all his work he shows complete mastery of handling black on white and at the same time of white on black.

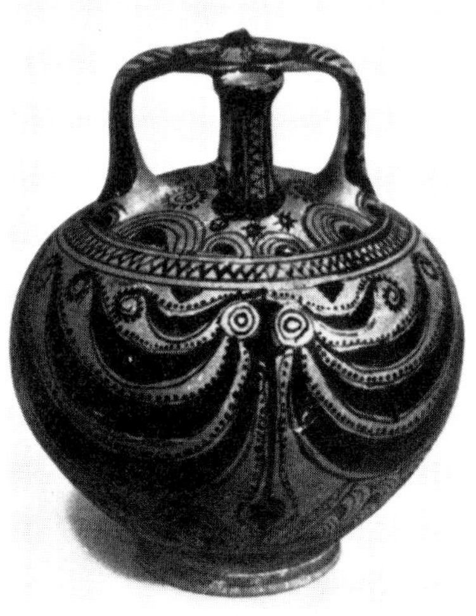

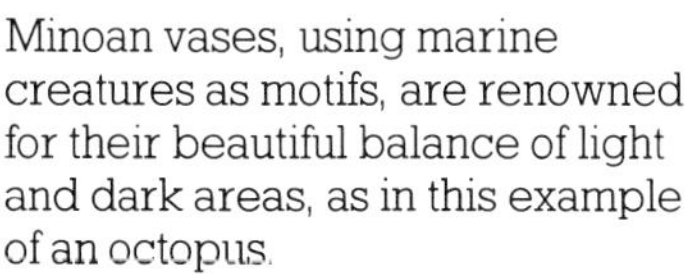

Minoan vases, using marine creatures as motifs, are renowned for their beautiful balance of light and dark areas, as in this example of an octopus.

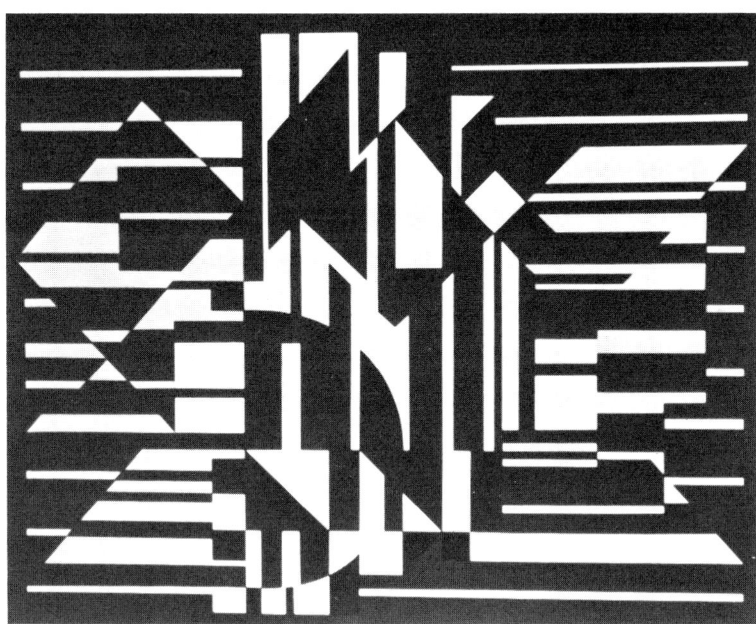

Horn: Victor Vasarely
So-called 'Op' artists, such as Victor Vasarely and Bridget Riley, often make the dark shapes exactly equal in size and shape to the light shapes – e.g. black and white lines of equal width. The result is that the black lines produce a white line after-image on the retina of the eye, and vice-versa. These ghostly after-images strive to superimpose themselves on to the original painting and as the eye fails to superimpose them exactly on to their original positions, a shifting, dazzling effect of movement results.

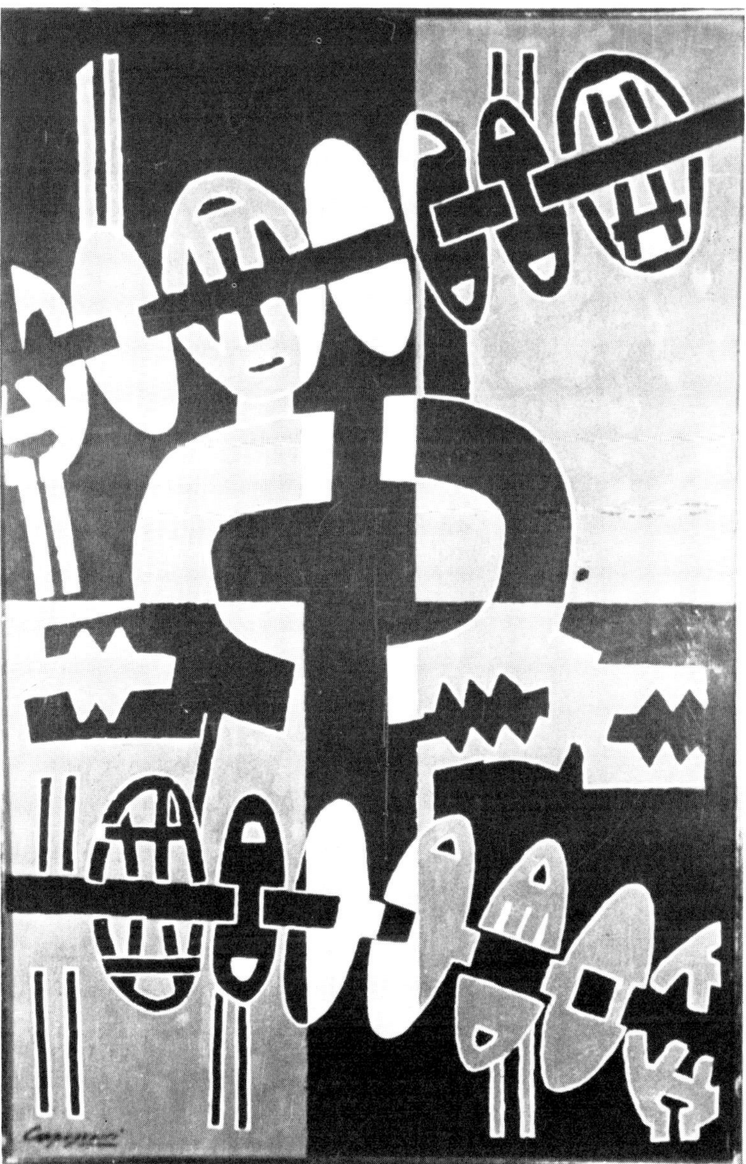

Surface 195: Giuseppe Capogrossi
In the interests of tonal pattern the artist may make use of the device known as counter-change – cutting shapes in half and using light shapes on the dark part and vice versa. This technique was exploited by both Picasso and Braque in their Cubist work, and subsequently became a cliché when employed by commercial designers of the 1920s and 1930s. Capogrossi uses strong value contrasts in this painting involving counter-change of related shapes.

TONE

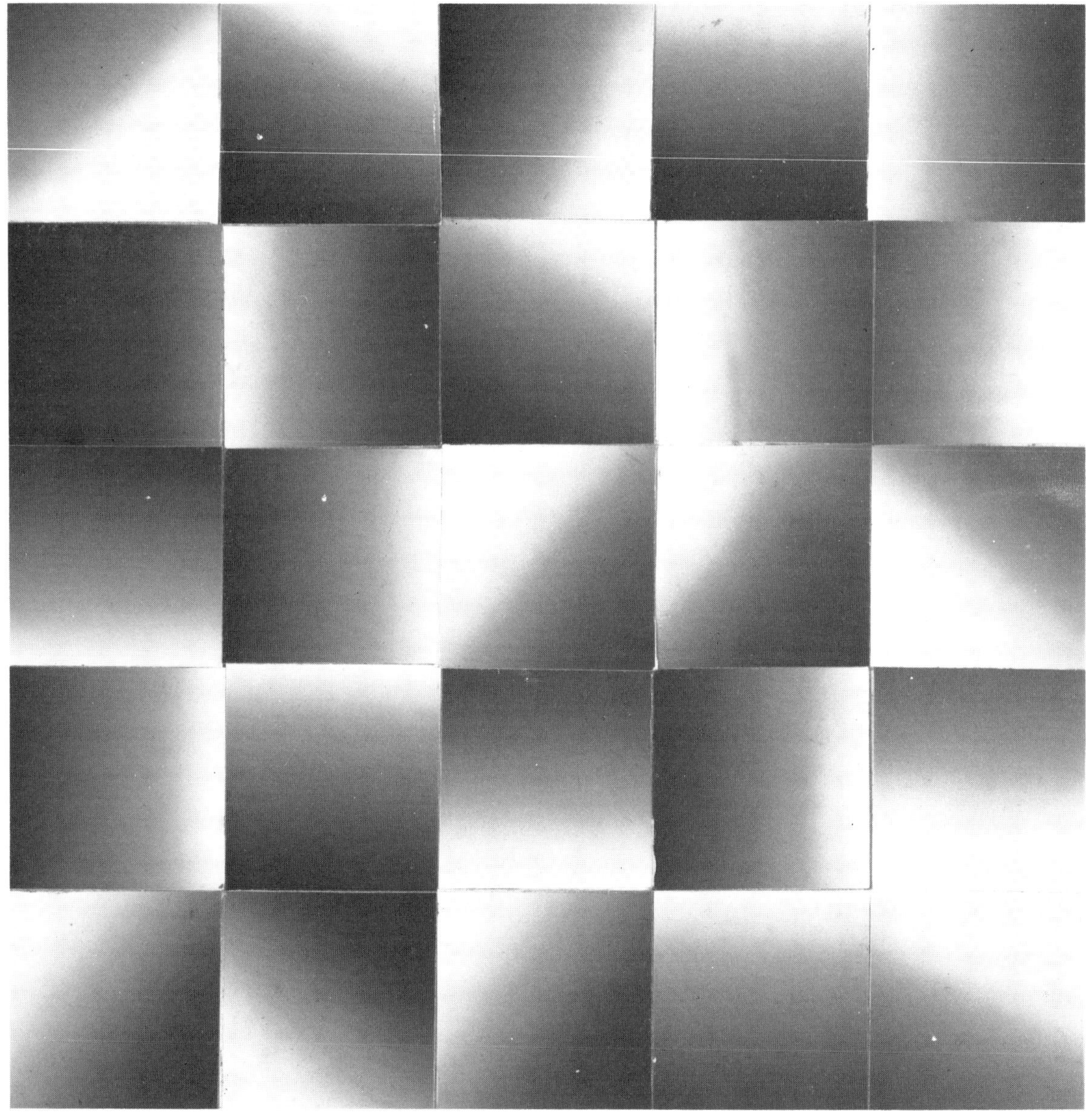

Tonal rhythms (diagram)
In this diagram the area has been divided into squares, each of which has been graduated in tone in a random way, resulting in the whole area appearing faceted; but as light parts and dark parts of the individual units coincide a series of unexpected rhythms is set up, breaking across the boundaries of the individual squares and linking parts together through their confluence of tones. With half-closed eyes the effect is more obvious.

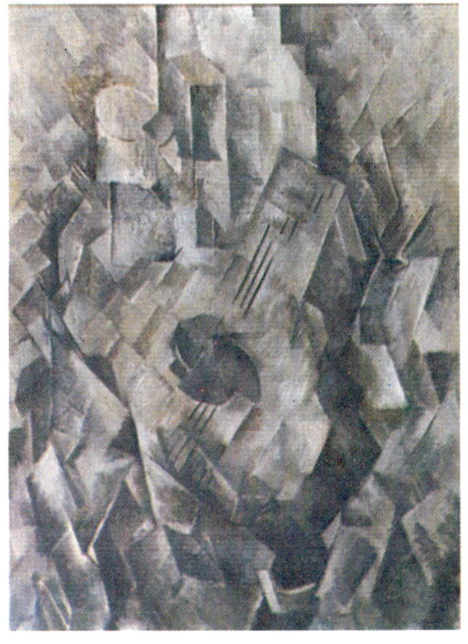

Mandolin: Georges Braque
The Cubists in their analytical phase made use of tone in this way, as may be seen in the work of Picasso, Braque and Gris, where tones graduate from the edges of faceted forms. During the early stages of Cubism the work of Picasso and Braque was very similar – they were 'like two mountaineers roped together'.

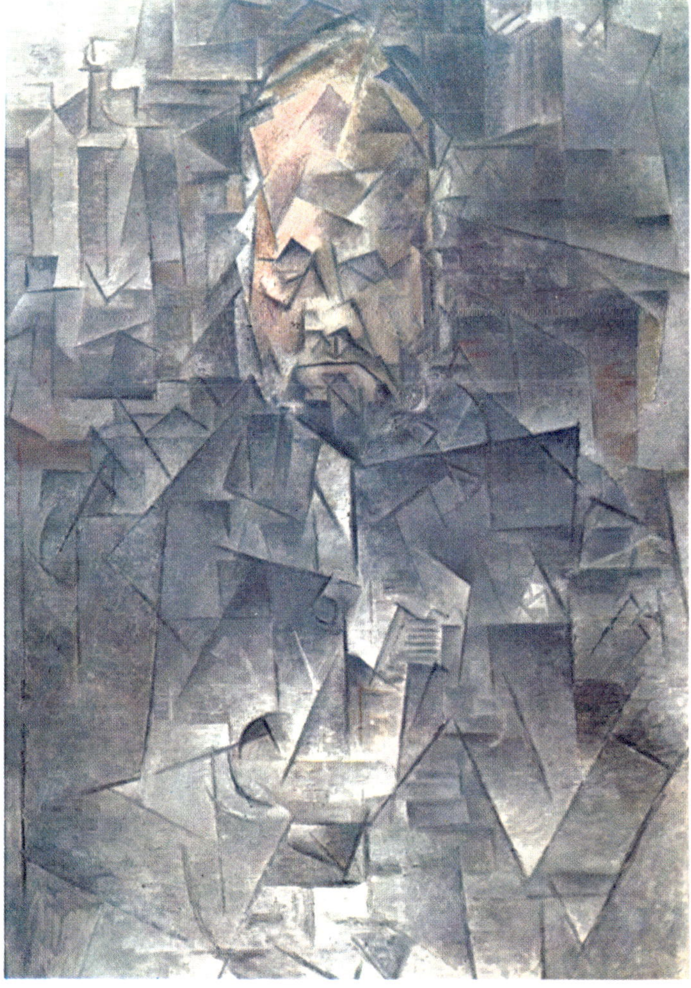

Ambroise Vollard: Pablo Picasso
Both Picasso and Braque made very little use of colour but relied on tone instead. The tones in these paintings help to describe the planes of various broken forms; but these planes themselves are not confined to the forms, and the tones – where they have a common tonality – break across individual planes to create unexpected rhythms.

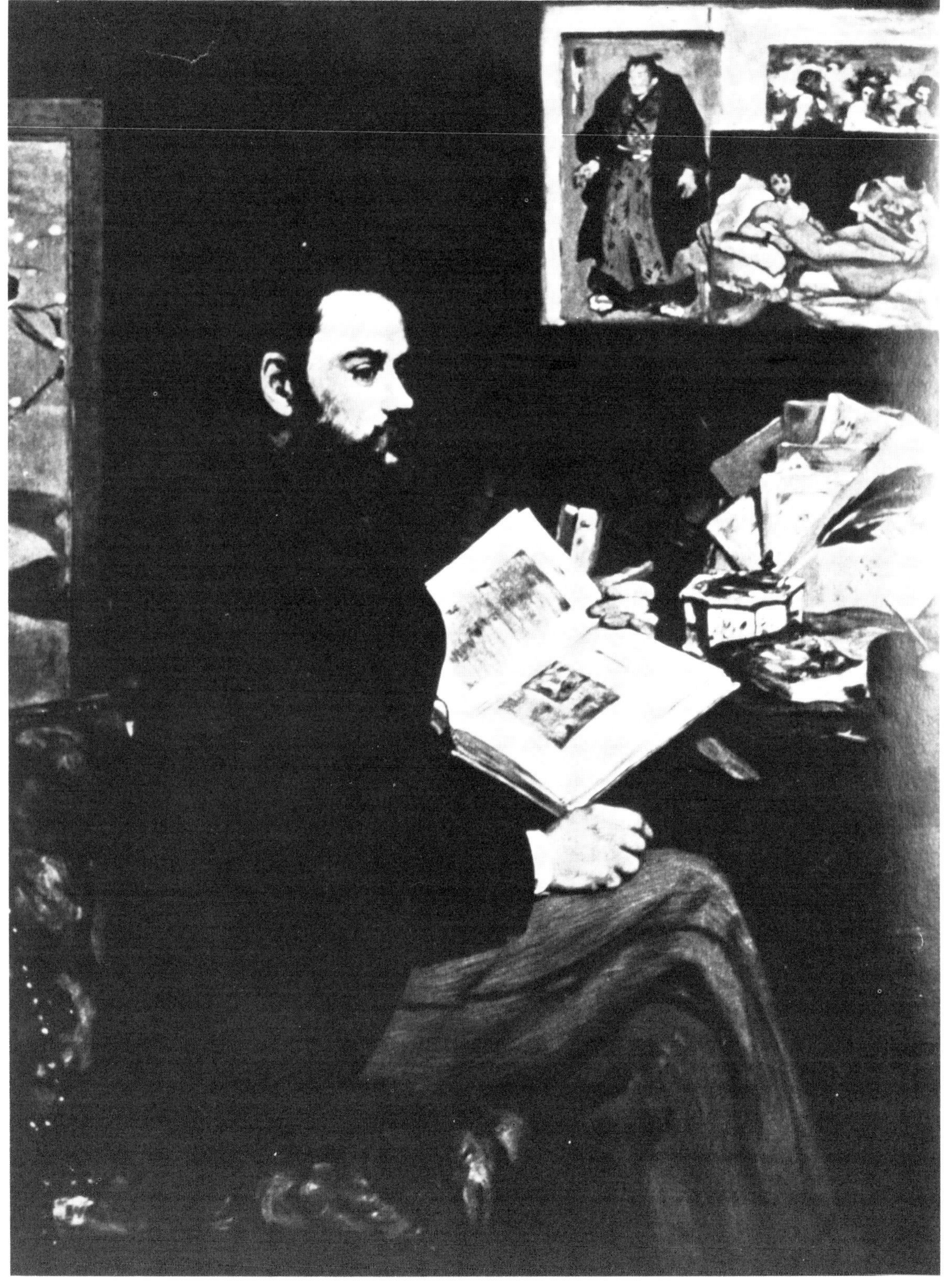

Tonality: the tonal concept

The Impressionists were influenced in various ways by the Japanese prints which were introduced into France during the nineteenth century. Some, such as Monet, Pissarro, and to a lesser extent Sisley, tended to put light above all and were prepared to sacrifice tonal pattern and formal composition for immediate sensation. These artists were interested in the spontaneity of the Japanese brushwork which expressed so much with apparently so little effort. But others of the group were impressed by the Japanese use of the silhouetted shape, a device which Toulouse-Lautrec found useful in giving visual impact to his posters.

◀ *Emile Zola*: Edouard Manet
This portrait of Emile Zola shows Manet's interest in the silhouette, and his interest in tone generally. In the background we can see an example of a similar use of silhouetted shape in the print by Utamaro. Also on the back wall is a tonal sketch for Manet's painting *Olympia* with black servant and white sheets; and behind that, as if Manet was comparing the two, we can just see a little of a tone study of Velazquez's painting *The Topers*. Why should Manet, a so-called French Impressionist, be studying Velazquez – a seventeenth-century Spanish realist? What have they in common? Some artists seem to have concentrated their talents and interest on line, some on tone, and others on colour.

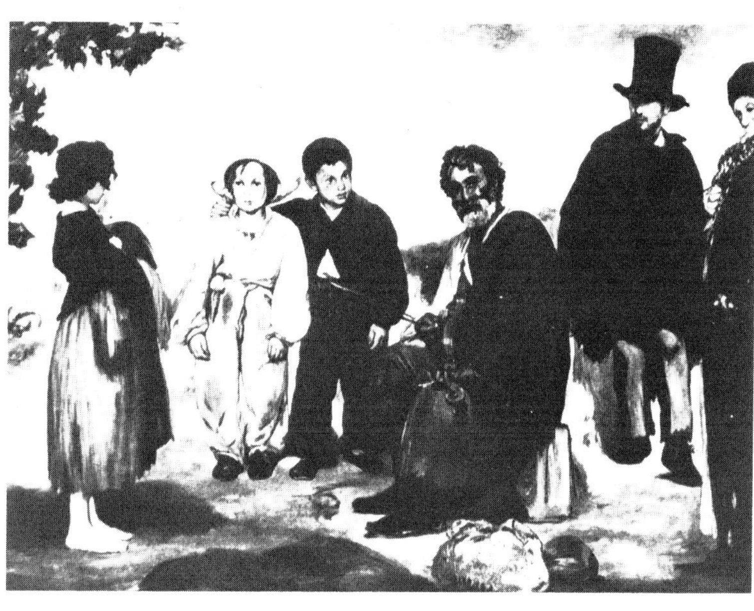

The Old Musician: Edouard Manet

We can see by comparing *The Topers* (left) with *The Old Musician* that Manet, like Velazquez, had a profound interest in tone. Both these artists have a similar sense of tonality, both employ the silhouetted shape and use the same tonal rango, which givoc rico to a certain sharpness of tonal contrast. It was largely the abruptness of tonal transitions which provoked the hostile reaction to Manet's *Déjeuner sur l'Herbe* rather than the indecency of what was a traditional subject.

The Topers: Diego Velazquez

COLOUR

'Colours are the children of light and light is their mother'. J. Itten, The Art of Colour.

The word 'colour' is used to describe a sensation received by the brain when the retina of the eye is stimulated by certain wavelengths of light. Although we tend to refer to 'colour' as if it exists as an entity in the outside world, since it is a sensation it only exists when there is someone present to experience the sensation.

As the light constantly varies the effect of colours, we receive from the world around us constant changes of colour sensation according to the weather and time of day. Although these variations are not easily perceived due to a phenomenon called colour constancy, Monet's two series, one of *Rouen Cathedral* and one of *Haystacks*, each show the same scene in the different colours caused by different lighting conditions.

The Spectrum (diagram)
Although in the first century A.D. the Stoic philosopher Seneca held angular glass rods against the light to produce a rainbow, it was Sir Isaac Newton in 1671/2 who demonstrated the origin of colour from white light, by passing a narrow beam through a prism. In the nineteenth century Ogden Rood showed by using magic lanterns that certain colours of light, if used in the right proportion, could be combined on a screen to produce white. The results of these scientific experiments were not lost on painters, who began to use the new chemical pigments of the spectral hues. For centuries artists had had only a narrow range of colours available, such as red and yellow ochres, metallic oxides from the earth, chalk or lime white, and black from soot or charcoal. The great cave paintings of prehistory use this limited palette – and these pigments from the earth are still a source of artists' colours, which have proved their permanence throughout the ages.

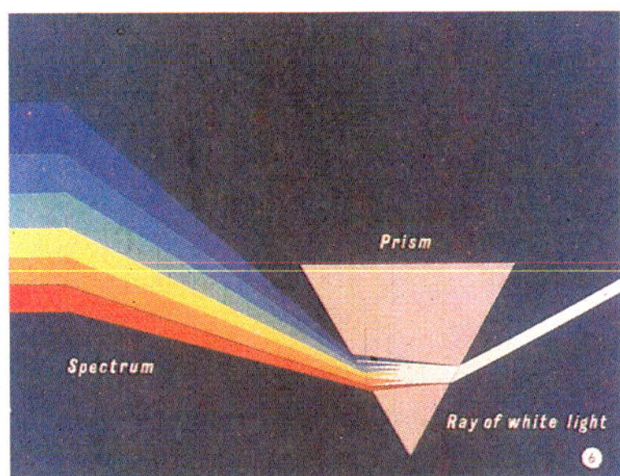

Bison. Cave painting, Altamira, Spain

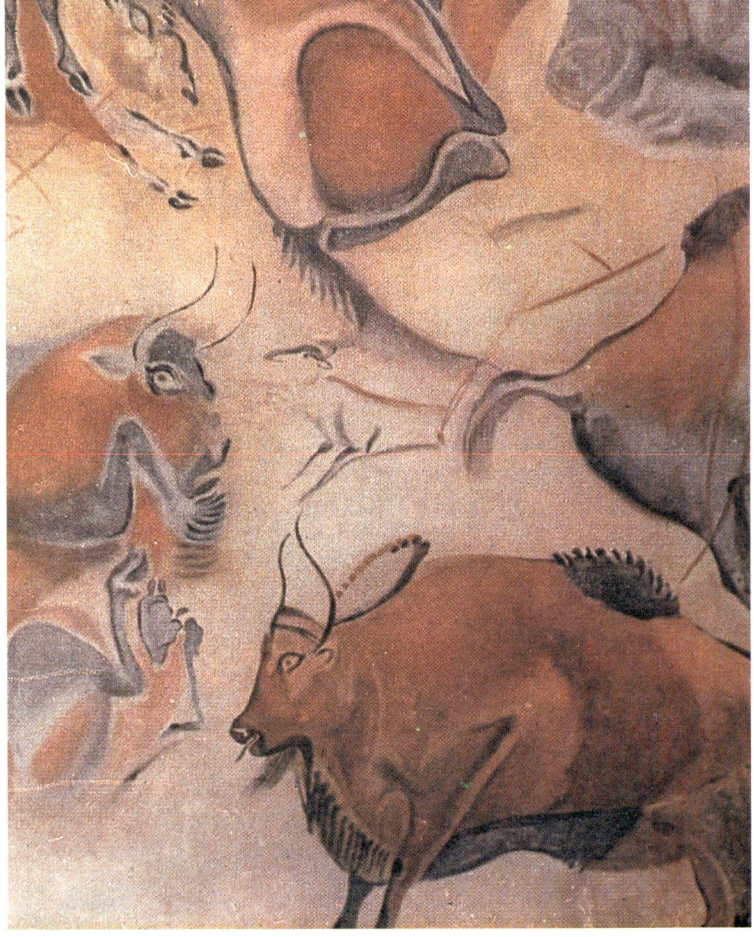

The use of the words 'brilliance' or 'intensity' to describe a particular hue brings us to the question of how we can visualize or classify the entire range of colour possibilities.

Democritus in Ancient Greece was one of the first to attempt a colour classification, but by the early eighteenth century it was realized that there were three fundamental dimensions: hue, value and intensity (or chroma).

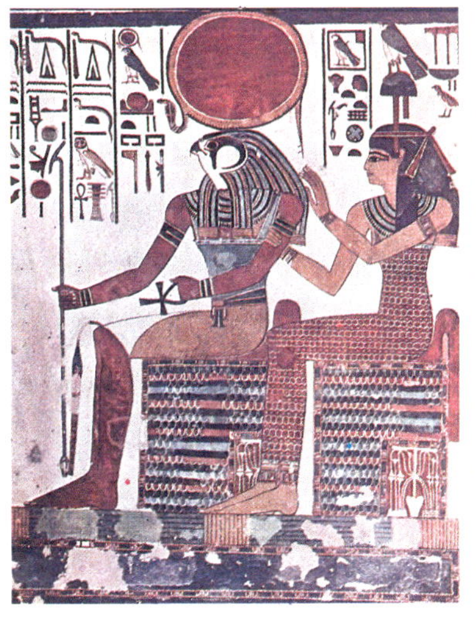

Tomb of Nefertari, Egypt
The semi-precious blue stone, lapis lazuli, known to the Egyptians, was ground to a fine powder to produce the brilliant blue known as ultramarine.

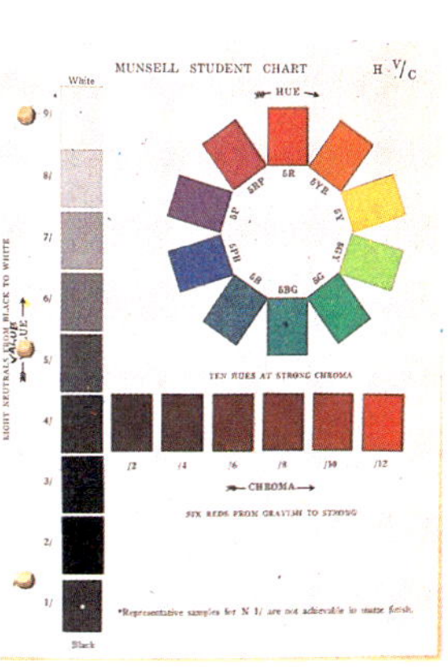

Hue, Value, Chroma: A. H. Munsell (diagram)
This illustration is a page from an early colour atlas first produced in 1905 by A. H. Munsell, an American art teacher. The circle as a colour diagram (a concept put forward by Newton in his *Opticks*, 1704) illustrates colours spaced at regular intervals in the same natural order of hue as in the rainbow. **Hue** may be described as the quality which distinguishes a red from an orange or a red from a green, and so on. **Value** (or tone value) is the degree of luminosity – or that quality which differentiates a dark yellow from a light yellow. The Munsell system classifies values from 1 to 10. **Chroma**, the degree of colourfulness, or saturation, strength, intensity or purity differentiates the dull from the bright colour, and under the Munsell system is numbered from 1 to 16.

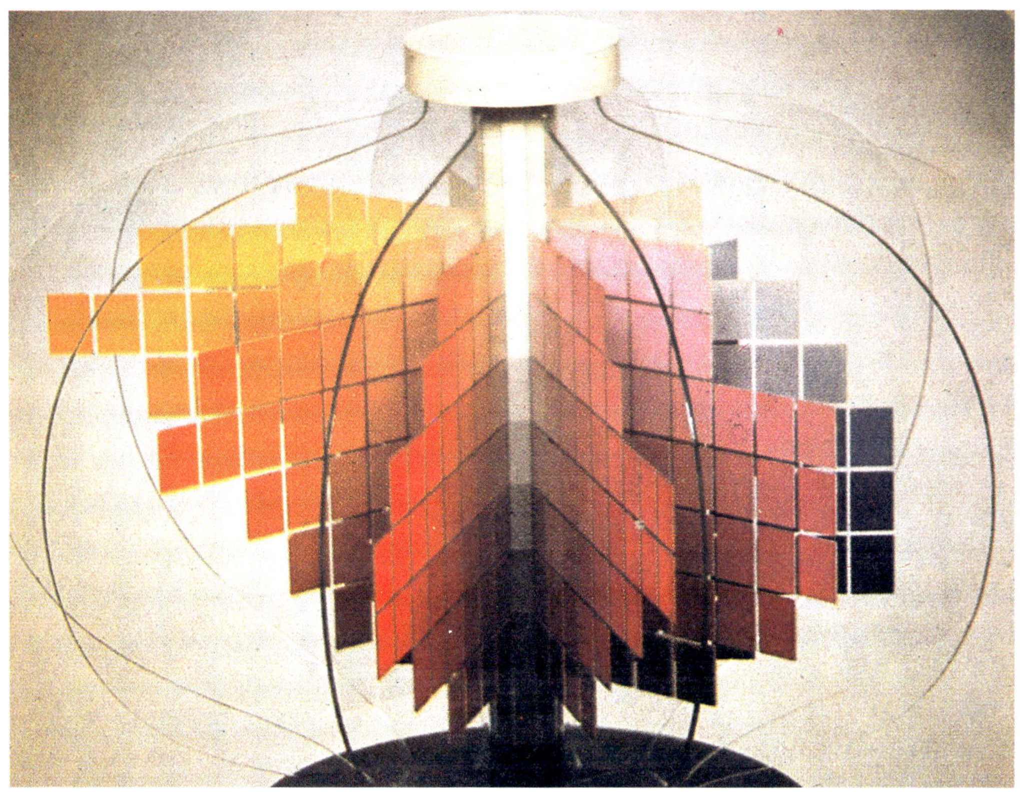

Colour solid: A. H. Munsell
Various attempts have been made to display colours on a three-dimensional form. This illustration of a Munsell colour solid enables us to grasp the concept of hue, value and chroma as the three dimensions of colour.

COLOUR

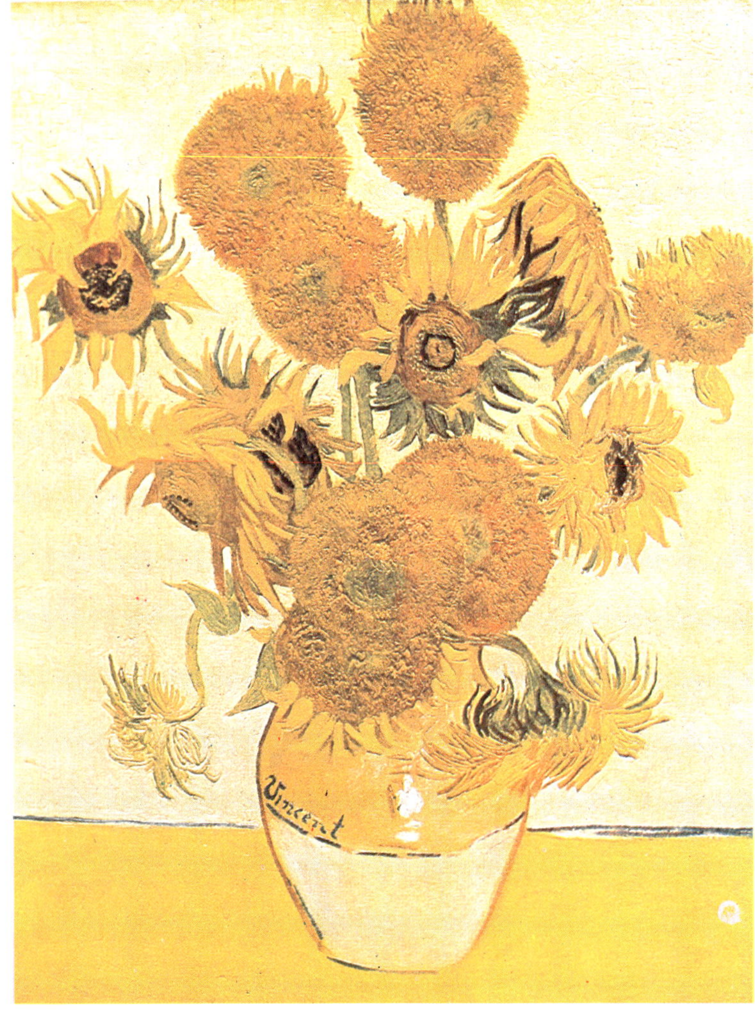

Sunflowers: Vincent van Gogh
Those hues which are adjacent, or close together, on the colour circle are said to be harmonious. Van Gogh, like his French Impressionist contemporaries, was well acquainted with recent research by the physicist Chevreul towards an understanding of the nature of colour. Here Van Gogh uses a range of yellows, from the deepest conceivable old gold at the lower end of the scale to bright clear yellow at the other end. All was designed to produce a sensation of gay and cheerful harmony as a warm welcome to his prospective visitor, Gauguin.

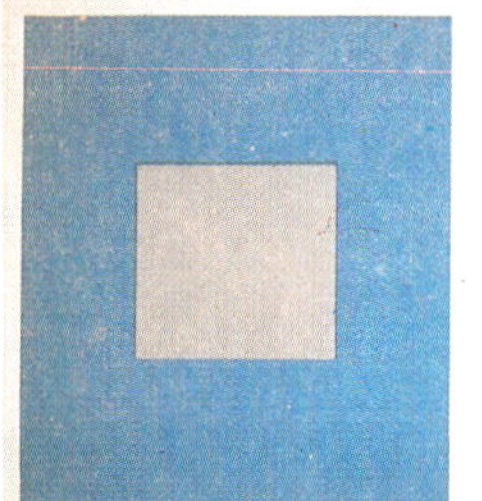

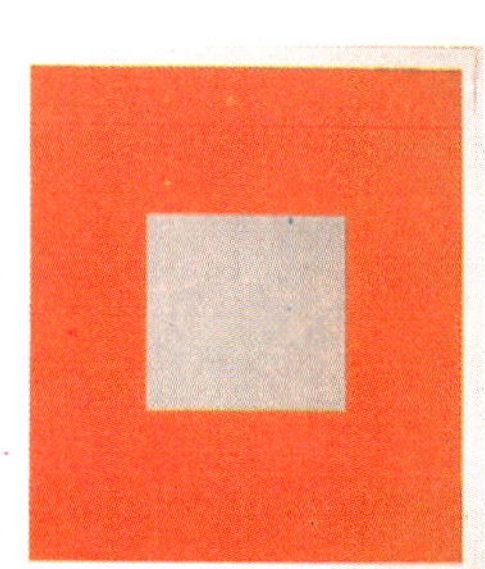

Complementaries: J. Itten (diagram)
Those hues which are opposite to each other on the colour circle are said to be complementary. If one looks at an area of a colour for a time, and then switches one's gaze to a white surface, the complementary colour may then be seen as a ghostly after-image floating against the white background. This diagram illustrates the fact that a grey surrounded by a colour tends to take on the complementary hue of that colour; so a grey surrounded by red will appear a greenish grey (a blueish green being the opposite colour to red) and vice versa.

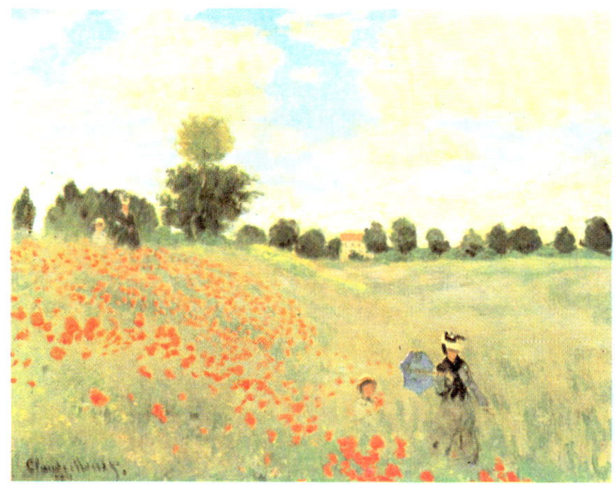

Field of Poppies: Claude Monet
Monet was no doubt well aware of this phenomenon which he has used to effect in this painting, where the red is strikingly bright against comparatively greyish greens. This effect of greenness is achieved not so much through the use of green paint, but as a complementary consequence of the proximity of the powerful reds. Had the green been painted with the same kind of strong colour as the reds, the result would have been garish and vulgar – instead of bright and full of colour.

Complementaries mixing to grey (diagram)
This beautiful range of colour shows the result of mixing two complementaries, blue and orange, through a series of steps – in each case the mid-colour is a grey (because two complementary hues when mixed neutralize each other). Grey is one of the most useful colours, and the artist is constantly called on to make the most delicate judgements – not of black versus white, but to distinguish between different greys of the kind illustrated here.

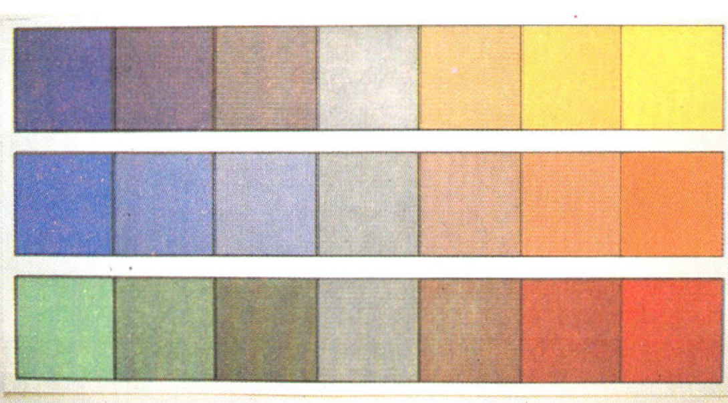

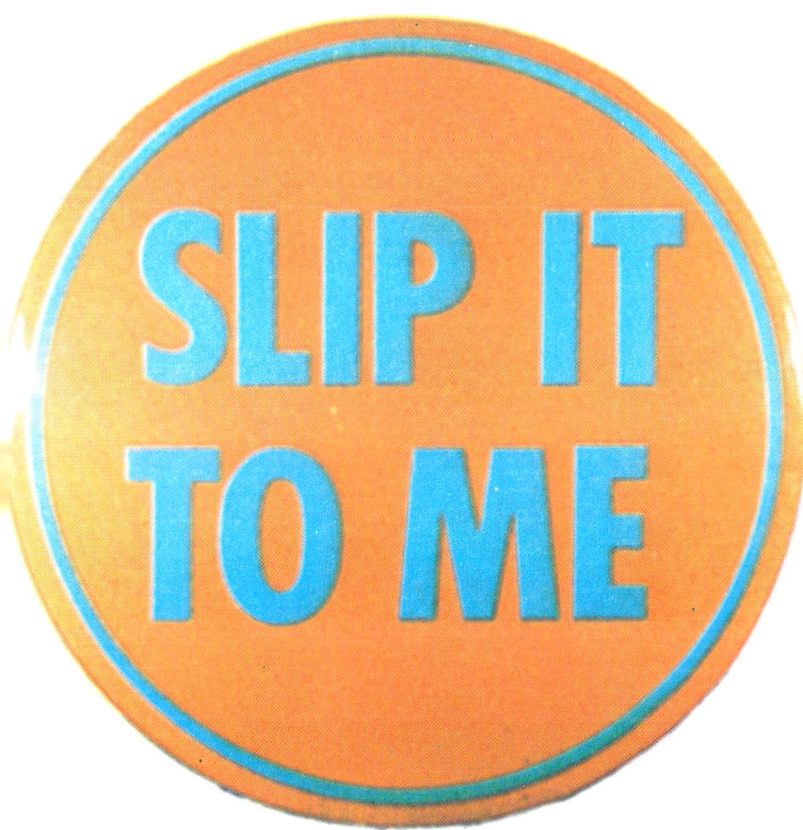

Epiphany: Richard Hamilton
This large circular painting owes its sense of immediate impact (one of the characteristics of so-called Pop Art) to the abrupt contrast of hue. Complementaries simultaneously opposing each other, as they do here, produce a violence of colour reaction which is in keeping with the general brashness and vulgarity of much of today's media messages. (We can now imagine what Monet's poppy field would look like if given the red/green simultaneous contrast treatment!)

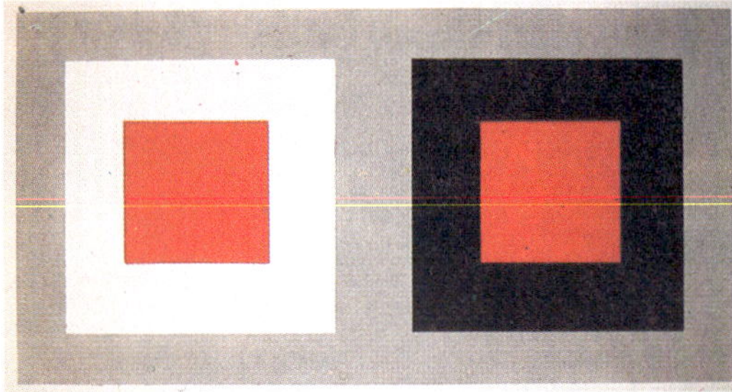

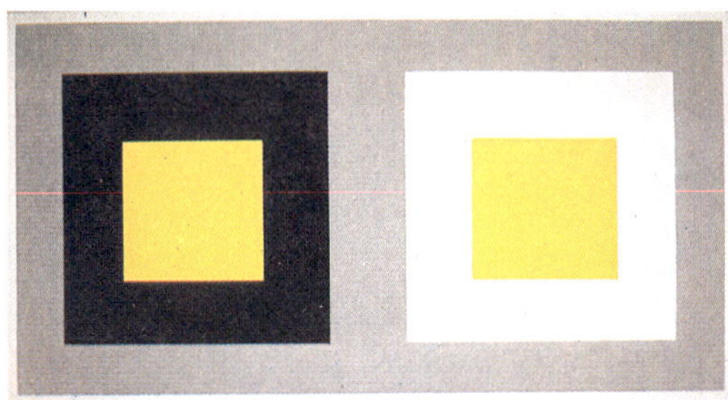

Colour values: J. Itten (diagram)
A colour appears lighter against a dark background, and vice versa. The red appears dark and comparatively dull against white, but against the black it is fiery and hot. Yellow is considerably more luminous against the dark background than against the light.

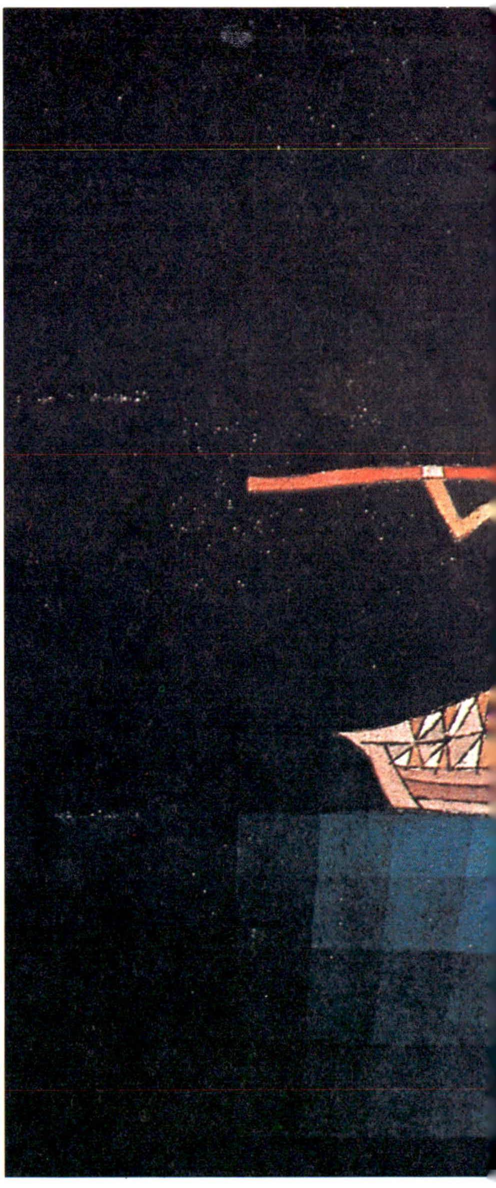

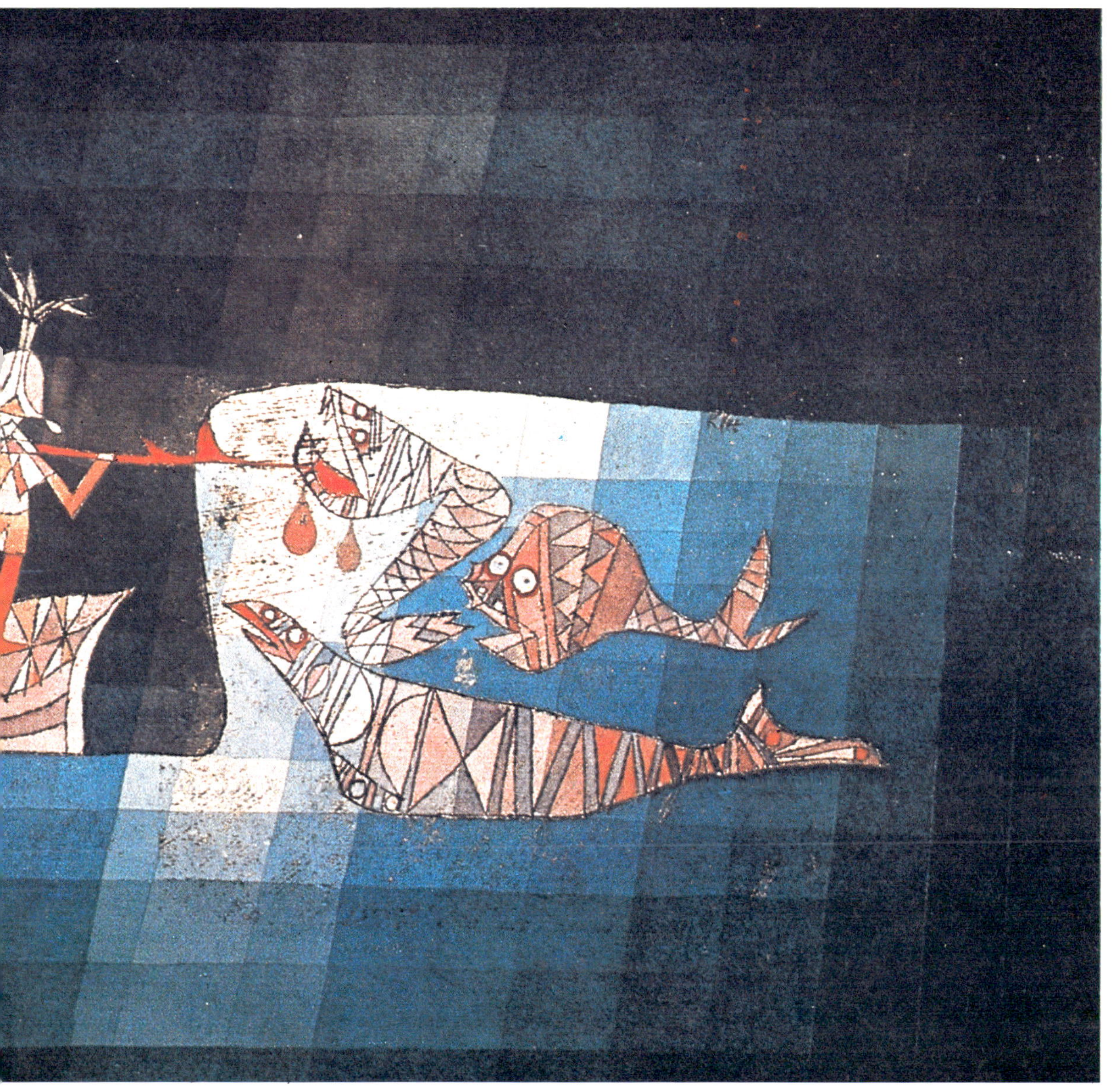

Battle Scene from the comic fantastic opera 'The Seafarer'. Paul Klee

This effect may be observed in this painting by Paul Klee, where the subtle change of value in the blue background creates a curious fluted effect, due to the edge of each tone appearing to become darker as it comes into contrast with a light tone. Klee uses the value changes of the background blue to create a kind of crossing spotlight effect – illuminating the protagonists in this stirring battle scene!

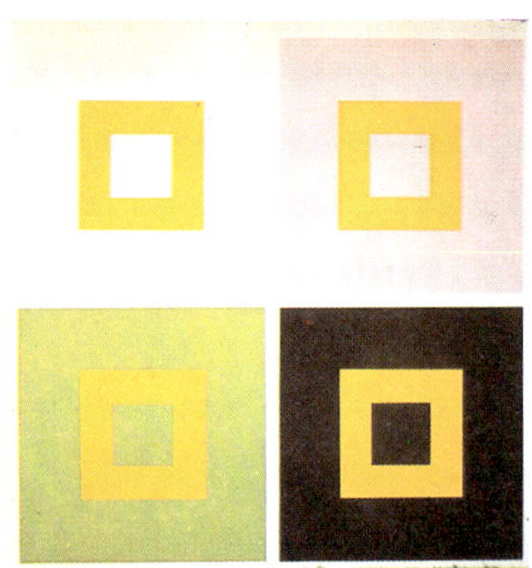

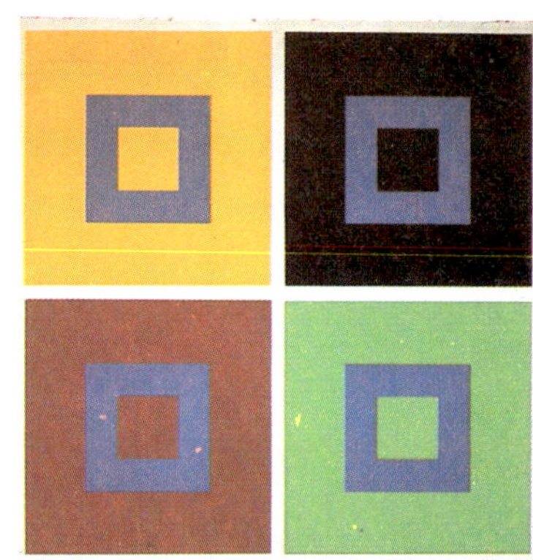

Chroma: J. Itten (diagrams)
Some of the most dramatic colour effects are due to contrast of chroma. Colour is always seen in relation to its surroundings: hue, value and/or chroma all change under different circumstances. All these yellows, printed in the same colour, have been altered by different juxtapositions. The yellow against white is dark and not particularly yellow (i.e. reduced in chroma); against pink of the same value the yellow takes on a greenish tinge (due to the simultaneous contrast against the suggestion of red). Against a green of darker value the yellow begins to glow and leans more towards orange (i.e. red) than before, but it is against the black that the chroma is most intense.

On yellow the blue appears very dark, whereas on black the blue suggests infinite distance and is radiant with light. On purple the blue changes to a quiet, undistinguished blue; whereas on a green of similar value maximum interreaction occurs, and the blue shifts towards red (i.e. opposite to green) creating a violet blue.

As a general rule a colour appears weaker against the strongest colour of the same hue, and stronger against the complementary.

Weeping Woman: Pablo Picasso
Some paintings make use of the fact that strong value contrast tends to overpower or reduce a colour's chroma, so that dark colours appear weaker in chroma against white, and vice versa. This principle may be used to harmonize or unify dark contrasting elements, by outlining in white, silver or gold. Alternatively, as in this painting by Picasso, heavy black lines are used to subdue and integrate violently conflicting light colours by isolating them. The sense of conflict remains, but our sensibility is not assailed by conflicting colour. The same principle is often employed in stained glass work, where the black lines of the leading are used to separate the colours.

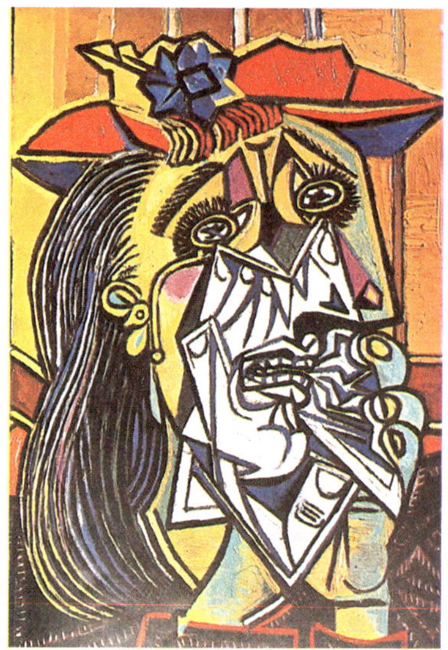

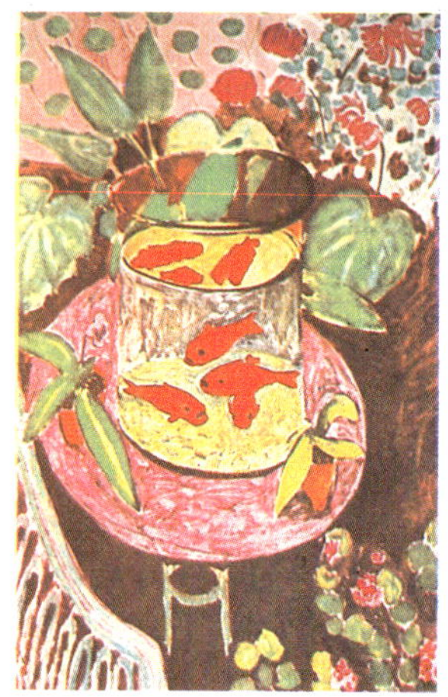

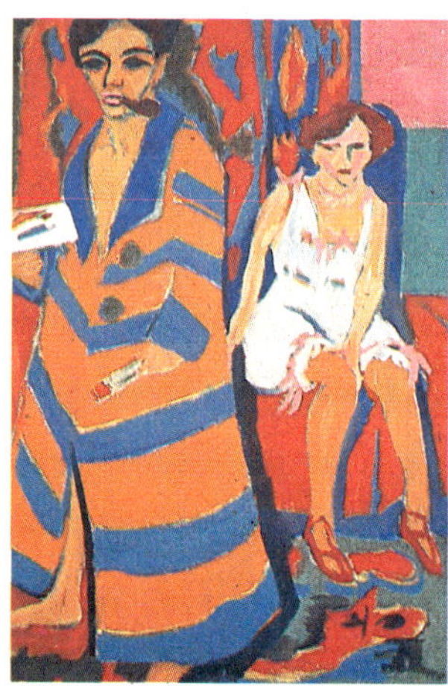

Goldfish: Henri Matisse
Self-portrait with Model: Ernst Kirchner
Both the Fauves and the Expressionists pushed colour to the extreme, and to get the ultimate in chromatic intensity they needed to use colours of much the same value and of complementary hue. Matisse uses the complementaries red and green at maximum intensity, and Ernst Kirchner chooses orange against blue to create maximum colour impact.

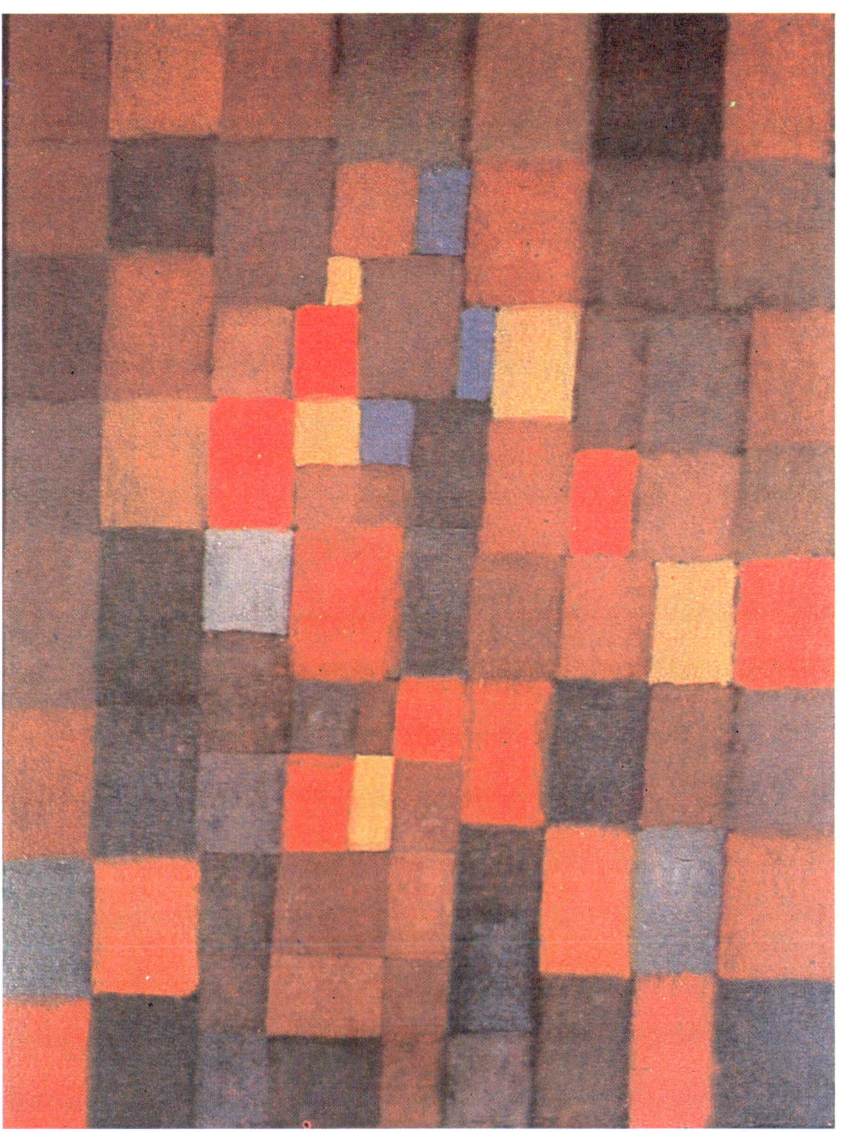

Architecture: Red, Yellow & Blue: Paul Klee

In his continuous investigation of the means at his disposal Klee pursued his search from point to line, to tone and colour. In this painting the placing of the strong red, yellow and blue in close proximity to each other, and the particular placing of this generative area in relation to the frame, are important to the balance of colour. From this initial premise Paul Klee leads us into a closely reasoned visual argument: that the other colours used will stem from these. Step by step he works towards the perimeter, permutating a series of warm brown greys, cool grey browns, and greyed yellows. Although these are very reduced in chroma compared to the starting colours, because they are often of the same value they enhance each other and take on a positive identity – instead of (as so easily might have happened) becoming just dull, muddy and indeterminate colours.

Colour as mood

Colour is capable of, and indeed largely responsible for, conveying emotional feeling, and colours are described by the same words as the feelings they convey. We speak of gay or cheerful colours, as well as sad or sombre ones. A grey day may depress the spirits and result in a feeling of the 'blues'.

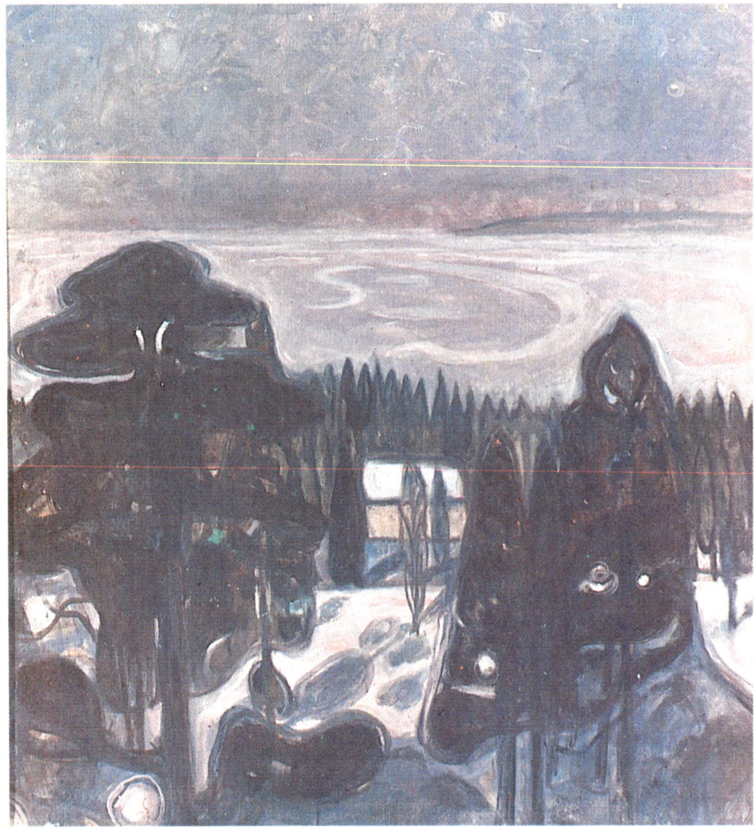

White Night: Edvard Munch
The blues not only express the coldness, loneliness, and silence of this empty landscape, but reflect the loneliness and silence of the painter himself: the endless Norwegian twilight becomes an expression of Munch's own existence.

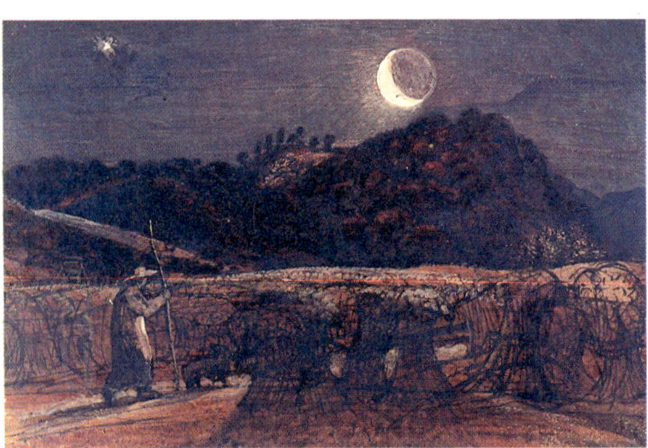

Cornfield by Moonlight with Evening Star: Samuel Palmer
What a different mood is conveyed by the warm colours of this moonlight landscape, seen on a warm summer night under the harvest moon. Imagine changing the predominantly warm colours of this scene to the cold colours of the Munch, and vice versa!

The Big Circus: Marc Chagall
Marc Chagall remembers colours; his memories are fragmentary, but essentially he remembers that fantastic world of the circus, in which anything could happen. All this is conveyed by his choice of colours, which bear no relation to the drab colours of everyday existence.

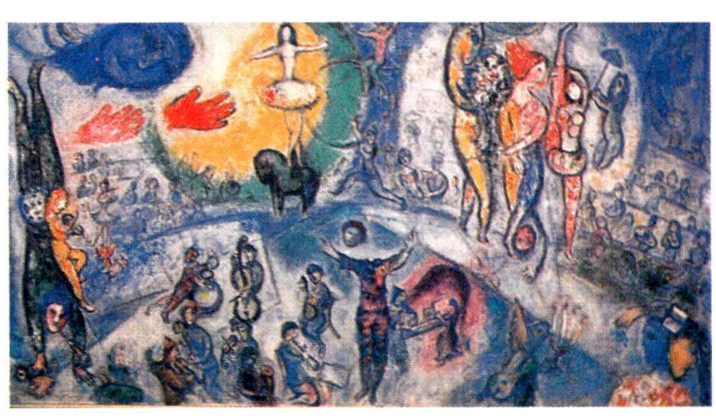

Colour as symbol

From ancient time colours have been used as symbols – red, with its association with blood, still speaks of danger; black has long represented death or evil. The phases of the moon were represented in early cultures by different colours, and for centuries colours have been considered as an influence of the heavenly bodies: e.g. silver belongs to the Moon, gold to the Sun, red to Mars, violet to Mercury. The four seasons, the four elements of the alchemist and the four 'humours' of the Greek doctor Hippocrates (the Melancholic, Phlegmatic, Choleric, and Sanguine) all have their characteristic colours. Medieval chivalry also attributed symbolic meaning to colours – in fact the symbolic role of colour throughout man's history is diverse and universal.

As is so often the case, Christianity gave ancient beliefs new meaning and so Christian colour symbolism gave new meanings to the ancient colours. The blue of the sky (symbol of Venus of Jupiter) was associated with the Virgin Mary as Queen of Heaven.

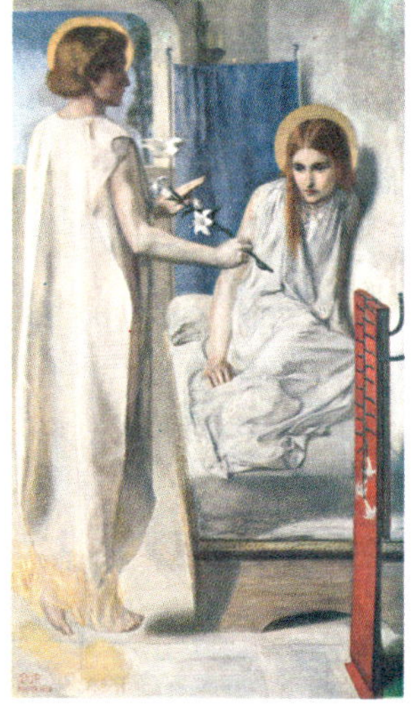

'Ecce Ancilla Domini': Dante Gabriel Rossetti
White (from earliest times associated with day and light, hence with the magical power to dispel black, i.e. night or darkness) became the colour for purification, holy virgins and brides. The overall colour impression we receive from this painting is of whiteness, creating a kind of spiritual plane with no disturbing influences from the colourful physical world of the flesh.

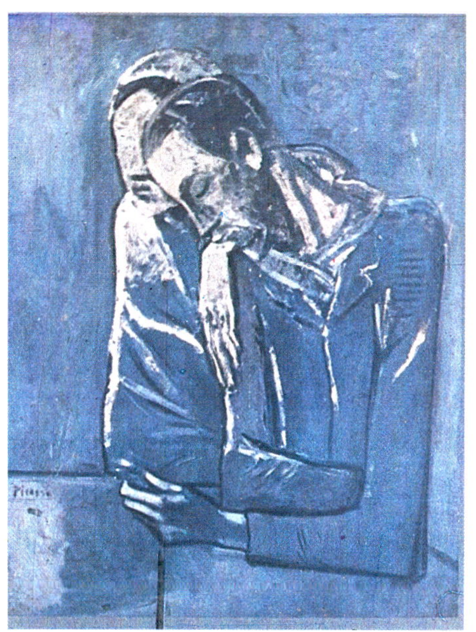

Les Miserables: Pablo Picasso
The poverty-stricken feeling of the figures and of the colour in this Picasso is typical of his 'Blue Period'.

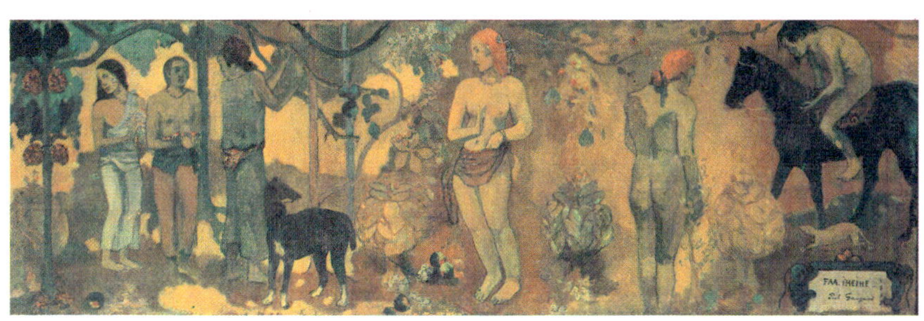

Nevermore: Paul Gauguin
The effect of the colours used in this painting is exactly opposite to that of the Rossetti. Here we are confronted with all the rich feast of colour of the physical world, and the flesh is the colour of bronze. Gauguin clearly stated his aims in a letter – 'I wanted to suggest by means of a simple nude a certain long-lost barbarian luxury. The whole is drowned in colours which are deliberatedly sombre and sad; it is neither silk nor velvet, nor batiste, nor gold which creates the luxury here but simply matter which has been enriched by the hand of an artist . . . ' Colour here is rich, exotic, spicy, and deeply resonant, like the half-heard, half-felt reverberation of a great drum. These dim colours from the past are brought to pulsating life by the sudden singing red and sulphurous yellow. Without these enrichments 'by the hand of an artist' the colours would simply be dull, not 'deliberately sombre and sad'.

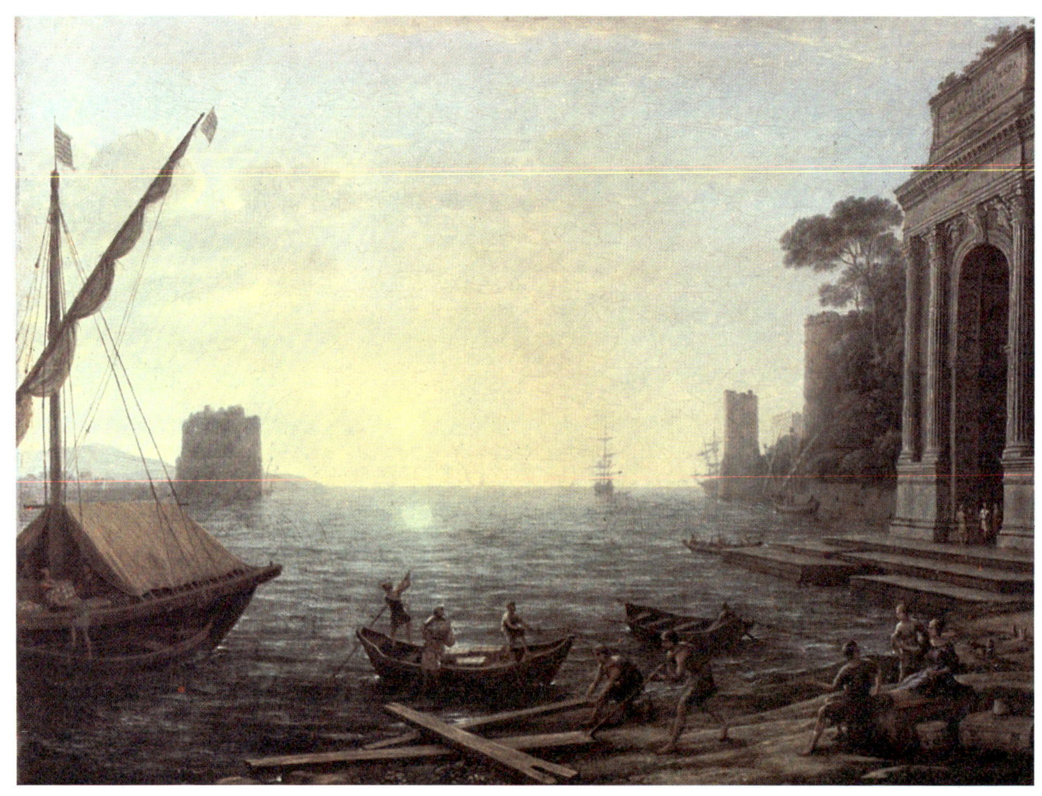

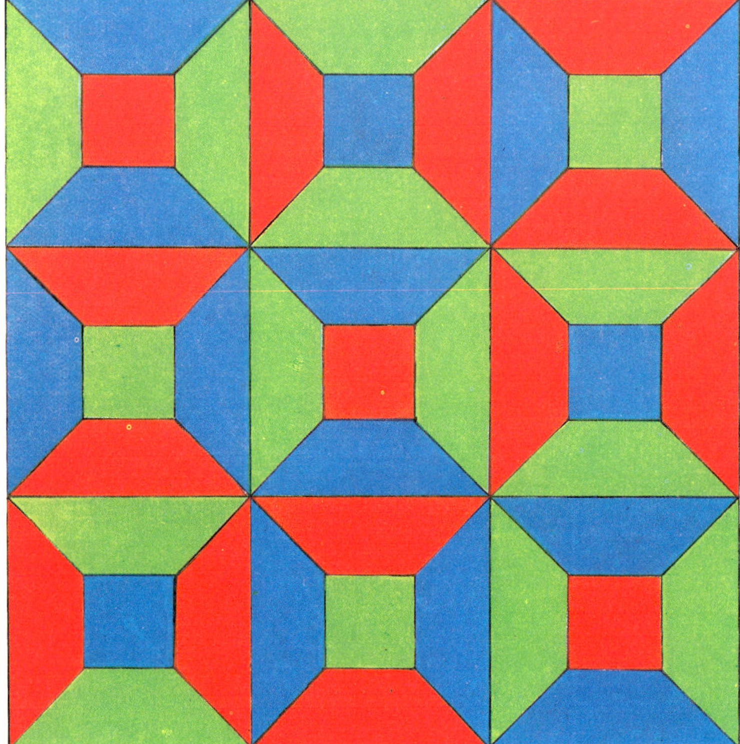

Harbour at Sunrise: Claude
It is often thought that blue tends to recede into a picture and red to advance. The quality of recession in this painting by Claude is clearly partly achieved by making the distant scene generally less coloured and by making the distant colours tend towards blue, i.e. as they would appear in nature due to the effect of the atmosphere. By simulating this effect he creates the illusion of distance.

Advancing and receding colour (diagram)
The ability of colours to advance or recede is not dependent on the individual colour – red, blue or any other – but on relationships between colours. By using a spatially ambiguous situation we can see that some colours sometimes tend to produce the effect of a truncated pyramid; at other times we are apparently looking into a box. All depends on surrounding colours.

Colour as space (aerial perspective)

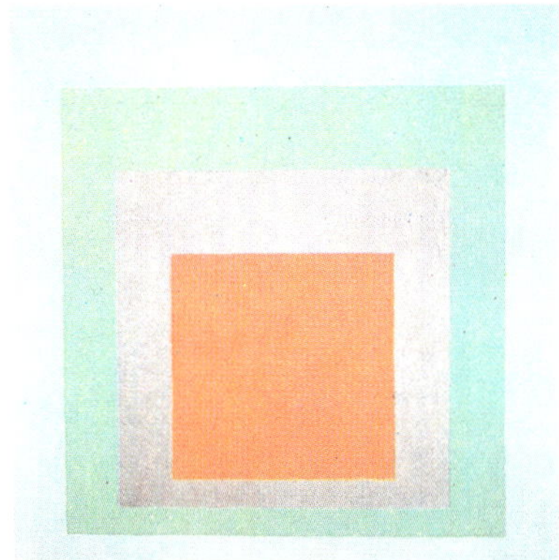

Homage to the Square: Josef Albers
In his series of paintings *Homage to the Square* Josef Albers made numerous experiments with colours, putting them into different relationships with each other, in an attempt to exploit fully the spatial quality of colour (and the difference between physical size and apparent size in differing situations).

Blossoming: Paul Klee
As our eye moves over the surface of this Klee, noticing the curious repetitive relationship of the blues (always paired and seen in juxtaposition with red), we find that the 'surface' begins to move backwards and forwards as some colours float towards us and others drift further away.

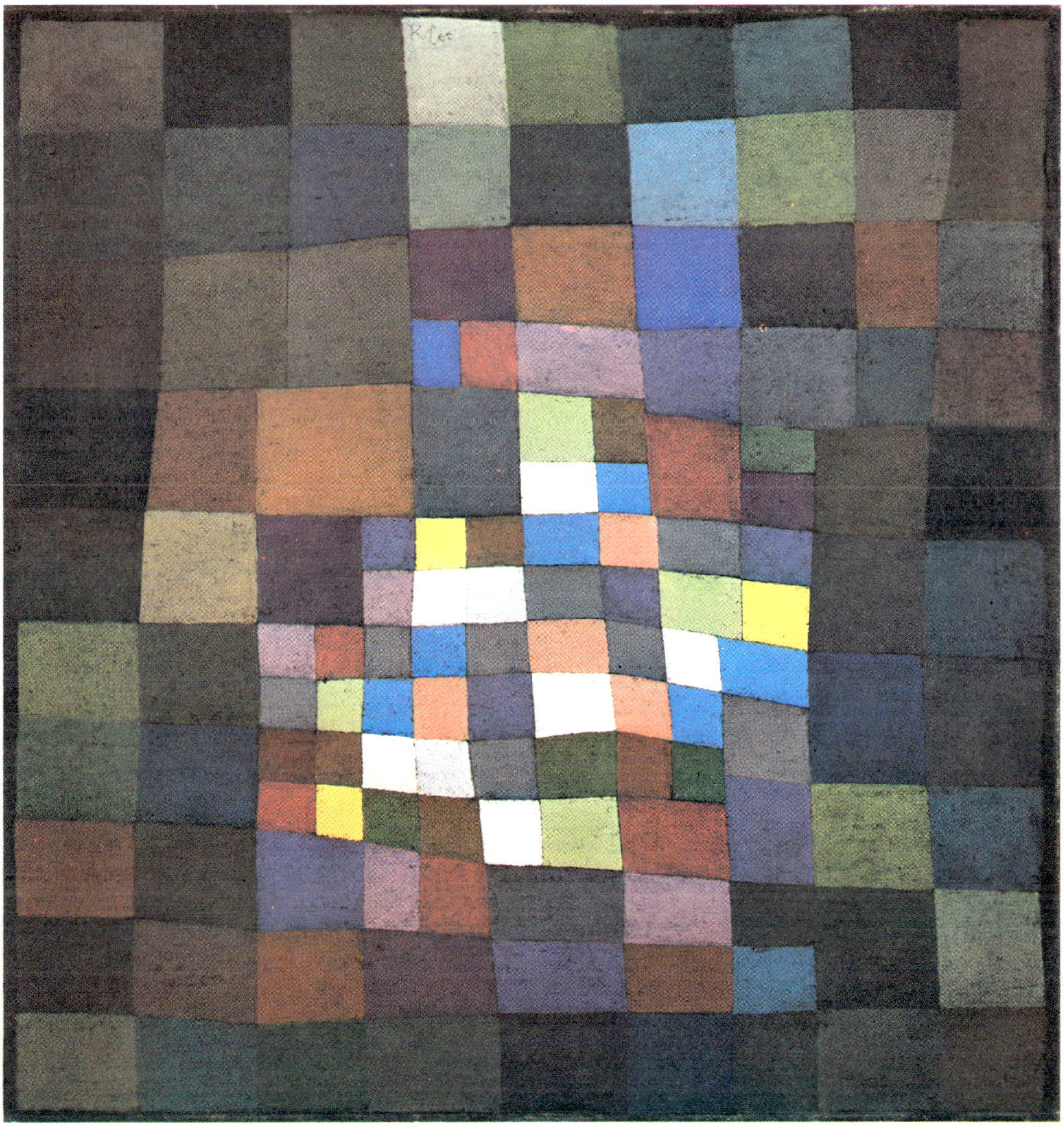

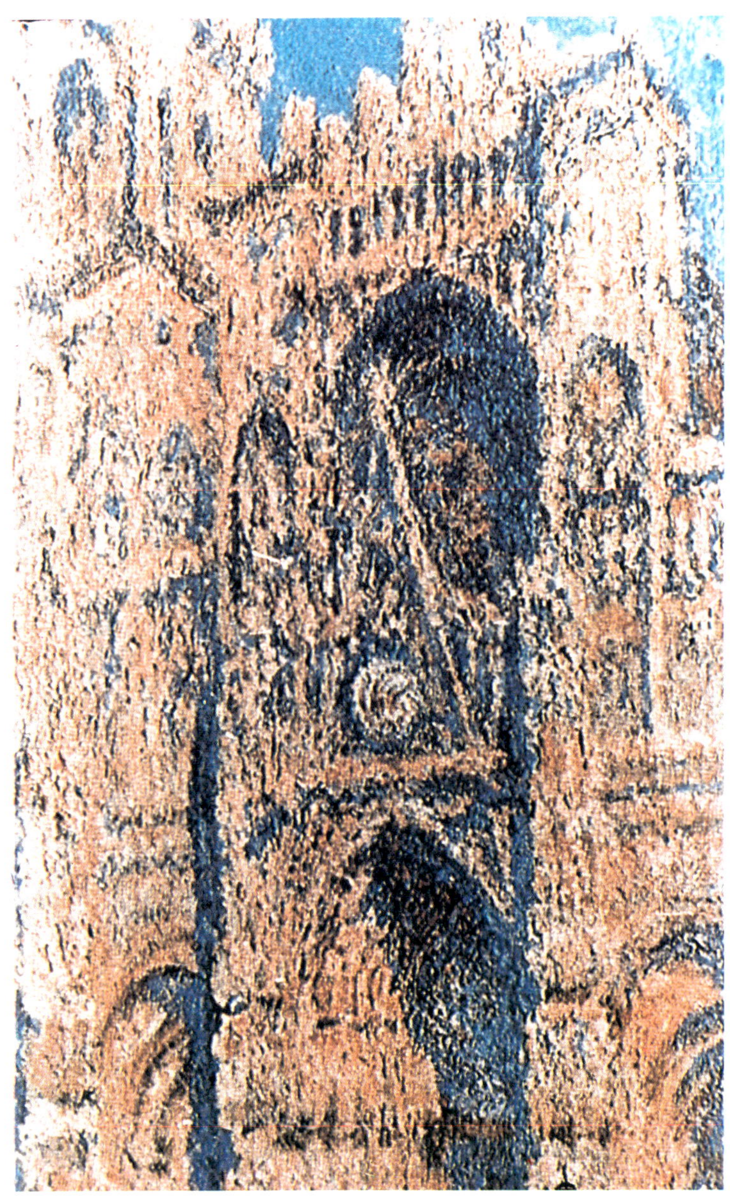

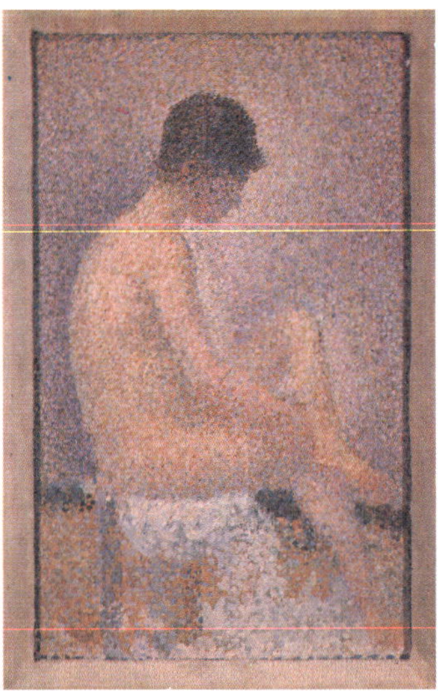

Seated Model in Profile: Georges Seurat
The logical conclusion of Impressionism – with its broken brush strokes endeavouring to create the immediacy of light, and with its insistence on the rainbow palette – would seem to be found in the work of the Pointillists, who reduced the broken touch of Impressionism to small dots of individual colours and attempted to put their observation of colour effects on to a scientific basis.

The intention is that when viewed from a distance, the light reflected from the individual touches shall fuse together on the retina of the eye to produce the required effect. Of course it was never the intention (as is so often erroneously stated) that blue and yellow dots be placed close together to produce green – an idea derived from the mixing of pigments, whereas Seurat was trying to create the effect of light. This misconception may easily be removed simply by looking at paintings by Seurat, when one can clearly see the use of green.

Rouen Cathedral in Full Sunlight: (detail) Claude Monet
Abandoning black and the faithful ochres and earths which had served painters for so long and so well, they plunged their brushes into the colours of the spectrum–the colours of light. This example from Monet's series of paintings of Rouen Cathedral shows the great façade dissolving into a myriad facets of jewelled mist. Gone is the sense of a mighty and permanent structure, and the authority of the Church; in its place we see a glittering momentary vision, which in a moment will disappear before our eyes to be replaced by another.

Colour as light and movement

As we have seen there is no colour without light, and as light changes so colour changes. Of all painters the French Impressionists were the most fascinated by the fleeting effects of light as it flickered over the surface of the everyday scene, transforming it into all the colours of the rainbow.

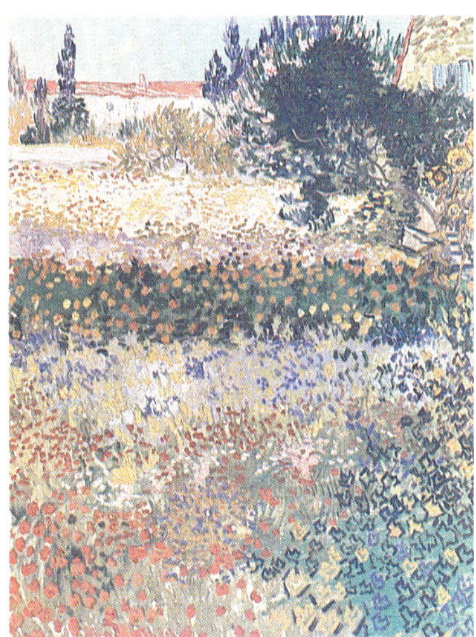

Flowering Garden: Vincent van Gogh
Van Gogh's work always expresses dynamic movement, often through his powerful brushwork which twists and turns as it finds its way through the thick paint. In this painting the movement of the colours is contrasted with the comparatively static forms of the composition – bands of changing colours dance their way into the distance between a framework of horizontals.

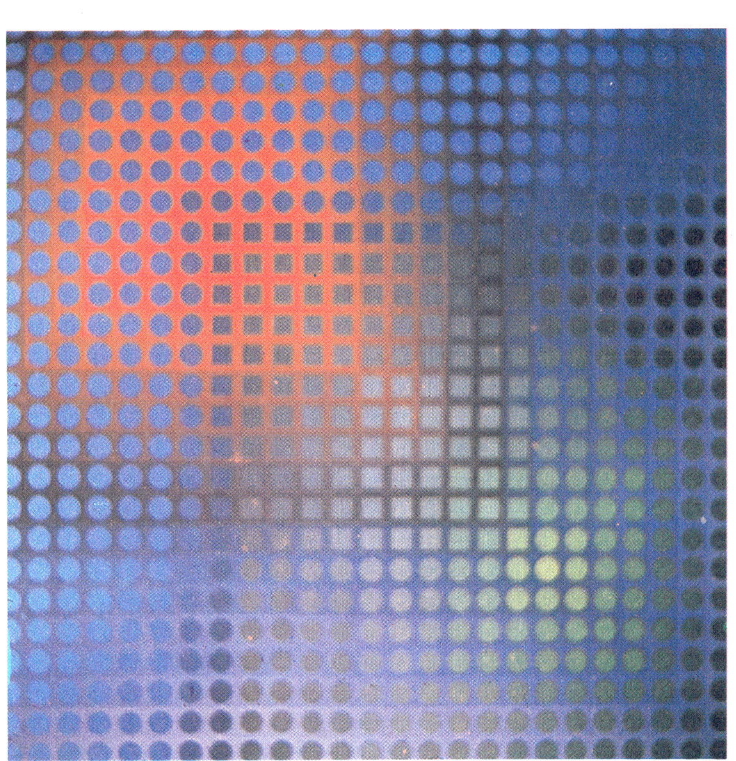

Arny: Victor Vasarely
'Op' artists do not try to represent movement so much as they try to create the appearance of movement, by bombarding the retina of the eye with alternate light/dark repetition so that the after-image of each shape becomes confused and difficult to focus, thereby resulting in a flickering sensation of movement.

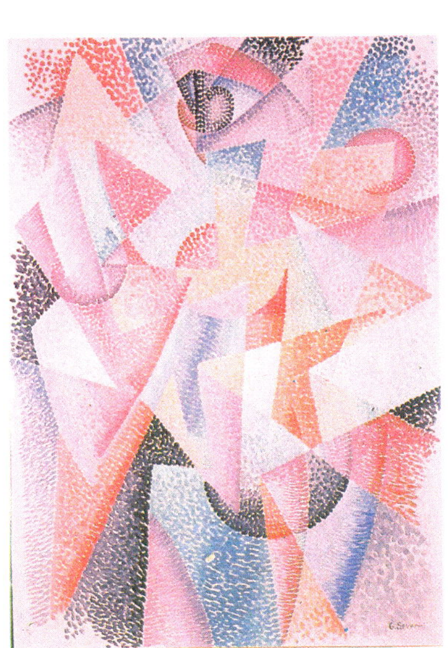

Movement of Luminous Forms in Space: Gino Severini
Futurism was essentially concerned with movement (and to the Futurists that meant speed – the latest thing in 1910!). All the elements of design were pressed into service in trying to express this idea, and in the forefront was the use of colour. Colour, like line, can express transparency by means of one colour overlapping, or being seen through, another, and thereby establishing the relationship between successive stages of a process seen at the same time – particularly evident in this painting by Severini.

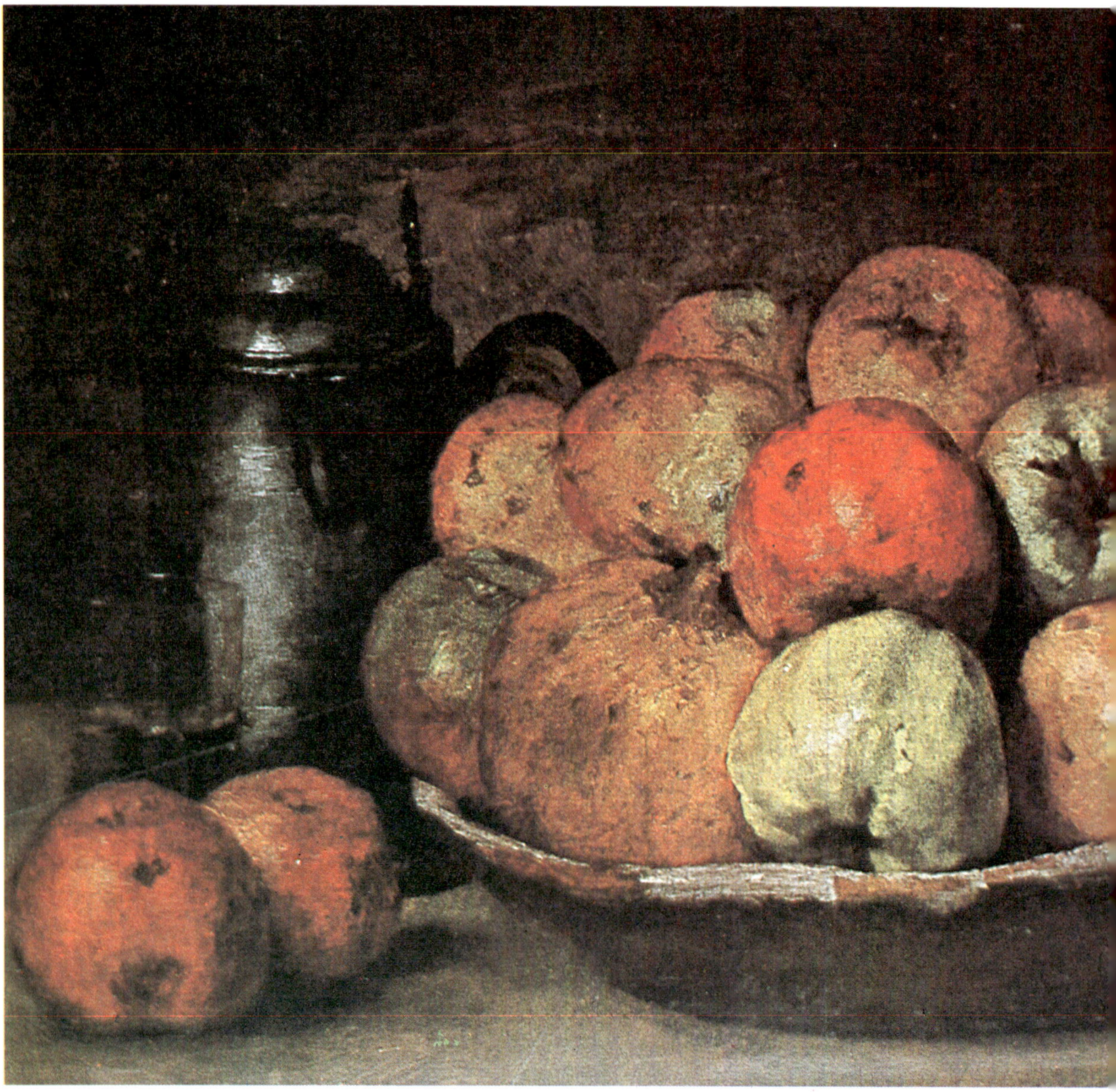

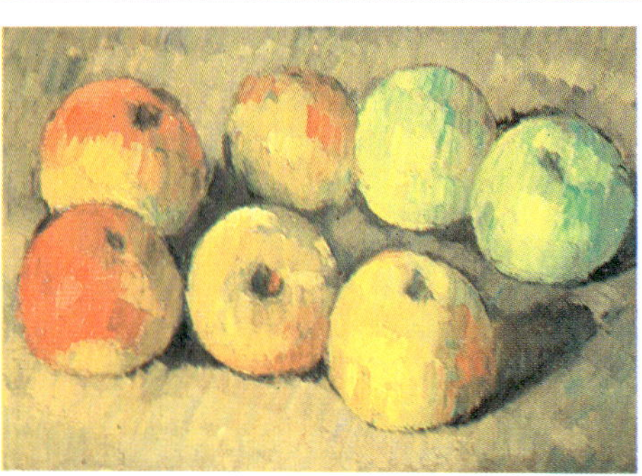

Apples: Paul Cézanne

Cézanne expresses his attitude to form in his famous dictum 'Quand la couleur est à sa richesse la forme est à sa plenitude', translated as 'When colour is at its richest form is at its fullest' i.e. most pronounced.

When we look at Courbet's apple we see form, with the addition of colour as a descriptive element: 'Here are solid apples, they are coloured red.' But when we look at the Cézanne form and colour are seen as one, i.e. colour is used to express the form of the red apple – Cézanne succeeds in uniting colour and form into a harmonious organization.

Colour as form

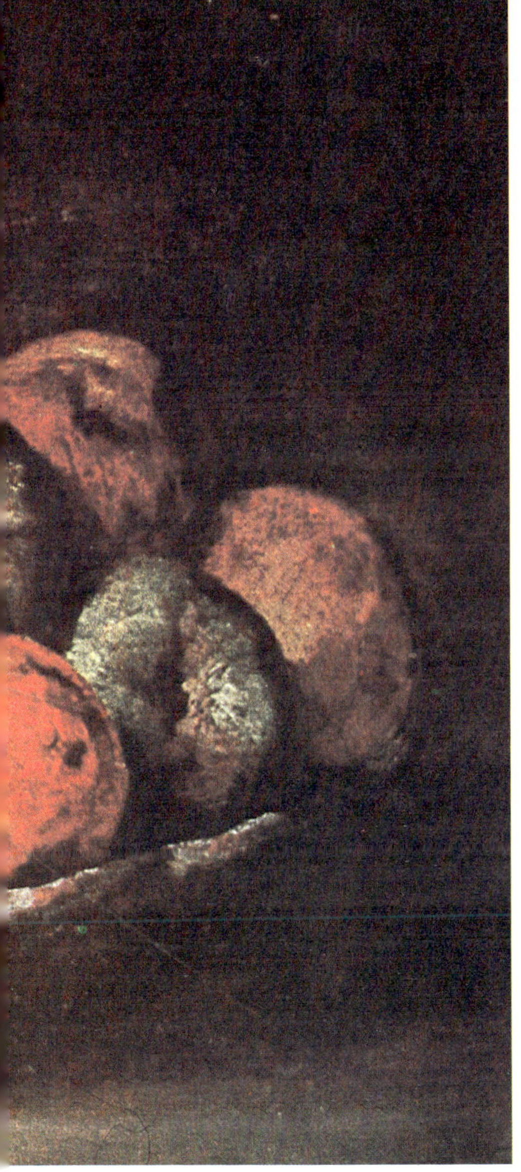

◀ *Still Life: Apples and Pomegranate*: Gustave Courbet
Courbet was a self-styled Realist painter, claiming that if you can't see it or touch it you can't paint it! In other words, he was preaching a doctrine of the primacy of form, and his painting of apples expresses this very clearly. Colour here is obviously subordinate to the demands of form. Tone, rather than colour, is used to model these forms to create the utmost feeling of plasticity. These are very solid apples indeed.

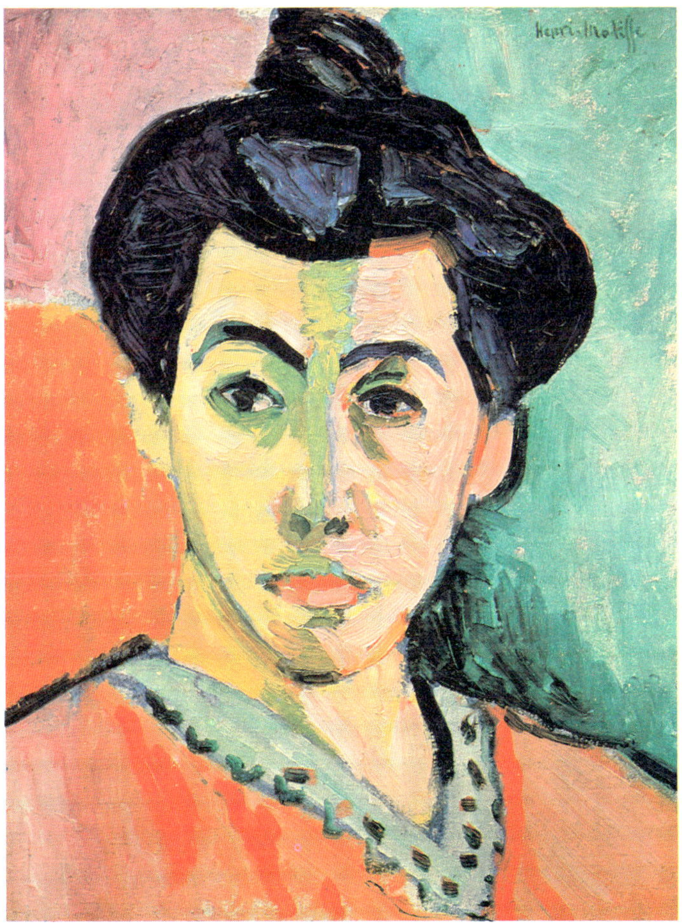

Portrait of Madame Matisse with Green Stripe: Henri Matisse
Whereas the Cubists adopted almost literally Cézanne's advice to treat Nature as geometric form, it seems to have been left to Matisse to interpret his views on the relationship between form and colour. In this early Fauve painting by Matisse, wherever the form is most pronounced (i.e. the parts nearest to the spectator, from which the form recedes on each side) there we find the strongest colour. Matisse (1869–1954) went on to spend his whole life exploring the rich and inexhaustible field of colour.

DRAWING

'Drawing well does not mean drawing correctly.' Note by Jawlensky quoted in *Das Kunstwerk II*, 1948.
'A study of drawings is not only the necessary basis of all scientific art criticism, it is the best training for the private sensibility.' H. Read.
'You cannot express life by copying laboriously natural appearances.' H. Speed.

Drawing has nothing to do with copying – it is essentially a creative activity, involving the intuitive faculty, and is a means of representing visual information about something seen or imagined, making use of subtle selection and emphasis.

The characteristics of drawing are governed by the following factors:

(1) The medium: drawings may be made in any medium or combination of media which will leave a mark on a surface, although pencil drawings on white paper are comparatively rare except among students and amateur draughtsmen. The artist's choice of media will depend on the scale that he wishes to work on, which aspect of the subject he wishes to emphasize, and the purpose for which he is making the drawing. The artist may decide to use a linear or tonal technique and will choose an appropriate medium for this purpose, e.g. pen/ink for line, or wash or chalk for tone.

(2) As well as deciding whether to express line or tone, or a combination of both, the artist decides which particular aspect of his subject he wishes to emphasize: he may wish to show the linear rhythms, the movement or basic geometry or possibly the anatomical aspect; alternatively it may be the tonal relationships or the form which he is seeking to express. There are very many different paths, but generally artists are single-minded in their pursuit of Truth.

(3) The final factor governing the character of a drawing is the purpose for which the drawing is being made. The drawing may be a preparation or study for work to be carried out in another medium, or it may be a rapid sketch, a record of a fleeting visual experience; or it may represent the final statement, and be a complete composition in itself.

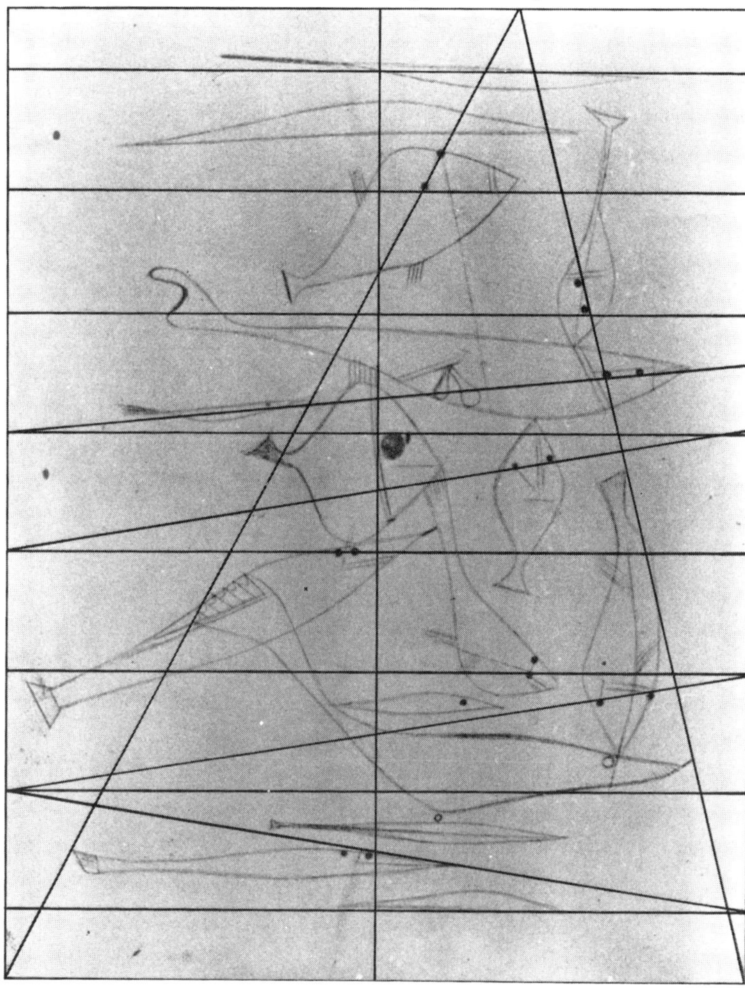

The Other Drawing for the Fish-picture: Paul Klee (diagram)
'Nodal points are points of support for different parts of the picture, and for the free space, e.g. the picture as a whole': *The Thinking Eye*, Paul Klee. By applying a simple analytical reasoning to the drawing, based on the premise that the fish with the eye larger than all the others is in the centre, we can see how Klee has arranged his 'nodal points' and then transfigured these points into fish.

The Point, and the point as movement

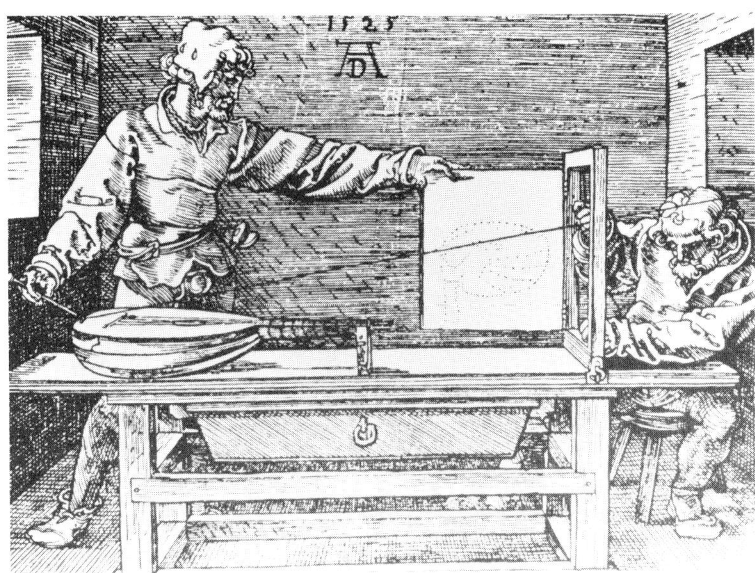

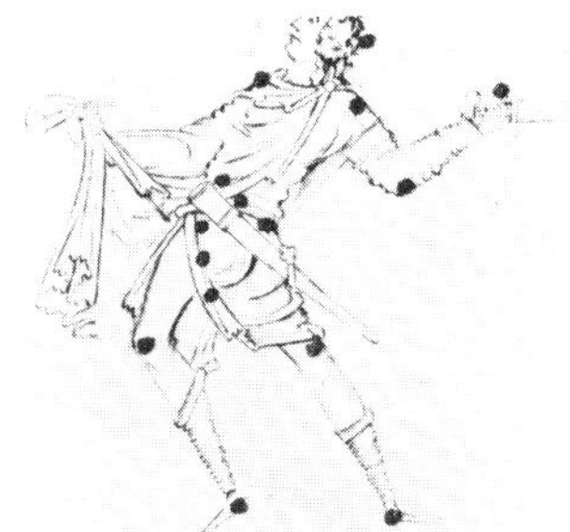

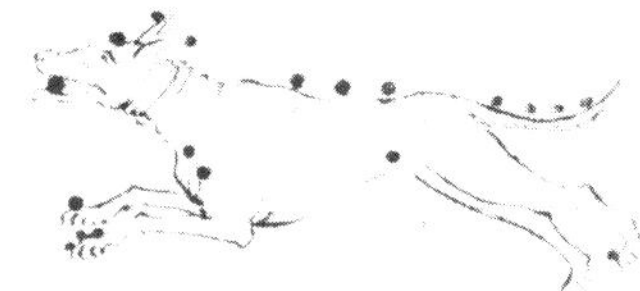

Treatise on measurement: Albrecht Dürer
This woodcut by Albrecht Dürer explains graphically the process of drawing from point to point. By means of referring salient points to co-ordinates on a grid, the artist is able to transfer them from three dimensions to two – thereby achieving a convincing foreshortening of the form of the lute.

Mediaeval manuscript
One of the simplest functions of the point, as we have seen, is to define a position in space. This mediaeval manuscript uses the point to identify the relative position of stars in this constellation. The line is used simply as additional visual identification and explanation.

View of La Crau from Montmajour: Vincent van Gogh
Van Gogh in all his work was always concerned with movement. All his drawings are charged with powerful energy, dynamically expressed and full of urgency. He often used a piece of sharpened wood dipped in ink to create a range of different point techniques, through which he expresses space, light and particularly movement.

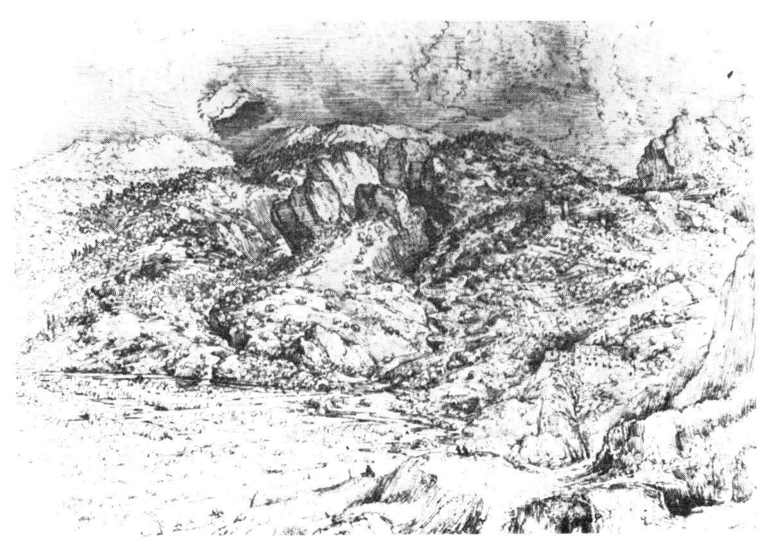

Landscape: Pieter Breughel
This drawing is also full of energy and movement. The trees suggested by the small units seem to swirl round the rocky features, leaving them in static isolation.

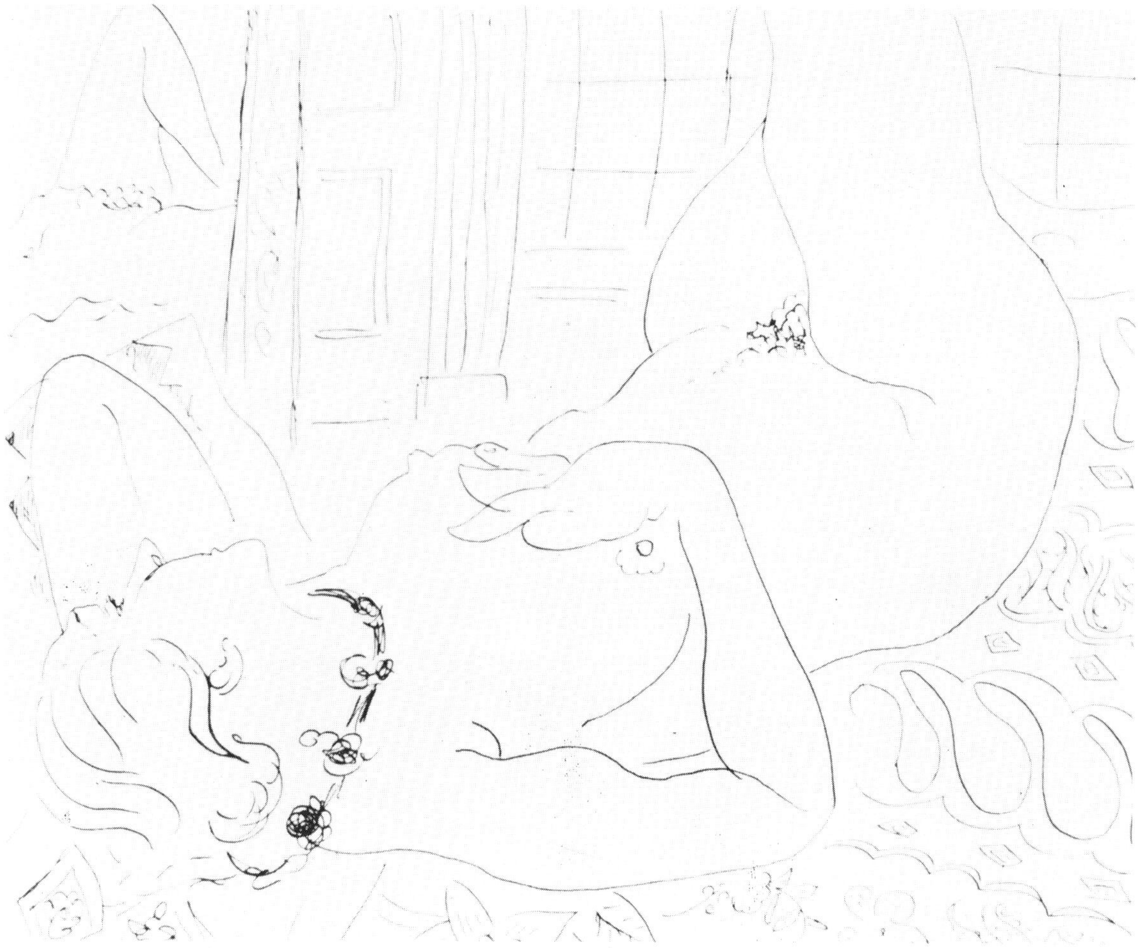

Nude: Henri Matisse
The drawings of Matisse, like his paintings, have a decorative calligraphic quality, seemingly achieved without effort. This meandering line describing the reclining nude so expressively is the end result of a gradual process of simplification, via a series of drawings which are traced one from another, simplifying each time.

Seated Nude: Pablo Picasso
Whereas Matisse uses the continuous unbroken line, Picasso also gives that impression; but on examination we find that there is no line in this very skilful drawing which is not broken. The more we look at this drawing the more we discover how little is drawn, in the sense that there are few marks on the paper, but Picasso has chosen just those marks to imply all that he has 'left out'. An astonishing *tour de force*.

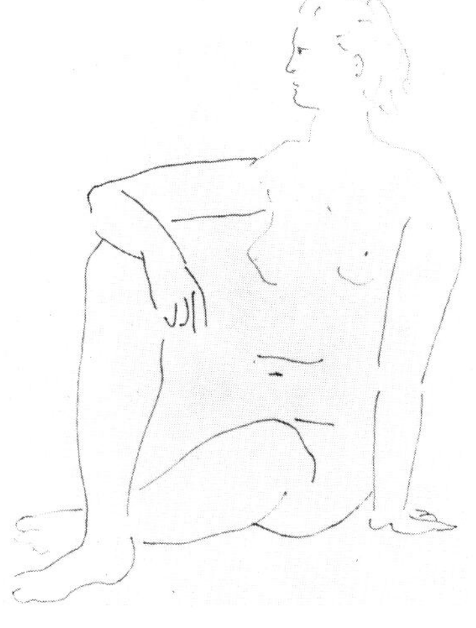

Line as movement

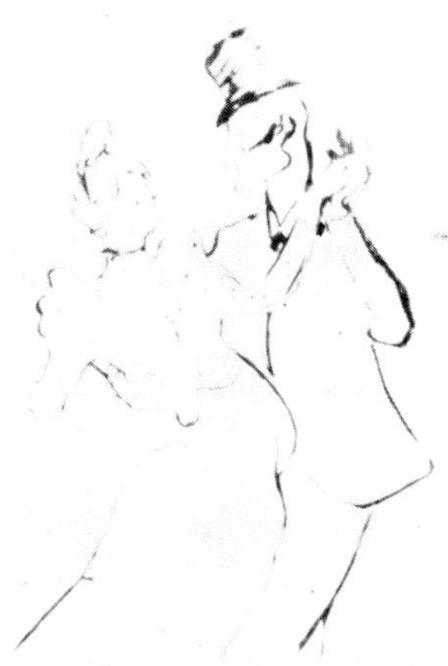

Dancers: Henri de Toulouse-Lautrec
This quick sketch of La Goulue and Valentin Le Désossé at the Moulin Rouge conveys, by brush line alone, the rippling quality of the dance of the 'boneless one'. Notice how the lines link the two figures, seeing them as one configuration rather than outlining each one separately.

Boats at Saintes-Maries: Vincent van Gogh
Solely by use of lines of differing weight and thickness, Van Gogh creates a swirling sea, lively boats, and everything imbued with a feeling of light and space.

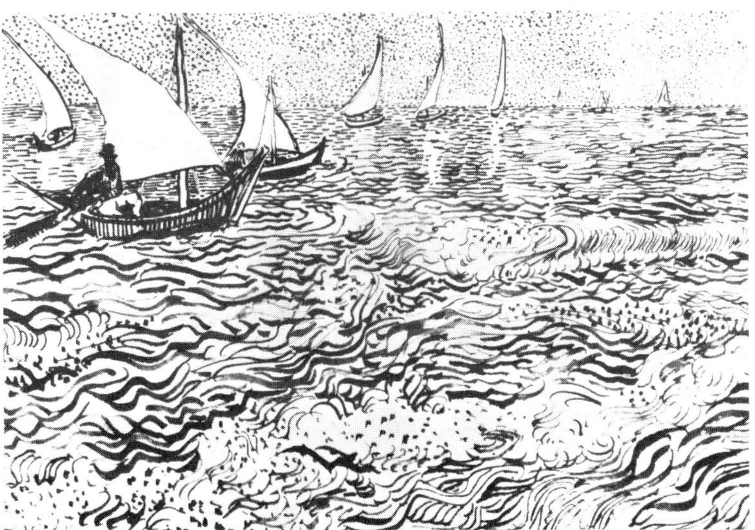

Allegorical figure: Abundance: Botticelli
Botticelli was a master of the languorous line – used here to suggest a dreamy drifting movement. His delicate use of the pen and the gentle touches of white create a figure half seen, half suggested. Notice how the central axis of the figure is paralleled by that of the cornucopia – a thinly veiled allusion to the idea of fertility.

Line as perspective and implied perspective

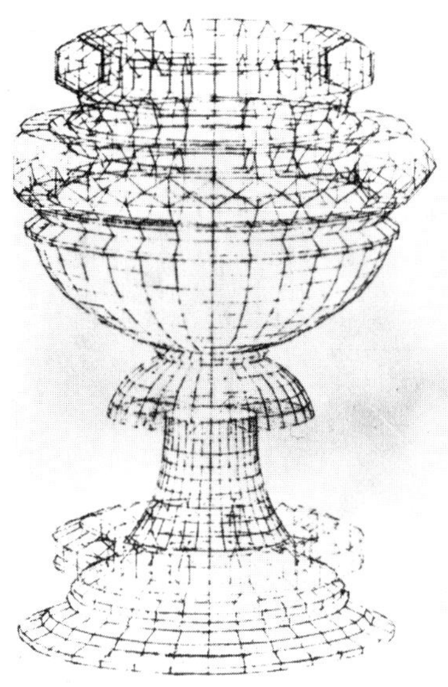

Chalice: Paolo Uccello
Uccello was fascinated by the 'new science' of perspective. This is a convincing solution to the problem of representing curved forms in perspective, which depends on the illusion that parallel lines meet at a point on the eye level. By dividing the continuously curving forms into facets Uccello creates the necessary parallels, and by further treating the chalice as a transparency he conveys, by line alone, a convincing sense of three dimensions.

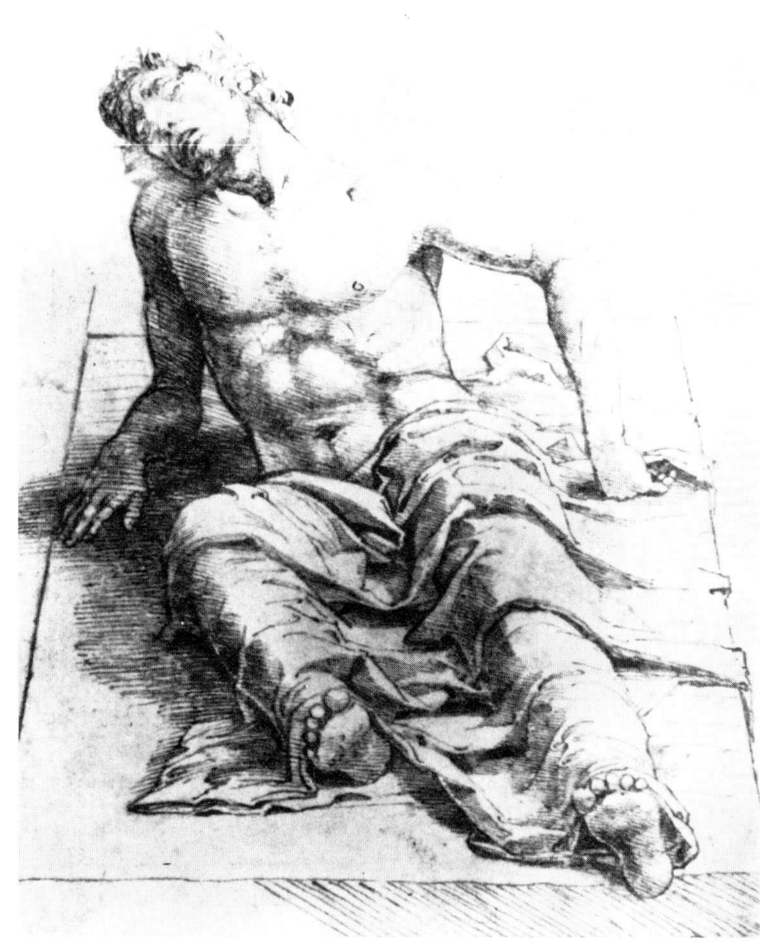

Man lying on a Stone Slab: Andrea Mantegna
Mantegna attempts a dramatic foreshortening, reminiscent of his *Dead Christ*. The plane on which the figure reclines is used to create the space in which the form will be placed. The realization of the form relies on emphasizing the folds of the drapery in order to create a series of 'squared-off' cylindrical forms. The drapery is also used to reinforce the realization of the plane on which the figure lies.

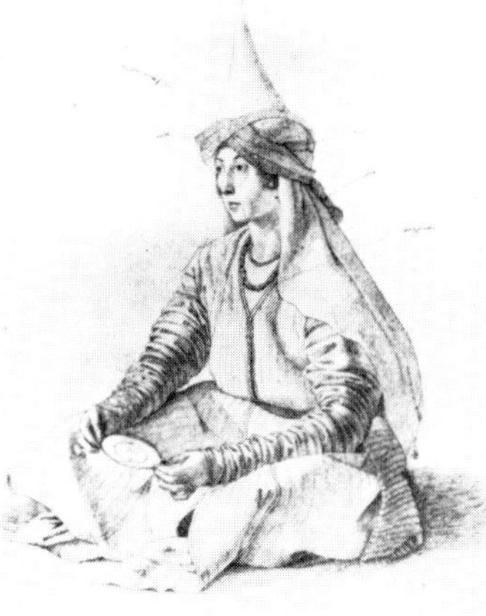

Turkish Woman: Jacopo Bellini
This three-quarter view seated figure expresses very clearly the idea of three-dimensional form, more through the implication of perspective than through any obvious reference. The clear realization of a flat plane occupying the area across the forearms, which is hinted at by analogy with the major axis of the saucer held between the fingers, is in turn a parallel plane to the implied floor on which the figure is seated.

Line as geometry

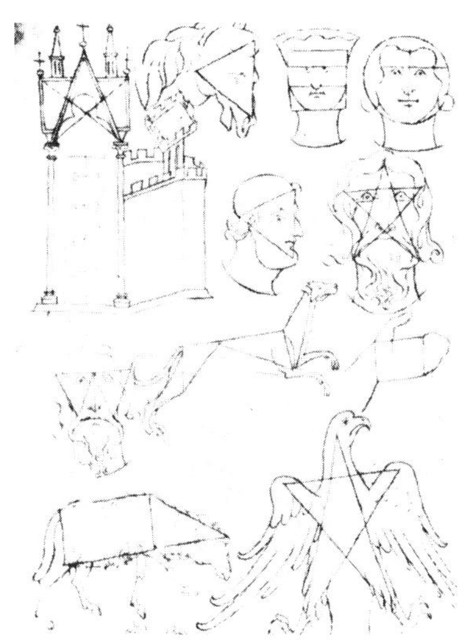

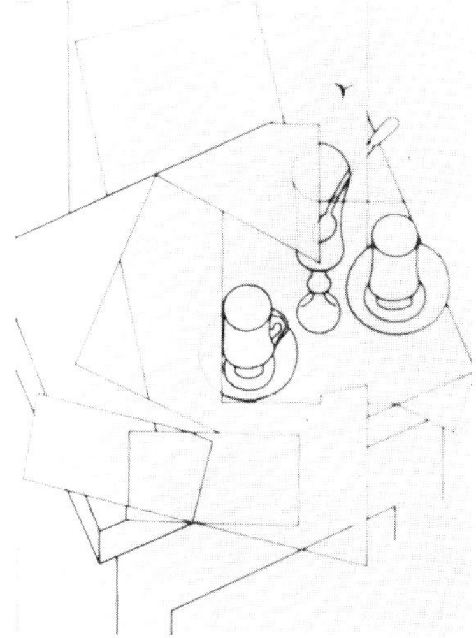

Drawing: Villard d'Honnecourt
These drawings are from the notebook of patterns (or patrons as they were sometimes called) of the thirteenth-century French architect Villard d'Honnecourt. The geometric schematization of animals and figures accords with the mediaeval concept of God's handiwork, reflecting God the Great Geometrician of the Universe. Villard uses a precise outlining technique suggesting a 'follow the easy steps' approach of the instructor.

Breakfast: Juan Gris
If we look at the underlying drawing of this painting by Juan Gris we find that the ellipses of the cups and glass are drawn as circles, that straight lines are apparently ruled, and that there is a predominance of rectilinear forms – all factors tending to emphasize the surface of the painting. Gris makes particular use of the broken straight line leaving us to bridge the gaps subconsciously. These continuities, although invisible, contribute to the feeling of logic and order inherent in this work.

Still Life Photograph and Three Analyses: Hannes Beckman

This photograph of a still life group, used during Kandinsky's drawing course (part of the Preliminary Course at the Bauhaus) gives a good idea of the basic realities of the drawing process – in this case the search for the basic geometric construction. Clearly the students were *not* asked to draw the basket, table etc. as a number of named *things* set before them, but to discover certain relationships inherent in the group.

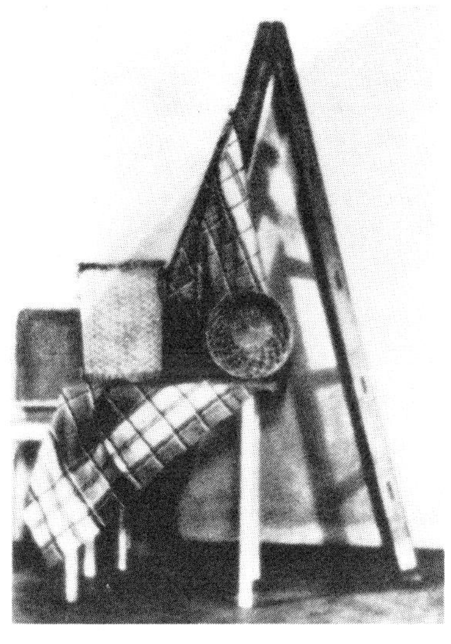

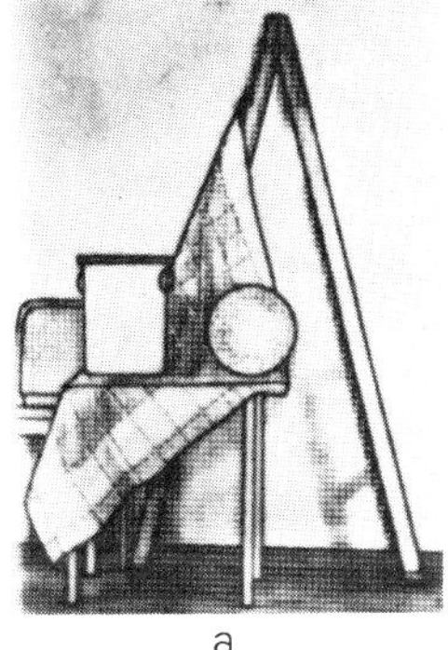

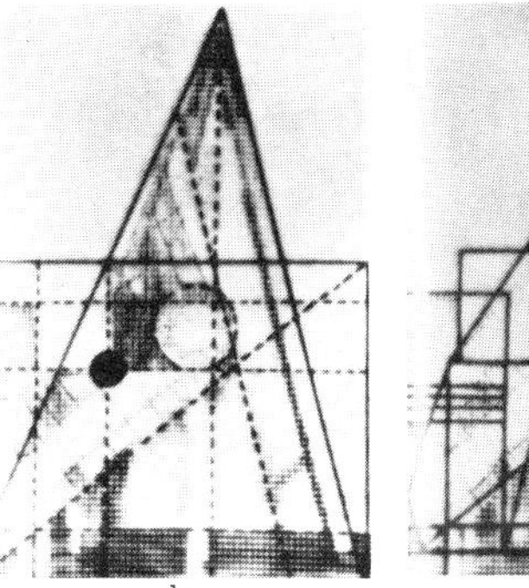

a b c

a) A drawing of the group is still concerned with the idea of perspective and not totally analytical.
b) This drawing is more concerned with linear thrusts or stresses, both main and subsidiary.
c) The final drawing relates thrusts to basic geometric construction.

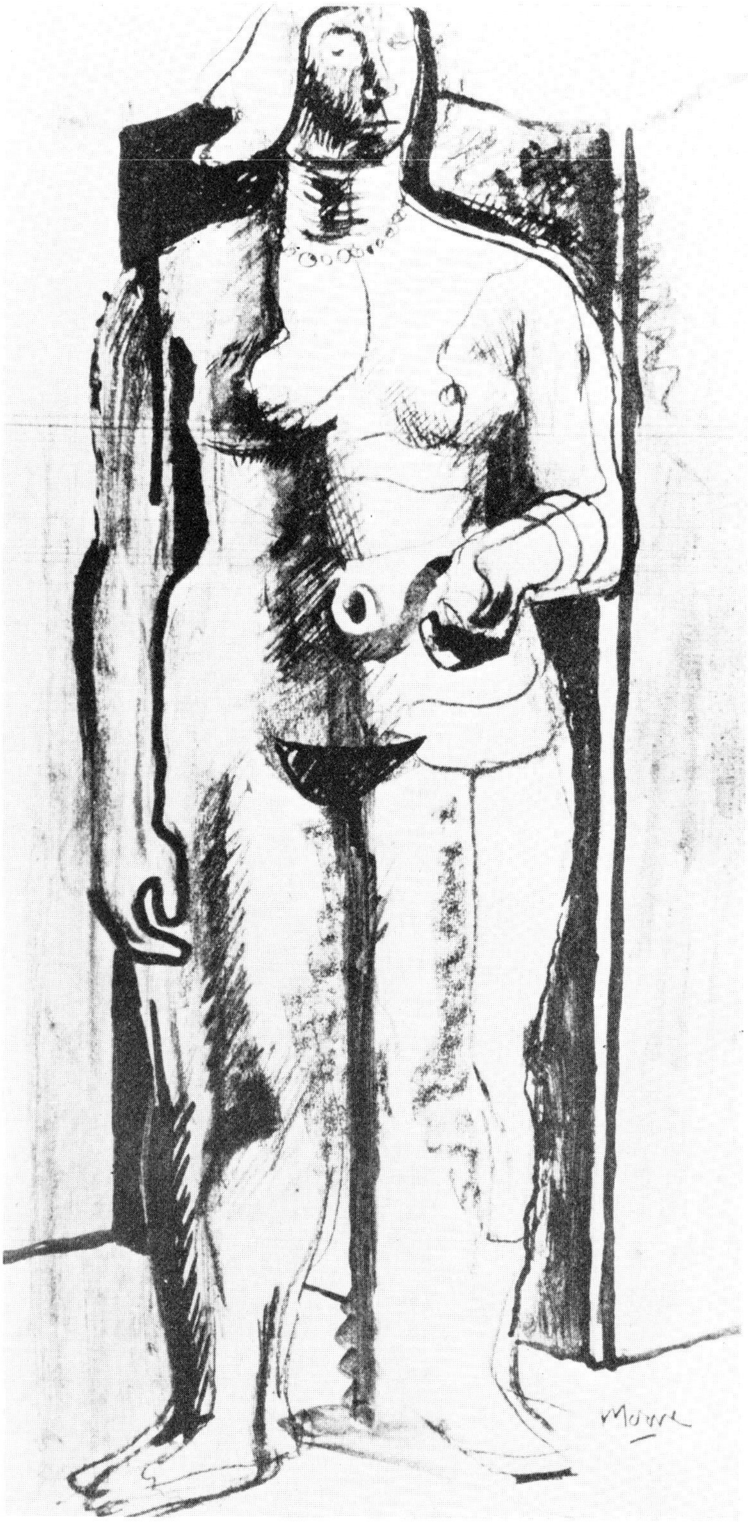

Standing Figure: Henry Moore
A powerful drawing by the sculptor Henry Moore emphasizing the weight and stability of the standing figure, standing four-square in space. The emphasis on form, i.e. roundness or squareness, is a result of the cross-sections – not only the minor lateral sections but also what amounts to the major vertical cross-sections of the figure, emphasized by Moore's use of heavy reinforcing tone.

Preparatory Drawing for the Esterhazy Madonna:
Raphael
Although at first sight the use of cross-section to create form is not so obvious in this group by Raphael, as we study it we find that all the forms are treated in the same way – created by the use of curved lines which are continually overlapped by others, creating a series of sections and projections.

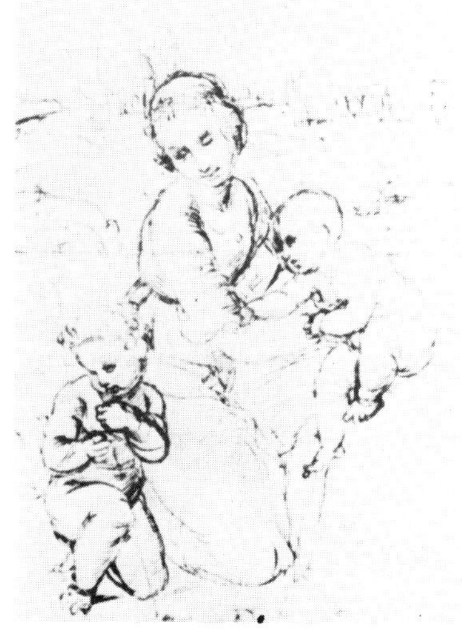

Line as form by direction of plane

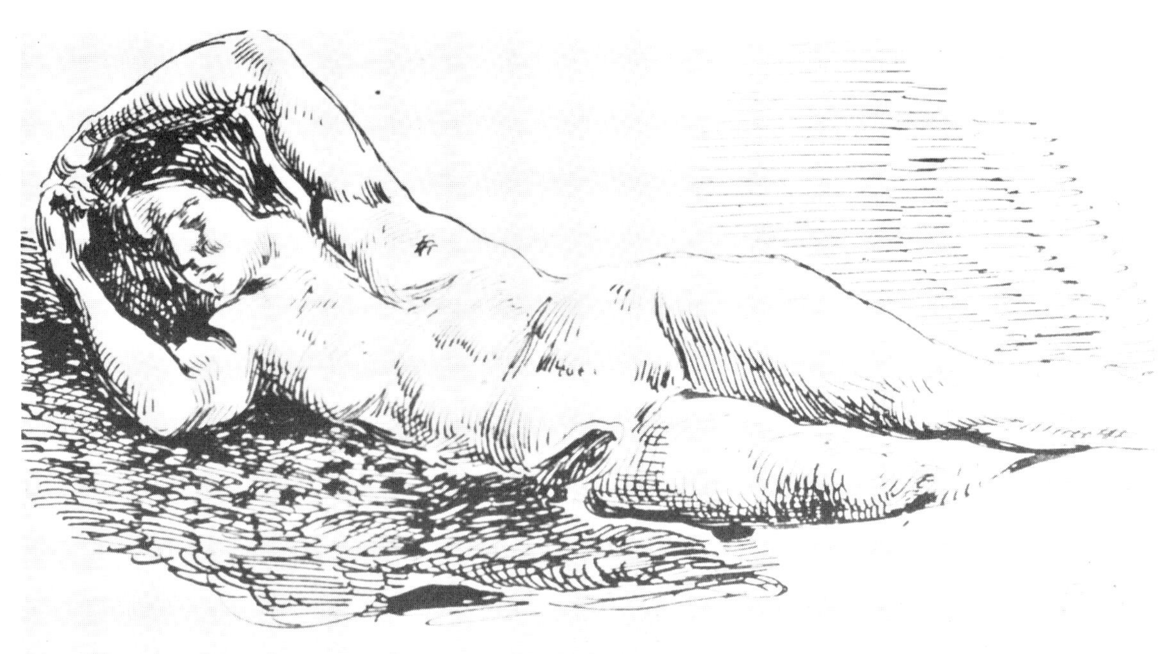

Nude Study: Eugène Delacroix
Another way in which artists use line as a means of suggesting form is clearly seen in this study by Delacroix, where the lines are used to indicate the direction of a particular plane notice the changing directions of lines on breast and knee. As well as indicating change of plane the lines also suggest light and shade, and this also contributes to the sense of form.

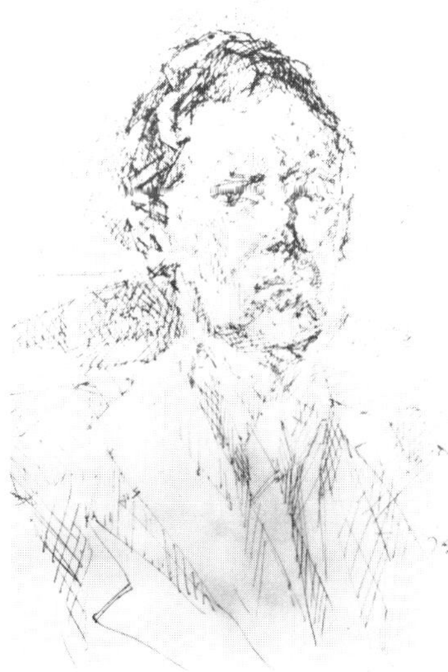

Portrait: Jacques Villon
Villon uses lines to break down the forms of the head into clearly defined planes which he relates to the surrounding space by consistency of treatment.

The Plea: Jean Louis Forain
Forain also expresses form by emphasis on the plane, but uses chalk or charcoal instead of ink. The forms are squared-off and very simplified, and a great deal more is suggested without actually being drawn.

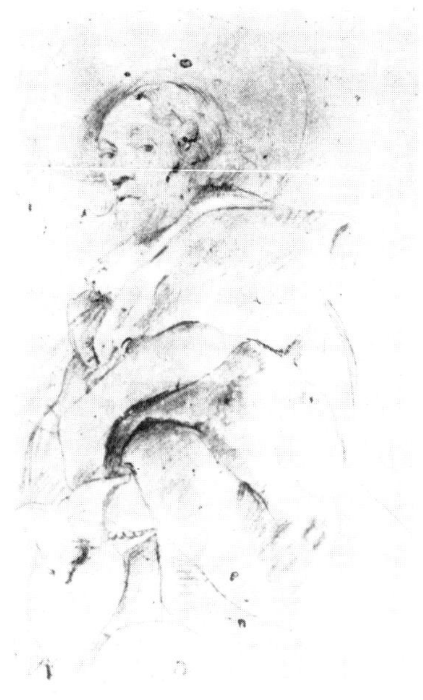

Self Portrait: Sir Peter Paul Rubens
The use of tone, seen in the drawing by Ingres, is also noticeable in this drawing by Rubens. Here tone is clearly not used as a means of describing the light or dark values of colours, or to imitate the effect of light on the forms, but only to raise one edge of a form in relief from its background.

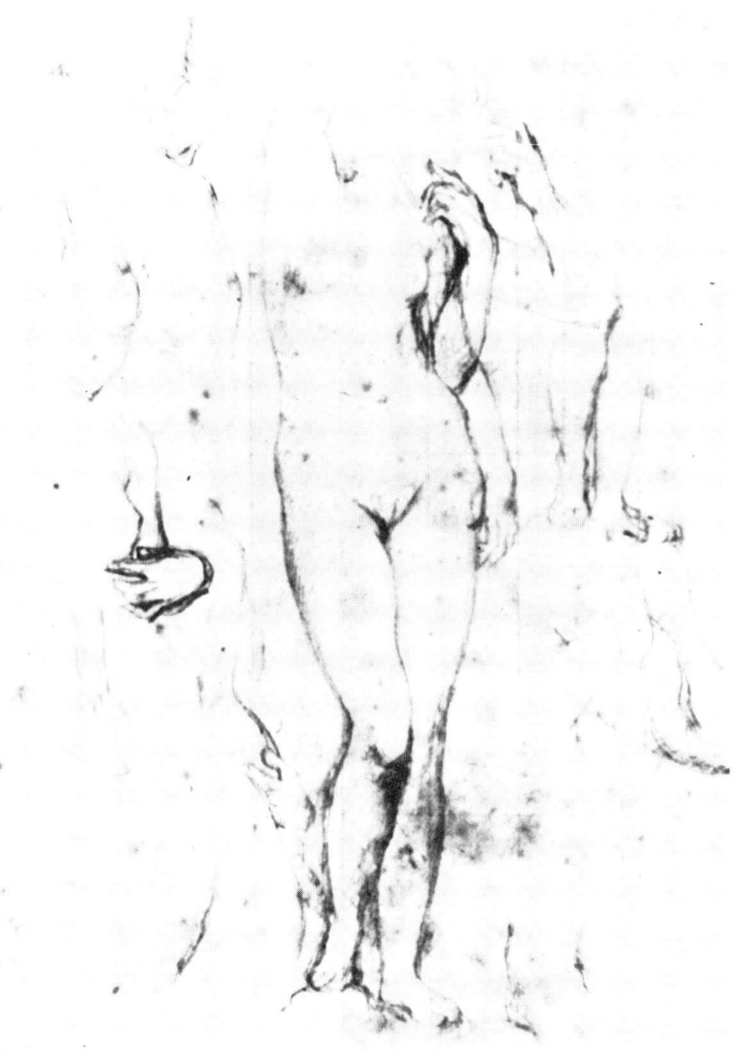

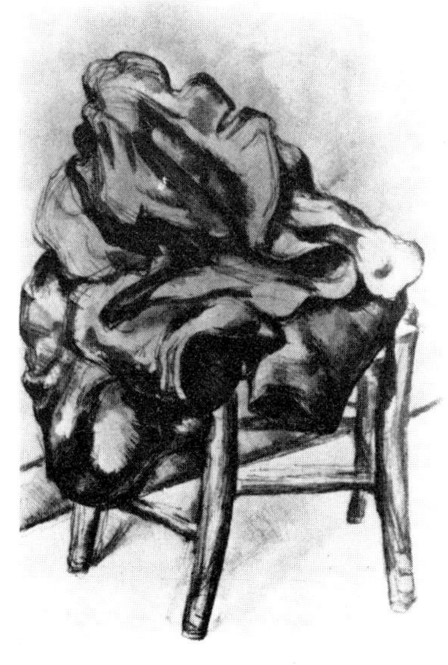

Drawing: Paul Cézanne
This process is carried to an extreme by Cézanne who uses tone rather sparingly in his drawings, selecting only sufficient to create a very limited sense of one form overlapping, or being in front of, another.

Study for *La Source*: J.A.D. Ingres
Ingres, as befits a great draughtsman, was a great believer in the importance of drawing – saying 'drawing is the probity of art', and 'a thing well drawn is well enough painted'. He also equated drawing with line – in this drawing the lines are very expressive. Tone is used very sparingly and simply as a means of indicating on which side of the line the tone occurs and at the same time the relative darkness of the tone.

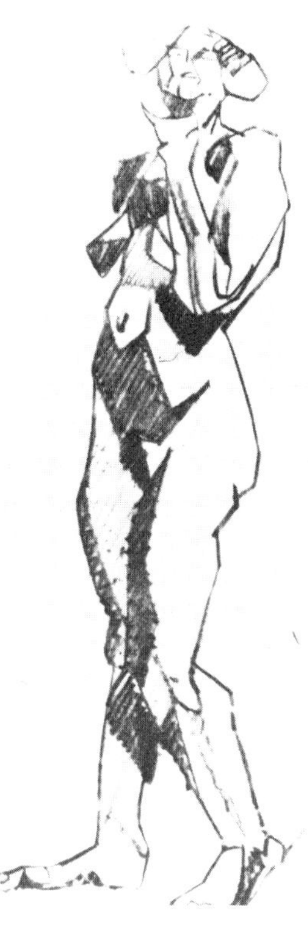

Nude: Henri Gaudier-Brzeska
As lines may be used to create differences of boundaries between planes and to create the illusion of light and shade on those planes, so tone can be used to define the difference between one plane and another. This standing nude by Henri Gaudier-Brzeska uses simplified tones to create the simplified forms expressed in terms of simplified planes.

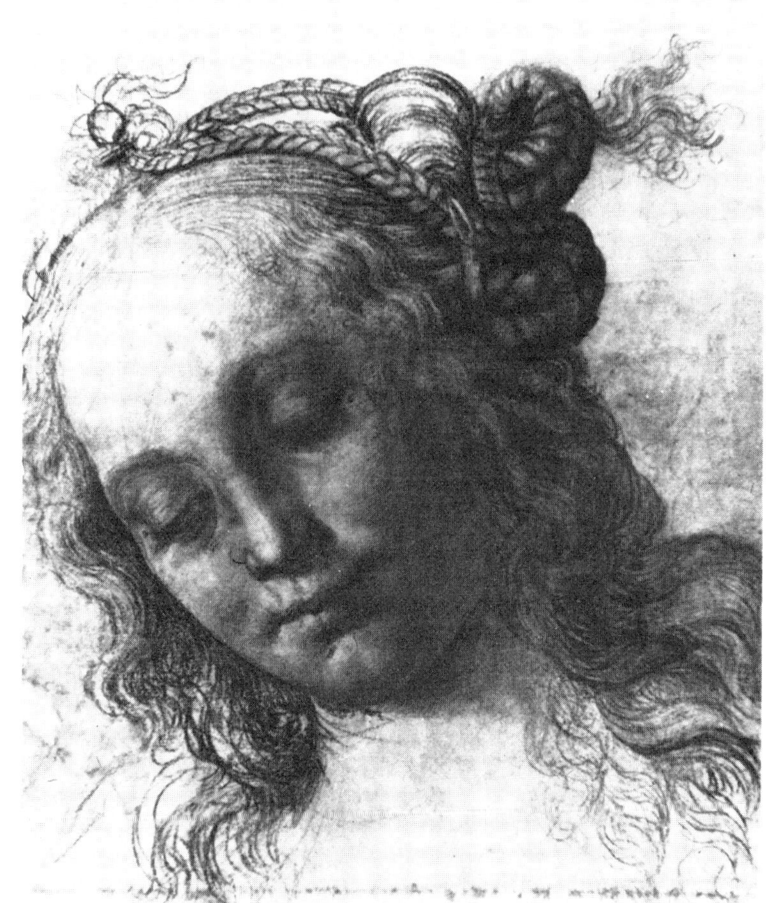

Head of a Woman with Elaborate Coiffure: Andrea del Verrocchio
Curious how different in result, yet similar in approach, is the head by Verrocchio (above) and that by Picasso (left). Both artists use the same concept, i.e. visualizing the head as an ovoid form and then fitting smaller geometric solids into this–eyes, mouth, nostrils and chin are all treated as spheres. The whole construction is then consistently lit from a particular direction and modelled up into an illusion of three dimensions by the use of tone.

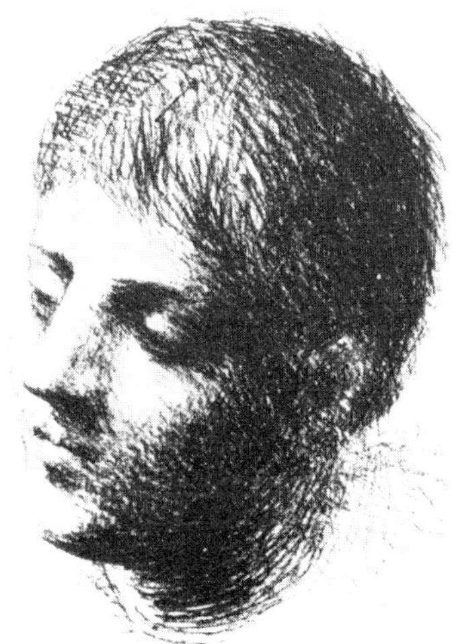

Head: Pablo Picasso

Tone as space and as value

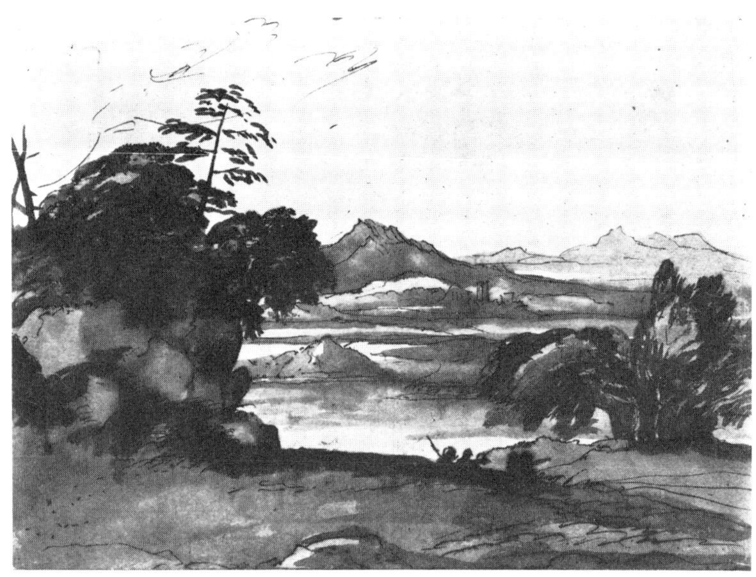

River Tiber: Claude
Claude uses broad, simple washes to create space, light and atmosphere. The strength of the tone is directly related to distance.

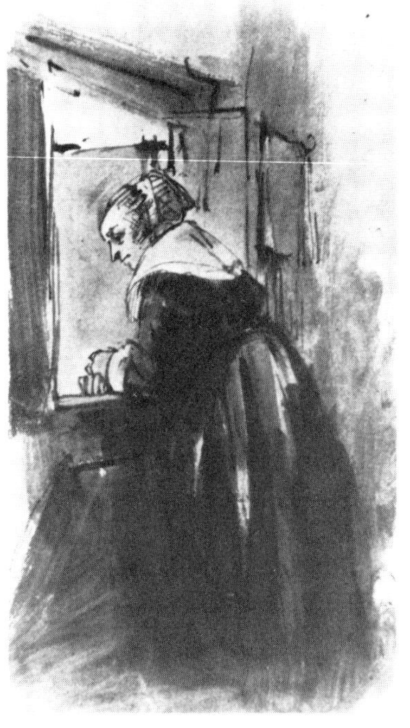

Figure Study: Rembrandt
With the utmost economy of means, simple broad strokes of wash and the minimum of lines, Rembrandt creates the whole atmosphere of this room, setting the woman leaning on the windowsill in the surrounding space. So little is drawn, so much expressed!

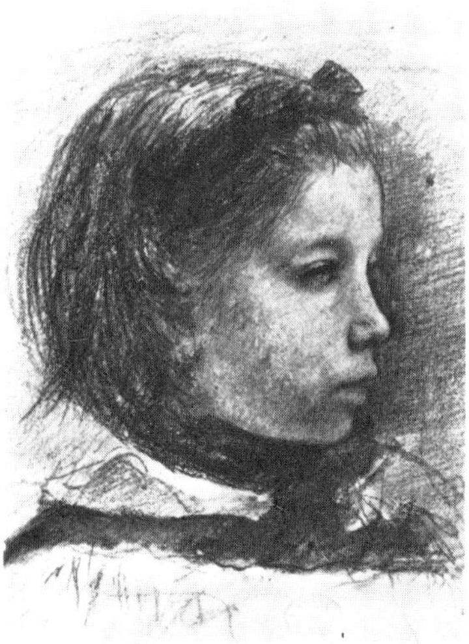

Portrait: Edgar Degas
In this very sensitively drawn portrait, the master draughtsman Degas uses tone not only to describe the form of the head but also the tone values of hair and clothes. Although Degas produced comparatively few portraits and was a very uncompromising draughtsman, it is clear that he was a fine portrait artist.

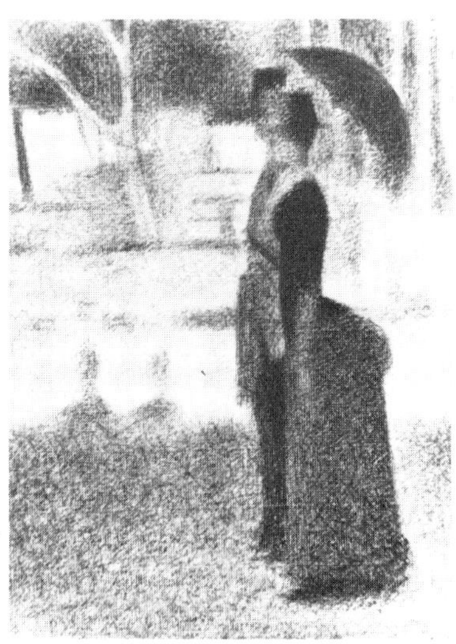

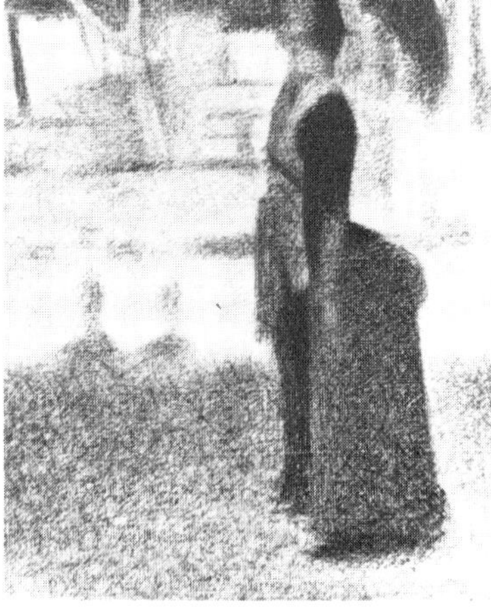

Promenading Couple: Georges Seurat
Working with black conté crayon on a paper with a fine vertical weave, Seurat concentrates on the tone values: other considerations, such as detail or line of movement, are all subordinate to his exacting search for tonal relationships, and the way that light affects these tones.

Tonal analysis

All drawing is by its very nature a process of analysis – some drawings analyse the relationship between points, some of lines to other lines: some (e.g. Mondrian) seek to analyse further, in order to arrive at only the significant *straight* lines.

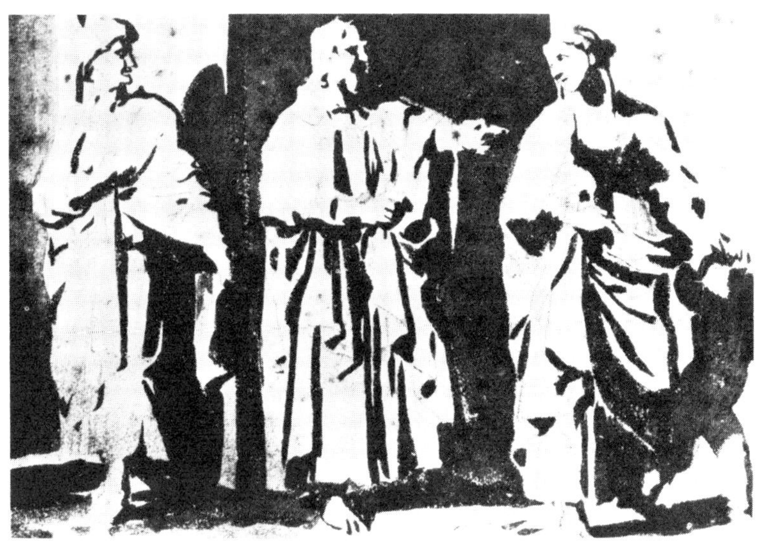

Study: Nicolas Poussin

In the case of this tonal analysis by Poussin, by using black ink he has sought to reduce the study to only two tones. In this way he can be sure of a satisfactory basic foundation for any subsequent tonal scheme. He is establishing the overall tonal effect of light and shade.

This kind of drastic tonal analysis as preparatory study is an approach followed by many artists. Constable, for example, made broad black and white sketches as part of the initial planning stages of his work.

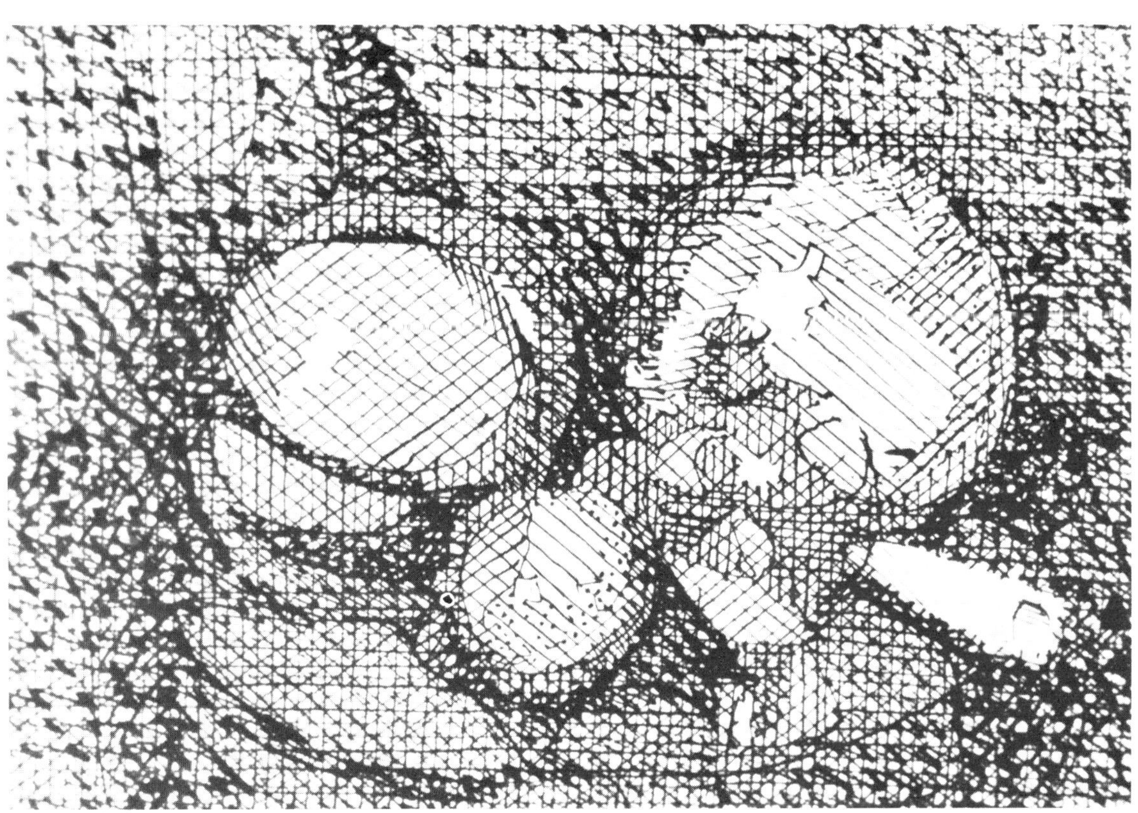

Still Life: Jacques Villon

Villon, using pen and ink, produces a systematic hatching of line which represents a simplification of the tone values of this still life group seen against a background. These tones are used to simplify the forms into separate planes. This drawing reveals very clearly the way in which the painter thinks – selecting a limited rank of tones of equal value, and organizing them with systematic intervals between them (as seen in the chapter on Tone).

COMPOSITION

'Remember that a picture – before being a horse, a nude, or some sort of anecdote – is essentially a flat surface covered with colours assembled in a certain order.' Maurice Denis.

Composition is a process of arranging and organizing those pictorial elements, so far considered separately, in order to produce a conceptual unity.

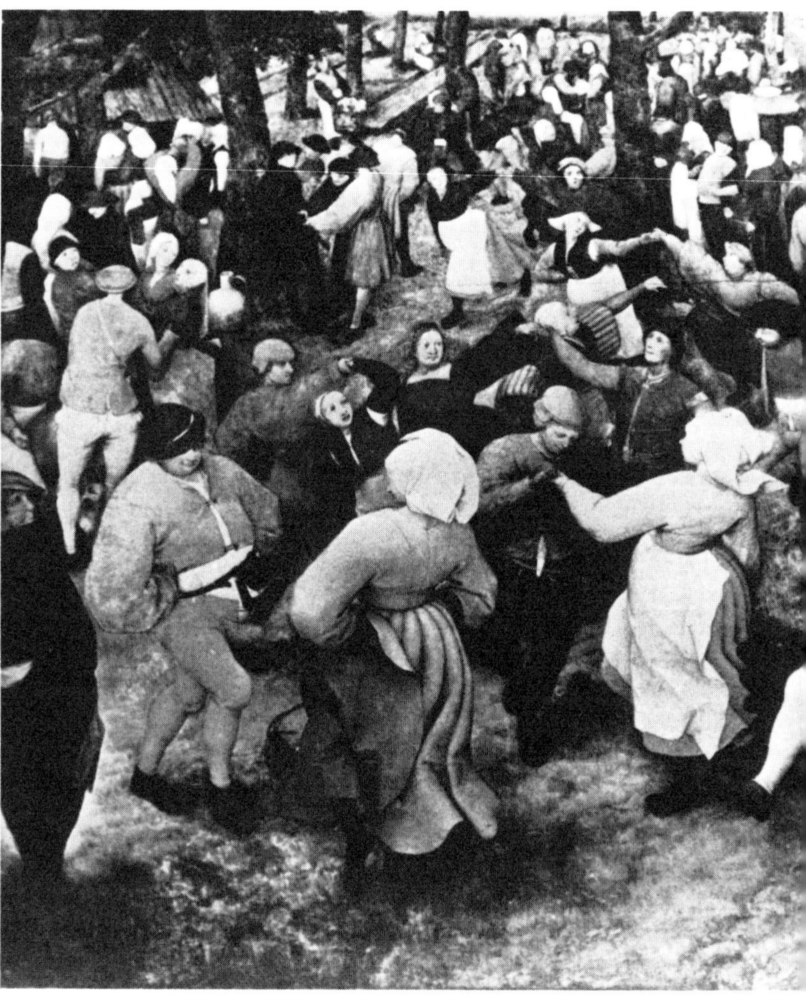

The Wedding Dance in the Open Air: Pieter Breughel
In Breughel's paintings, dancing– particularly when accompanied by the music of bagpipes – is generally associated with sin; and in this painting the underlying subject is the sin of lust, the idea of the wedding being seen as a pretext for sex rather than a sacrament. (In searching for suitably clear reproductions of this painting – the original is in Detroit – I consulted an Italian book entitled *Brvegel* by G. G. Görlich (Milan, 1945) only to find that the sin of lust had reaped a grim retribution – all the codpieces had been removed by the publishers, and thus a good deal of the point of the painting had been lost!)

Points (above right)
This diagram illustrates the distribution of heads in the composition, seen simply as repeating units of different sizes – but in all the apparent confusion of the dance, we find a group of foreground figures (black points) whose heads describe a regular rhythmical rise and fall. They are seen against the counterpoint rhythm of the mid-distance figures (grey points) and all this is framed by the more compact groupings of the distant crowd.

Analysis of composition

There is no better way of gaining understanding and deepening appreciation of painting than by looking at actual paintings; seeing the quality of the painted surface – the texture and brushwork – rather than looking at reproductions, which are often reduced to the same tiny scale, and (whatever the original medium) reduced to coloured inks on paper.

So we should take every opportunity to *see* the painting, rather than read the book of the painting (even this one!) since words can only interpret, and in so doing most of the meaning is lost. But when visiting galleries or exhibitions we should try to look at only some of the works on view. To look at all the works in an average exhibition would be too exhausting, since, as we have realized, looking demands conscious effort. So we should spend a little time – say three or four minutes – looking at our selected painting. After all, it took a good deal longer to paint it; and as Whistler said, the experience of a lifetime to express it.

However, we may prepare ourselves for the time when we have the opportunity to see the actual works, by continuing our analysis of some aspects of the elements of composition.

Having considered some different ways of looking at different kinds of paintings by different artists, it may now be useful to look at *one* painting from some different points of view.

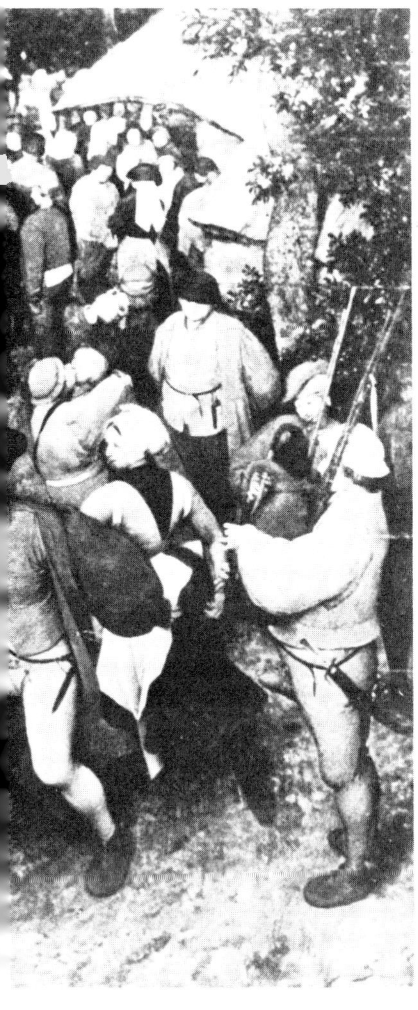

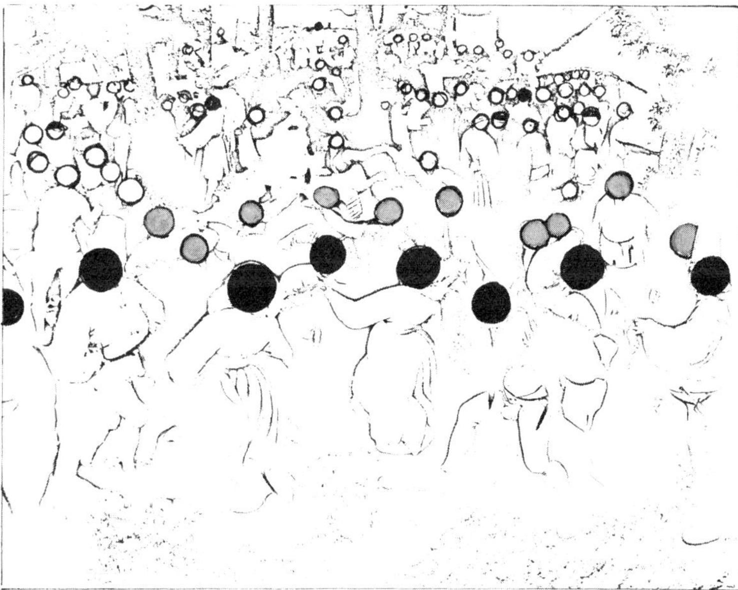

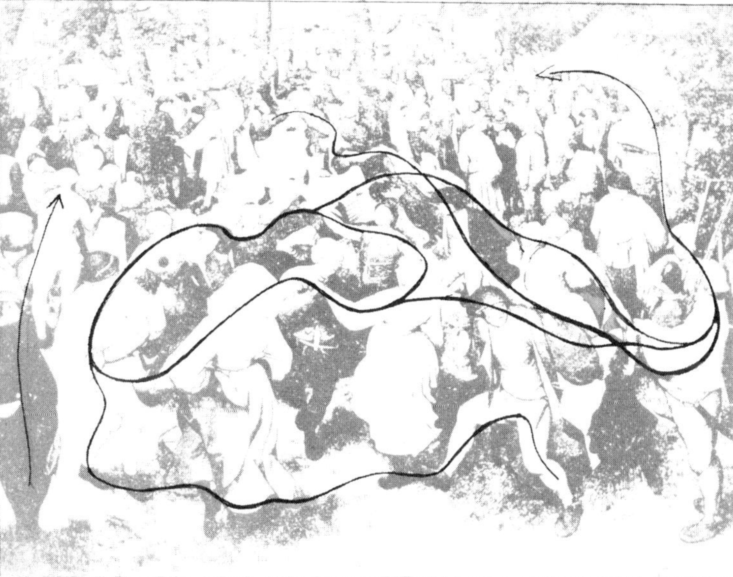

Linear rhythms
The linear thrusts and linking movements are important and complex. Legs and arms are used to bridge the gaps between dancers, and linear rhythms are used to link the foreground, middle distance and background.

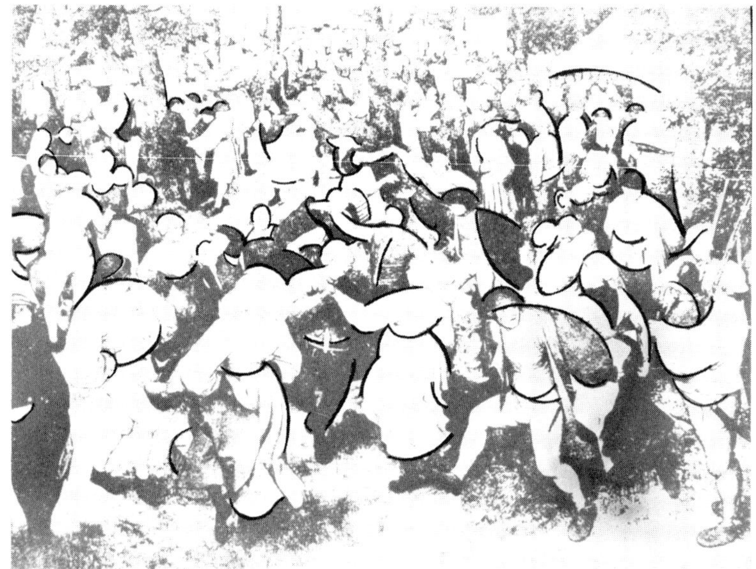

Curved line analysis
By emphasizing the curved lines we can see how they link up one with another and thereby link one shape to another. Breughel creates a set of short, jerky, individual movements which are seen as taking their place in a much broader group activity.

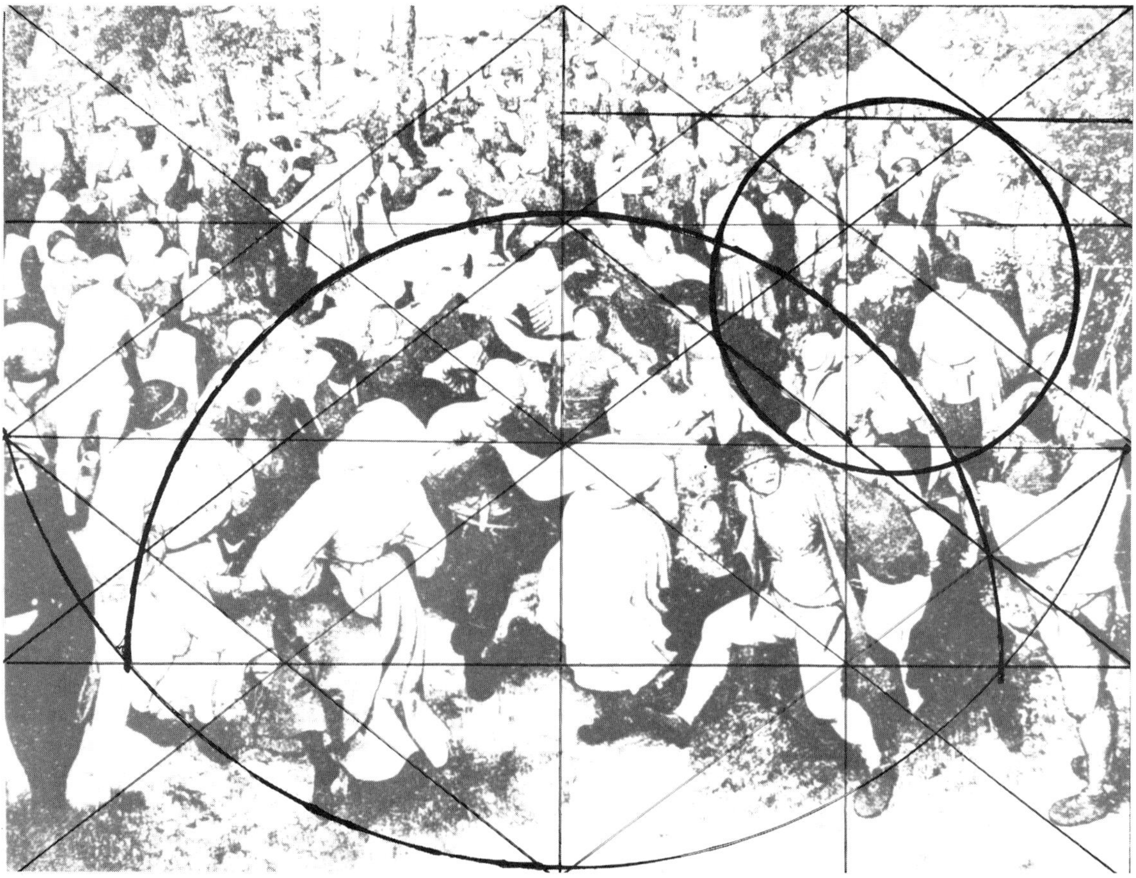

Tone analysis
Seen in black and white only, we can appreciate how Breughel has created a strong, lively, and vigorous pattern in keeping with the subject. Dark and light shapes are balanced from front to back of the picture, with the larger dark/light areas being nearer and the smaller light/darks further away.

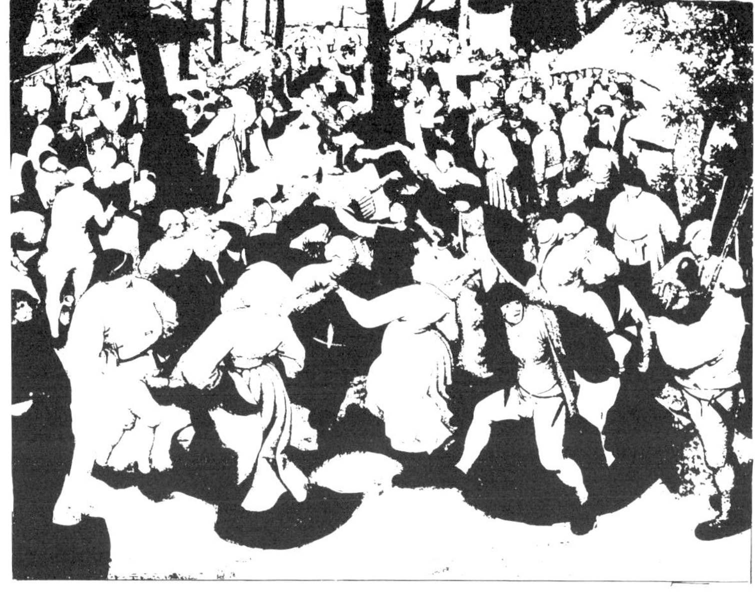

Three-tone analysis
By looking at the painting in three tones it becomes clear how the artist has kept his tonal scale basically simple, thereby creating that sense of ordered relationship which music, dance and painting have in common.

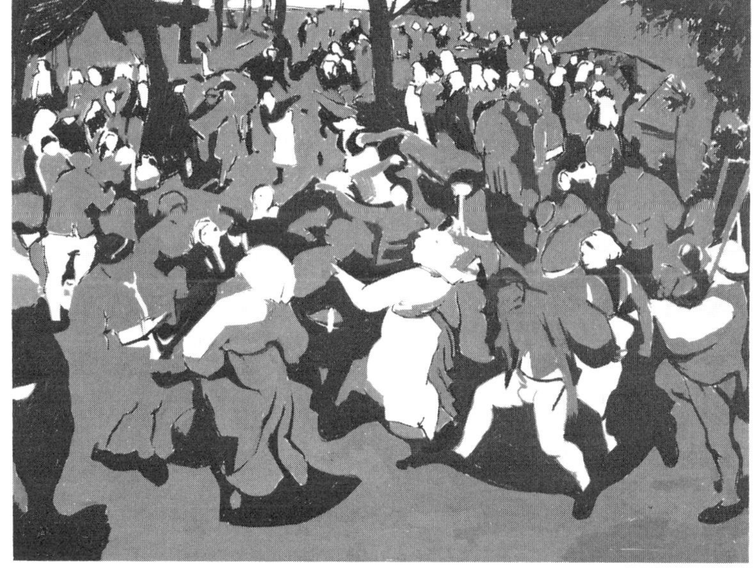

Geometric construction (left)
Breughel's use of geometry as the basis of his composition is both simple and ingenious (as in *The Parable of the Blind*, see page 77). By using a high eye level, as in many of his works, he is able to convey a suggestion of a plan view; the basic arrangement of figures on plan is more easily understood. The figures comprising foreground and middle-distance groups are dancing in a circle on plan, the centre of which is based on 'the centre' of the painting. Generally, this painting – although giving the appearance of a lively informality – is organized quite regularly on a geometric construction.

Acknowledgements

The publishers wish to thank the following owners and institutions for permission to reproduce pictures in their possession (Key: page number; a = above, b = below, L = left, R = right):
Amsterdam: Collection National Museum Vincent van Gogh, 113bL; Stedelijk Museum, 79. Arezzo: Soprintenza per i beni ambientali, archtettonici, artistici e storici, 34. Athens: 67R. Barcelona: Museo d'Art de Catalunya, 85b. Basel: Kunstmuseum, 47a, 78b. Bern: Foundation Hermann and Margrit Rupf, Museum of Fine Arts, 55b; Paul Klee Foundation, Museum of Fine Arts, 103a. Buffalo: Allbright-Knox Art Gallery, 36L. Cambridge, Mass.: Fogg Art Museum, Harvard University, 27a. Cleveland, Ohio: The Cleveland Museum of Art, 51. Copenhagen: Statens Museum for Kunst, 111. Detroit: Institute of Arts, 124. Dublin: The Board of Trinity College, 42. Florence: Galleria degli Uffizi, 26, 50, 75, 76; Sta Maria Novella, 58; Sta Croce, 72; Gabinetto Disegni e Stampe degli Uffizi, 116aL, 118R. The Hague: Collection Haags Gemeentemuseum, 30b, 30aL. Hamburg: Kunsthalle, 102bR. London: reproduced by Courtesy of the Trustees of the British Museum, 71b, 115aR, 116aR, 116b, 121aR, 122aL; Courtauld Institute Galleries, 88; reproduced by courtesy of the Trustees, The National Gallery, 19a, 28, 29, 40a, 40bR, 43a, 49, 98a, 110a; The Tate Gallery, 31, 93a, 105aL, 105b. Madrid: Museo del Prado, 83a, 95b. Milan: Convent of Sta Maria delle Grazie, 18; Pinacoteca di Brera, 55a, 62a, 93b. Moscow: the Pushkin Museum, 93b, 102aL. Munich: Bayerische Staatsgemäldesammlung, Alte Pinakothek, 27a, 41, 106a. Naples: Museo e Galleria Nazionale di Capodimonte, 77. New York: The Justin K. Thannhauser Collection, the Solomon R. Guggenheim Museum (Photo R. Mates), 115b; Metropolitan Museum of Art, 68; Museum of Modern Art, 23, 45; Sidney Janis Gallery, 30aR. Oslo: Nasjonalgalleriet, 104a. Padua: Capella degli Scrovegni, 19b, 56/7. Paris: Museum of Modern Art, 44; Musée National du Louvre, 60/1, 65a, 73, 80, 84, 113bR; Musée National du Louvre–Jeu de Paume, 21, 63a, 89b, 94, 108R. Philadelphia: The Louise and Walter Arensberg Collection, Philadelphia Museum of Art, 36R. Ravenna: Basilica di S Vitale, 22bL. Rhode Island: School of Design, 87b. Rome: S Luigi dei Francesi, 82. Sansepulcro: Pinacoteca Communale, 74. Urbino: Galleria Nazionale delle Marche, Palazzo Ducale, 59a. Washington: Chester Dale Collection, National Gallery of Art, 95a. Winterthur: Kunstmuseum, 107b. Zürich: Kunsthaus, 36R. Private collections: 3, 13R, 24, 27b, 35, 53, 61a, 65b, 83bL, 101, 103b, 104bL, 105aR, 109aL, 110b, 119a, 122bR.